Silence, Civility, and Sanity

Silence, Civility, and Sanity

Hope for Humanity in a Digital Age

Stephanie Bennett

LEXINGTON BOOKS
Lanham • Boulder • New York • London

Published by Lexington Books
An imprint of The Rowman & Littlefield Publishing Group, Inc.
4501 Forbes Boulevard, Suite 200, Lanham, Maryland 20706
www.rowman.com

86-90 Paul Street, London EC2A 4NE

Copyright © 2022 by The Rowman & Littlefield Publishing Group, Inc.

All rights reserved. No part of this book may be reproduced in any form or by any electronic or mechanical means, including information storage and retrieval systems, without written permission from the publisher, except by a reviewer who may quote passages in a review.

British Library Cataloguing in Publication Information Available

Library of Congress Cataloging-in-Publication Data

Names: Bennett, Stephanie Anne, author.
Title: Silence, civility, and sanity : hope for humanity in a digital age / Stephanie Bennett.
Description: Lanham : Lexington Books, [2022] | Includes bibliographical references.
Identifiers: LCCN 2021062620 (print) | LCCN 2021062621 (ebook) | ISBN 9781793639882 (cloth) | ISBN 9781793639905 (paper) | ISBN 9781793639899 (ebook)
Subjects: LCSH: Silence—Social aspects. | Interpersonal communication. | Courtesy. | Communication—Moral and ethical aspects.
Classification: LCC BJ1499.S5 B46 2022 (print) | LCC BJ1499.S5 (ebook) | DDC 302.2—dc23/eng/20220210
LC record available at https://lccn.loc.gov/2021062620
  LC ebook record available at https://lccn.loc.gov/2021062621

Dedicated to my beloved son
Matthew Earl Bennett
1984–2019

Contents

Acknowledgments	ix
Foreword *Clifford G. Christians*	xi
Introduction *Stephanie Bennett*	1
Chapter 1: Why Silence?	7
Chapter 2: Contemplative Silence	17
Chapter 3: Attentive Silence	43
Chapter 4: Ontological Silence	71
Chapter 5: Phantom Silence	101
Chapter 6: Relational Silence	119
Chapter 7: Ethical Silence	139
Chapter 8: Unhealthy Silence	157
Bibliography	179
Index	185
About the Author	195

Acknowledgments

Writing a book of this sort is never accomplished alone. The research, writing, and many drafts require patience, persistence, and support. My dear colleagues and friends Geri Forsberg, Darlene Graves, Corey Anton, Alex Wainer, Tom St. Antoine, Paul Garrison, David Gill, and Quentin Schultze must be acknowledged here in that capacity for each has taken time to speak into my work and supported me through the early drafts. I am honored to know and work with each of them. I am thankful as well to Nicolette Amstutz, who encouraged me from the start to begin this venture. To carry this project through to completion I am blessed to have a husband, children, and grandchildren who have cheered me on. Even when I have been focused on the screen more than I wish to be, their ongoing love and affection have kept me inspired and mindful of that which matters most in life. Over the years encouragement has come from several key and very dear professors and friends, but none more than my brother in shalom, Dr. Clifford G. Christians. As a role model there is none better than he; as a friend, none richer. His generous spirit and tenacious advocacy for all his students has not only inspired me to think more critically and carefully about the purest goals of higher education but encouraged me to stay true to the grand questions that advance my studies and stir my soul. Many thanks to this fine colleague for helping me to define and articulate the larger work to which this project belongs. There are so many others as well, too many to mention, but to whom I owe a great debt of gratitude for seeing something in me worth developing. Michael Graves, Jack Keeler, Eleanor Novek, and Don Swanson—graduate professors who have left an indelible mark on my heart and intellect: thank you all. Finally, I would be remiss not to mention those who have gone before me, friends I have never met but whose work has informed my thinking for the last thirty years: Jacques Ellul, Walter Ong, Neil Postman, Henri Nouwen, Jeanne Guyon, Francis—the *Poverello* from Assisi—and Thomas Merton. There are many others, but these true souls have been my companions as I pore through their works and continue to glean from their wisdom.

Peace and every good.
—Stephanie Bennett

Foreword

Clifford G. Christians

This beautifully written book is a promising classic in the philosophy of language repertoire. The author demonstrates, with uncontestable clarity, that the philosophy of language is high-end theory for transforming communication studies. The humanistic philosophy of language establishes foundational concepts such as human existence in ontological terms, humans as lingual beings, and language as universally symbolic. The moral philosophy of silence becomes an existential modality in chapter 7 never before created in communication ethics. The philosophical literature on language and mind is a resource that enables *Silence, Civility, and Sanity* to take the phenomenon of mobile media seriously without technological determinism, thereby contradicting the subject-object dichotomy of network society research.

To demonstrate conclusively that this intelligent book is a permanent landmark in the philosophy-of-language genre, the history of philosophical reflection on language warrants elaboration. The Vedas in India in 1000 BC, the Jewish tradition from Buber to Levinas, and the *Analects* of Confucius are philosophical treasures on the theory of language. Philosophers of language from antiquity to the present have produced inveterate dissections of the dialogic, speech acts, and representation. Cassirer's four-volume *Philosophy of Symbolic Forms*, Langer's *Philosophy in a New Key*, Bakhtin's *Dialogic Imagination*, and *Peirce on Signs* have no equal. For Wittgenstein, Austin, and Searle, oral and written language are central for comprehending human life. Karl Jaspers *Existenz* philosophy is a treatise on human communication. William Ernest Hocking, chair of Harvard's philosophy department, was the chief architect of social responsibility theory in the 1940s. Jürgen Habermas made communicative action central to his philosophy. Gadamer, Ricoeur, MacIntyre, and Benhabib illustrate humanistic theorizing that advances communication studies from the interpersonal to digital. Instead of cryptic references at various points non-essential to the content, author Bennett integrates the philosophy-of-language material into a compelling argument about silence, civility, and sanity. When the philosophy of language is understood across geography and history, three properties of human existence are entailed by its trajectories: ontology, hermeneutics, and normativity. In the remarkable substance of this book, the identical conceptual world is advanced: the universal human species in ontological terms, the interpretive mode of philosophical hermeneutics, and the normative ideal of authentic identity.

In philosophy-of-language scholarship, human existence is understood as intersubjectively primordial. This book joins the tradition of language and society in making the phenomenon of human intersubjectivity philosophically interesting. The core argument in both venues is that awareness of ourselves as distinctive beings-in-the-world arises from our lingual relationships through which we belong to *Homo sapiens* as a unique species. Meaningfulness comes not from individual speech acts, but from our common linguisticality. This book's trenchant review of the media ecology paradigm makes transparent that the lingual realm uncovers dimensions of reality not accessible to other animations. People are born into a linguistic system of values and meanings through which they know themselves ontologically as beings-in-lingual-relations. For Hans-Georg Gadamer, language is the medium that originates interactive enclaves of human valuing, with this book developing Kenneth Burke's literature-as-equipment-for-living to deepen human situatedness.

Rather than viewing language in terms of static linguistic signs, as true of classical philology, language in Gadamer is an active presence in the constitutive structure of existence. He reflects Martin Heidegger's early classic *Being and Time*, where existential Being becomes philosophy's preoccupation. In these terms, essences cannot be determinative of humankind; Being-in-the-world is the primary given. An essential human nature that defines discrete entities as rational represents an aggregative ontology without requiring communal consciousness. The conceptual issue is the relational reality as a complex of congruent dimensions. At strategic junctures in the book's argument, Jacques Ellul's scholarship is the counterpoint to the fragmentation and atomism of the technological era. In the provocative theorizing of Thomas Merton's *Seeds of Contemplation* and Jeanne Guyon's *Union with God* in chapter 2, Neil Postman in chapters 3 and 5, Martin Buber in chapter 4, and Kenneth Burke throughout, human agents are never separated from the representational. The verbal domain derives its meaning from the contexts humans themselves create. The structures and activities constitutive of the human condition are determinative. We know ourselves through our lingual experience. Language is not a vehicle of private meaning as the epistemology of rational individualism assumes. In penetrating terms, Stephanie Bennett and Hans-Georg Gadamer represent literary theorists who amplify the ontological dimensions of societies expressing their common humanity in language.

Philosophical hermeneutics sees the lingual as the defining characteristic of the human order, language referring in expansive terms to the full range of symbolic forms. The primary constituents of human livelihood are religion, myth, art, science, and history; symbol is the bond that sustains these creations. Philosophical hermeneutics gives intra- and inter-relationships precedence and, therefore, presumes that meaning and perspicacity are based on histories of prior belongingness. Given that language is the framework for human exchange, symbols create what humans view as reality. Literary and ethnographic interpretations are the imaginative forms in which knowledge is produced worldwide.

Susanne Langer calls the symbolic theory of language *Philosophy in a New Key*. Symbolization is the core idea for understanding the philosophy of mind. Symbolic transformation is the distinctive activity of the human species. In his four-volume *Philosophy of Symbolic Forms*, Ernst Cassirer identified people's unique capacity to generate symbolic structures for replacing both naturalistic neurophysiology and Cartesian subjectivism. The central question is the nature of symbolic representation and how it functions in its various transformations in human existence. As Walter Ong establishes in chapter 1, communication technology's symbolic mediations into various patterns resolutely impacts the structure of human consciousness and redesigns human meaning-making.

Because the symbolic realm is an exclusive property of *Homo sapiens*, humans alone of living creatures possess the creative mind, the wherewithal to reconstruct the world of emic and etic phenomena. Our symbolic linguistic beingness means that interpretation is the key to understanding humans, their capacities, and cultural formation. *Silence, Civility, and Sanity* is explicit about the interpretive modality, operating in concert with Paul Ricoeur's *Interpretation Theory*. For both books, interpretation is not inquiry for the sake of epistemic certainty, but dialogue with human civilizations past and present. Self-understanding is not directly autonomous, but a decoding of symbolic forms across cultures. The varied perspectives in everyday communities of interactive beings are the literary connections in chapters 2 and 6, integrating "Ontological Silence" and "Ethical Silence" while rightfully emphasizing non-instrumental discernment and mutuality.

In the philosophy of language as symbolic, cultures are lingual composites that organize reality; therefore, human relations are inherently normative. Values direct the ends of societal practice and consequently make life meaningful. Communities are lingual phenomena, not because the linguistic modality is neutral, but in social bondedness the moral life is experienced and moral vocabularies articulated. The conceptual foundation of normativity is formed of the universal features and capacities of human existence. As made explicit in chapter 1, the scholars' primary obligation is understanding the way humans arbitrate their lifeworld. Therefore, the character of human livelihood is the centerpiece of normative claims. Chapters 2 and 3 elaborate this humanistic grounding; social relations are normative since humans are cognitively interconnected with others. As Ricoeur elaborates, in creating life together humans consciously comprehend their selfhood and recognize their entailed commitments to others. In his view, whenever we are honest with our psychological felicity, we realize in contrast to individual rights that promises are inscribed in our *Verstehen* of human interaction. Comparable to Ricoeur, this book's elaboration on civility demonstrates that normative ideals are constructed from paradigmatic models of norms that humans observe and their reflections on them.

Silence, Civility, and Sanity is a philosophy-of-language leader in normative theorizing. The author recognizes that the issue is not the certainty of knowledge but theoretical cognition as an inquiry into the meaning of metanarratives. Likewise, in Gadamer's *Truth and Method*, theory is embedded in life and theorizing discloses the fundamental conditions of existential reality. With language situating us in actuality, deliberation is understood as reconstructing experience symbolically. The suggestiveness of theoretical postulates derives from the interpretive context that human culture symbolizes. This humanities perspective concerned with living meaningfully replaces the Enlightenment idea that the mind reflects impartially. Normative reasoning is not logically deductive, independently developing norms as propositions and secondarily applying the normative to specialized domains. In linear reasoning, should the original assertion be considered hypothetically true, the conclusion is true by syllogism. Disengaged scientific ascriptions are deductible in that the conclusions are self-evidentiary, contained within the premises. Contrariwise, the humanities version of theoretical modeling in this book aims for meaningful action instead of technical description. The empirical remains grafted into human experience rather than evolving into canons, regression vectors, and statistical correlations. Theories are not scholastic theorems of numerative precision, but theorizing is construed as the power of the imagination to give us an inside perspective on reality.

Over its history, the philosophy of language has emphasized two broad questions, the interdependence between language and mind, and between language and the world. In the language-mind relationship, speakers use language to express the cerebral. In the language-world relationship, the philosophical issue centers on meanings and how they can be known. In normative theorizing about the permanent questions, the philosophy of language follows what Cassirer developed in *The Logic of the Humanities*. Language and mind and language and society are not dualisms with relationships that need to be specified; they are interactive modes of human existence. As with normative theorizing in Stephanie Bennett's chapter 4, language represents the meaning and purpose of the common, lingual world in which humans exist. Dialogic lineage, not vacuous autonomy, is primordial to the human order. Therefore, natural language rather than the artificial language of mathematical logic is the mode of human understanding. Instead of instrumentalism's statistics or epistemologies of linear induction and hierarchical deduction, her book develops authenticity from the natural languages of human interaction.

Thomas Kuhn's *The Structure of Scientific Revolutions* is a classic in the philosophy-of-language's normativity. Theories as paradigm constructions are a complex mixture of politics, creativity, intuition, and beliefs. The chapters of *Silence, Civility, and Sanity* represent normative theorizing in these terms. From their perspective, questions of methodology are secondary to the substrative beliefs that guide theoreticians in epistemologically fundamental ways. In fact, this book's comprehensive treatment of Jacques Ellul's scholarship is an instructive illustration of normative theorizing as paradigm construction. For Ellul, the technological phenomenon is intertwined with the structure of human being, with *la technique* the determining factor in his ontology. If *la technique* dominates, machines are sacralized, with machine-like efficiency infusing industry, politics, education, religion, and medicine. When the technologies of industrialized societies have multiplied into an objectified order, the human-machine interface imperils personal rapport. For Kuhn, and Ellul in this book, theories are paradigm constructions rather than the normal science of verifying propositions redacted from ersatz hypotheses.

This book's sophisticated version of normative theorizing is Stephanie Bennett's foundation for discerning truth in given historical situations. As a normative theorist of the humanities, she unveils meaningful portraits of the human condition by integrating multiple levels of meaning accumulation. Establishing the truth modality in this book is a compelling substitute for interpretativeness conditioned by ideology and commonplaces.

In putting enlightened normative theorizing to work, chapter 7's "Ethical Silence" is a brilliant model of moral depth. The standard well-being of *eudaimonia* is primitive in comparison. Relational obligation is premised on human intersubjectivity as necessary, but in this book relational obligation differs from substantive responsibility. Substantive accountability derives its force from claims made about the formal properties of mortal interdependence. "Ethical Silence" takes seriously humanity's formal properties. It, therefore, is an advanced version of moral philosophy, not a juridical conception but an expressive-collaborative model. Regarding the latter, responsibilities understood dialectically give more content to assertions cross-culturally regarding what people owe each other—hence, this book's ethics of moral depth.

Dwelling in the philosophy of language anchors "Ethical Silence." In *The Question concerning Technology*, Heidegger summarized his existentialism as dwelling instead of building: "Only if we are capable of dwelling, only then can we build." To dwell, to be set at peace, means to exist with equilibrium within the dwellingness. The character of dwelling is rootedness. Dwelling is a reprieve for clarifying the ontological. In Clemenica Rodríguez, dwellings are fissures in the mediascape, meditative arenas rooted in the oral-aural and unprofessional. Dwelling places enrich human existence, with the technological paradigm pre-empting human being for itself. Chapter 7's foundational dwelling is lingually disparate with ontology its realizing framework.

Contingency and evil are adversaries that no one can eliminate. The obstacles of contingency and wickedness are uncontrollable, but aspiring humans are able to cultivate a judicious attitude toward them. This disposition is moral depth. People of moral depth penetrate below the surface and understand the world that appearances manifest. Moral depth comes from an enlarged view of our circumstances as clarified by normative theorizing. The moral depth of "Ethical Silence" is the safeguard against persistent adversaries inherent in the human condition cataloged in chapter 8. The conceptual foundation of social bondedness establishes a credible moral philosophy that reflects the globe's cultural diversity and complexity.

In contrast to technology as neutral from René Descartes to Norbert Wiener, this book understands technology as a cultural process in which human existence is established. Technology is not first of all a product or tool, that is, a noun; therefore, this domain is a verb phenomenon, the grammatical category of action. Technologies are an inseparable, irreducible component of ontology. The definition of technology as ontologically cultural is entailed by the humanistic philosophy of language. In the neutrality perspective, causality is reduced to efficient cause. If digital transmission is understood functionally, causality is limited to what the research on effects can calibrate. The philosophy-of-language paradigm defines agency in contextual terms to replace the thinness of disinterested functionalism. The philosophy-of-language perspective avoids the logical mistake of conflating cultural diversity with moral relativism. From David Hume's *An Enquiry concerning Human Understanding* to G. E. Moore's *Principia Ethica*, we have recognized the fallacy of deriving ought statements from description. To assert prescriptive claims from an experiential base entails the fallacy of confused categories.

Contrary to this philosophical confusion, having diverse cultures interpreted through normative theories follows the intellectual strategy of Jürgen Habermas's *Moral Consciousness and Communicative Action*. Habermas presupposes that language is fundamental to society and, therefore, the basic characteristics of language are universal. He argues that the principle of universalization acts as a rule of argumentation and is taken for granted in human discourse. For him, denying this fact involves a performative contradiction; that is, one cannot assume this position without contradicting the rules tacitly accepted in communicative interaction. For normative theory, as with moral consciousness in Habermas's discourse ethics, universals are the bridging principle that make cross-cultural research efficacious.

Reflecting Habermasian terms regarding universals, this erudite book is a premiere illustration of faith-based scholarship and its core belief that reality is not merely raw material but a coherent whole, an intelligible order that makes theorizing intelligible. Thus, theories arise from and explain our foundational beliefs about the world. Cogitation is impossible without a given. Presuppositions, the pretheoretical, represent the researcher's belief regarding the worthwhile. Human knowledge is incoherent if there is infinite regression. From this perspective, questions of method are secondary to the belief system that guides theoreticians in epistemologically fundamental ways. Theories are interpretive schemes for elaborating basic values. In the humanities, theory is grounded in presuppositions; therefore, theories in Habermas and Bennett include their assumptions about reality. In William Urban's contention against Paul Tillich's total symbolization in *The Theology of Culture*, Tillich is convinced that all knowledge cannot be of a symbolic character, but must be limited by a non-symbolic ground of being. Bennett and Habermas insist on such a nonnegotiable ultimate that substantiates the possibility of truth statements with multiple realizations.

Along with Habermas's communicative rationality, *Silence, Civility, and Sanity* is astute in disputing moral relativism by developing an alternative consciousness to the technocratic worldview. This book is an electrifying composite of luminaries who work productively with concepts, authored by an academic of faith at home with the ideational. Its momentous philosophy of language demonstrates that communication studies can be equipped for the globalized twenty-first century. It is a showcase that our substantive trajectories now and in the future are ontology, hermeneutics, and normativity.

Introduction

Stephanie Bennett

In the last three decades the world has become immersed in a media environment that favors speed, anonymity, and increased social connection, but along with the fun and fascination there has been fallout. Russian hackers, malicious software viruses, phishing expeditions, fake news, and Internet trolls are but a few of the phrases that have become commonplace and dogged our lives. While these factors are not the only ones that contribute to the polarized divisions and deepening tensions around the world, they exacerbate the ability to hold a meaningful conversation with someone who does not share the same view as our own. The undoing of reasoned speech and thoughtfully articulated ideas has moved across the spectrum from challenging to nearly impossible.

Thankfully, the news is not all bad. In fact, despite trends suggesting democracy is flailing, religious affiliation at an all-time low, and empathy decreasing, some signs that the pendulum is beginning to swing back to center have begun to emerge. Fifteen years after the emergence of Facebook and its progeny some of the original positivity surrounding the rhetoric of *greater connection* has worn thin. In the States, there are congressional hearings. (At least they are talking about the problems.) Another sign is dotted along the byways of popular culture. Consider Morgan Neville's 2018 blockbuster documentary about the life and mission of Fred Rogers, *Won't You Be My Neighbor?* Typically, the words "blockbuster" and "documentary" are not found in the same sentence. This one—featuring public television's Mister Rogers's distinctive brand of radical kindness and soft, graceful, abnormally slow pace—grossed $22.8 million. Or, *The Social Dilemma*, another documentary featuring tech-insiders' revelations about the manipulative features of social media. In early 2020, the film was seen by 38 million people, nabbing the number 1 spot in Netflix's lineup the month it was released.[1] The documentary revealed the built-in, addictive properties of media outlets like Facebook, Instagram, and Twitter, warning the public of the open manipulation used by developers of the platforms. These few examples do not alter the deeply problematic aspects of the current communication environment or change the confrontational tone of public discourse, but they are signs that awareness is on the rise. There are other signs as well, however small. Yet I wonder, is the pendulum *really* swinging? Are we ready to return to a more civil social discourse? To do so will take more than talking about it. It will take more than awareness of the growing public mistrust of social media. It will take effort, determination, and commitment to the beauty of our humanness.

As a participant-observer whose research is at the crossroads of communication, technology, and social life for the last 25 years, I am now ready to speak boldly about the need for course correction, and to frame what is happening in our eroding public sphere as more than a passing trend. My approach is what some have called outreach scholarship, a combination of commentary heavily informed by years of research in a style that is (hopefully) not too stiff. Many of the thinkers and scholars quoted in my early research were proponents of what was then called CMC (Computer Mediated Communication) who have since changed their stance regarding the promise and overall efficacy of online communication. This, in light of the increasing ubiquity of digital dominance, is now being brought to the attention of the wider public.

To move toward reclamation of civil communication and healthy public conversation we must take a focused look at the reasons behind the demise of meaningful discourse. But a focused look is just the foundation. It will then take collective determination to steer the ship of national discourse away from the icebergs that threaten relational solvency and the demise of a democratic public. Among the many solutions one might offer, there exists one that is quite invisible. *Silence.* This underpinning of speech is immediately counterintuitive, but there is much room for the demure Sister of Speech to support such an effort, and this book is an attempt to uncover it. In recovering a greater sense of human community and reclaim conversation, we need to start at the foundation. Enter, Silence.

How might our wordy world of words regain some semblance of sanity *and* might that most underrated element of speech—silence—be in a position to help? At first blush one might ponder this word and think about how much we need the opposite of silence. Voices raised in bold bravery, rich in rhetorical eloquence, inspiring others to stand and speak for the good, the right, and the just; this is needed now more than ever, right? Indeed; words *are* needed. Being able to communicate effectively is at the center of strong relationships. Whether at home, work, or in the wider world, speech skills are nothing less than crucial to a civil society. Why, then, a whole book detailing the importance of silence, particularly when the cultural moment is needing boldness and so much of import continues to be left unsaid?

Part of the answer to these questions comes precisely because of this cultural moment. In the wide wake of broken communication and diligent attempts at dialogue that fail, silence can help. In chapter 1 we begin to explore these questions and discuss the place of silence as a communicational good, laying the groundwork for conversational efficacy in both public and private spaces. Chapter 2 digs more deeply into the part intrapersonal silence plays in the history of contemplative prayer, pointing toward ways we might apply such practices to our own lives. Chapter 3 explores the immense importance of Attentive Silence, that which is needed to effectively listen, and what it means to bring this silence into a conversation. In chapter 4 we turn again to a more reflective use of silence, this time exploring the ways it currently frames our collective sense of self in business, education, mental health, and spirituality. This treatment of silence is ontological.

Moving to chapter 5 we examine the current communication landscape in light of media history and begin to peel away the layers of technological advancement that can obscure perception. This is Phantom Silence—a discussion of noise that poses as silence, fills the semantic environment— noise we hardly know is there. Chapter 6 moves again toward the particular, focusing on interpersonal communication to discover ways silence may be used to support relational intimacy and long-lasting friendships. Then, while examining the way an increased pace affects our ability to make sense of the present flow of information, chapter 7 explores some of the ethical dimensions of silence, diving more deeply into its moral implications for a civil society. In the concluding chapter 8, we look at some of the abuses of silence, examining ways that silence is not the right choice in relationship talk and cultural dialogue. Here we revisit the efficacy of the spoken word, providing insight to the inherited power of the word and its abuses. This chapter summarizes dialogue with an eye toward the future. What are the implications of a world without the necessary boundaries of silence? How can the dialectic of speech and silence better inform our ways of being in the world? Can we be more intentional about using the reflective properties of silence to better inform our speech, foster well-being, and build bonds of trust in our relationships? I believe we can; thus, the reason for undertaking such a book project. However, a formula for this endeavor will not be found in these pages, for one does not exist. Instead, these pages are an invitation to a discussion of the immense (and often under-utilized) role silence can play in nudging our world forward in hopeful anticipation of greater civility, stronger relationships, and more patient, respectful honoring of our differences.

Although most assuredly a communication focus, this book explores underpinnings of silence that are deeply philosophical and interdisciplinary.

The social implications involved in the relationship between silence and speech have been addressed in 20th-century scholarship through a variety of disciplines. In particular, the fields of communication (Scott, 2000, 1993; Schultze, 2000, 1976; Soukup, 1993; Rhodes, 1993; Wolvin, 1993), psychology (Gergen, 1991; Murray, 2000; Tannen and Saville-Troike, 1985; Schutz, 1966), philosophy (Heidegger, 1971; Langer, 1942; Picard, 1948; Wittgenstein, 1922), theology (Buber, 1970; Kelly, 1941; Merton, 1947), and sociology (Giddens, 1995; Turkle, 1995) are among those that have addressed the way in which the environment and the words used to communicate form meaning and create culture.

Applying appropriate use of silence as a communication tool is something that has long been left to the mystics and religious studies. But today, in the midst of an entirely new media environment, there is fresh reason to mine its depths. In fact, the need to make connections between the empowerment of the spoken word and the proper measure of silence may never have been as important as it is today. Bold speech, a necessary remedy to thwart the infectious disease of manipulative, rude, and unsavory public discourse, requires courage and determination, but without the riches of silence what begins with well-intentioned desire to converse too easily ends up with insults and a war of words.

The conciliatory benefits of silence along with the moments of breath that provide time for reasoned response, particularly when two parties attempt to discuss opposing positions, are threaded throughout the pages of this book. Focusing on selfhood and relationship development rather than strategic political communication or public address, I will lay the groundwork for a return to more reasoned public discourse overall, a renewal of civility, and a path on which to make and maintain well-balanced relationships in the family, workplace, and community.

As digitality expands and fascination with the television begins to ebb, we see the explosion of images and noise through multiple screens that now follow us into every meeting and event. Henri Nouwen (1932–1996) observed this in the later part of the 20th century when he wrote of the time "when silence was normal and a lot of racket disturbed us. But today, noise is the normal fare and silence, strange as it may seem, has become the real disturbance."[2] Half a century later the situation has expanded with noise levels at an all-time high and noise-related stress exacerbated.

What is interesting and perhaps most unique about these technological advancements is that as applications and software converge, the tools for conversation are becoming increasingly associated with entertainment and favor the shortcuts and substitutions for conversations of substance. An example of this is what is taking place as cell phones morph from mobile telephony to the center of daily interactions. The cell phone is no longer just a telephone

one carries. *It is a world.* The office, the church service, the classroom, the bank—even the family table—find their sturdy places of social interaction upended by the sleek metal and graphite dimensions of our smart phones. Simultaneous viewing of the latest episode of one's favorite video while taking an online course is no longer impossible. Watching "the big game" during a religious service or even during a dinner date is rude, but not unheard of. One may shrink back from the idea of multi-tasking during the most important times of building relationship; nevertheless, these social anomalies are now becoming part of common practice.

Online gaming has become a massively successful business. The most recent models of the cell phone are now associated with 5G speed and interactivity that allow the average person using the device to engage seamlessly in digital gaming with multiple players across continents. Images snapped and archived in the cloud make pictures, videos, and downloaded music available 24/7, almost everywhere in the nation. Thus, as we look carefully at the social and relational implications of using PMM in everyday situations, new eyes are required, eyes that not only acknowledge the ongoing convergence of media, but view it from the sharp lens of history, considering the way older forms of communication and media have shaped and influenced the world.

To do so, the reader will become familiar with the ontological implications of digital media as they intersect with Jacques Ellul's concept of *la technique*, Walter J. Ong's discussion of orality and literacy, and the work of other notable media ecologists such as Neil Postman (1931–2003), Marshall McLuhan (1911–1980), James Carey (1934–2006), Clifford Christians (1939–present), and other communication scholars who approach study from a media ecologist perspective. These giants in the field of communication and media studies offer careful analyses, adding to the growing body of literature to interpret and help navigate the streams of change that our technological innovations are creating in the media landscape. As we explore these paths of transformation, we will do so with an eye to the future and strong reliance on the great river of knowledge that flows from the wealth of those who have gone before us and explored related questions. We do so looking for ways to maintain (and in many cases recover) civil, open dialogue and the colorful, vibrant gift of free speech along with the foundational goods necessary to maintain cultural solidarity and healthy public discourse.

Finally, it must be noted that more than silence and excellent communication skills are needed to bring our public discourse back into focus. We must wake up—*wake up* and remember the things that make our society work; restore the communication behavior that makes our relationships strong; renew those practices that help us walk in emotional equilibrium and find commonplaces that create a starting point for civil, respectful conversation.

In terms of the interpersonal, we may bemoan the throwaway attitude that's emerged in the West toward love and friendship, but at our core the longing for relationships that are stable and sure is a commonplace. We all need people we can depend upon. We need safe, trusted places to share heartfelt—even boisterous—opinions without fear of rejection. This book represents an effort toward reaching these goals and is offered with hope to help readers re-*member* ourselves as integral parts of the human community. It is time for re-*member*-ing what is increasingly dismembered and seemingly lost in our nation and our world—a collective care and concern for each other. Life, liberty, joy, hope, the pursuit of happiness: who does not desire these for their children? We have more in common than we realize. Let us go forward then, together.

NOTES

1. Forbes presents facts substantiating the milestone this status was for the major media conglomerate, Netflix. September 2020 was the first time a documentary came out on top on the most watched movies or television shows ever. Travis Bean. "The Social Dilemma Is about to Become the First Documentary . . . to Achieve This Incredible Milestone," Forbes, Sept. 24th 2020, [March 2, 2021] https://www.forbes.com/sites/travisbean/2020/09/24/the-social-dilemma-is-about-to-become-the-first-documentary-on-netflix-to-achieve-this-incredible-milestone/?sh=626f695622f2

2. Henri Nouwen. *Open Hands.* p. 36.

Chapter 1

Why Silence?

Silence is rarely seen as a gift, particularly as it requires so much time to become an able and skilled speaker. Its golden properties are metaphoric and mostly appear lacking in luster, especially for those of us living in a media-centric culture of chatter. But personal mobile media [PMM] have so dramatically altered the semantic environment that a new appreciation for silence –with a resurgence in contemplative practices—is beginning to emerge. Apps that schedule a reflective pause into our day, books about slowing down, and many mindfulness practices are flooding the marketplace. It appears there is a growing consciousness of silence.

From a theoretical standpoint, silence appears as the necessary rests and pauses that occur in conversational patterns, but as a part of communication practice, silence is much more. Regular silent practices have been shown to be effective for every part of human development and behavior. Along with alleviating stress, improving memory, and stimulating neurogenesis, silence has long been a practice that creates necessary mental space for reflection, analysis, critical thinking, focus, and intimacy.[1] In this way it is a most necessary component to speech. Without silence, the ability to engage in fruitful dialogue is a notion that largely remains in the realms of the Ideal. One must listen quietly to understanding the other.

Many fields of study address the worth of such silence, from medicine and psychology to philosophy, education, religion, literature, and communication, but whether it is formally addressed or not, silence is always in the room. While I do plan to touch upon these intersecting areas of research, my aim here is specifically with the communicational functions of silence in our current age of personal mobile media. Speech and silence are sisters, their dialectical involvement a necessity in meaning-making. Our digital media have engendered a paradigmatic shift in communication practices and, even more essentially, in who we are. The changes are nothing short of revolutionary. It is there that we must begin.

SPEECH AND FREEDOM

Speech is in our bones. In a culture of free expression such as is enjoyed in western democracies, it is not only difficult to understand the potential benefits of silence, but it is also a challenge to put them to use. This may be particularly so in a democratic Republic such as the United States where the battle for free speech was hard won and emerged as a constitutional right after a bloody war with England. In the States free speech is protected and most have never known what it means to be in the world without it. In fact, free speech is so central in the US it is seen as panacea for just about everything. If something doesn't look right, speak up. If someone pronounces something incorrectly, speak up. If there is an opinion we don't quite like, speak up. Speech is our right, our privilege. But, like the proverbial child born with a silver spoon in her mouth, we of great speaking privilege do not often see any other option in the face of conflict. We speak. We shout. We demand. We believe it is *our right*. So easily we move from the right to raucous rage. With voices raised, one interrupting the other, impatience follows; tempers flare. Often the result of the impulse to speak devolves to a cacophony of pontification, words that simply do not work to effect necessary, positive change. Instead of reasoned debate we are left with rants, raves, and prognostications, all doing deeper damage to divide and destroy.

May the gift and privilege of free speech never be undermined, but more than free speech is needed for a people to stay healthy and strong. Return to vibrant public dialogue requires an apprehension of the common good and a deeper understanding that living in peaceful equanimity with others requires more than just standing together against a common threat such as war, communism, or fascism. We in the West walk in a milieu of free speech, but to regain its power in maintaining active and hearty public discourse it is necessary to be *for* a common good, *for*, that is, each other. Without the positivity of being *for* rather than *against*, we inadvertently and too easily use the power of free speech in self-defeating ways. Free speech is a responsibility; when we neglect it, manners are trampled and the propensity to speak diminishes. Instead of important, necessary cultural change and social equanimity, opposing parties find themselves at an impasse, stuck in a sticky web of words. When not attended to, a civilized people too easily find themselves one step away from chaos or collective "insanity." This is the current state of affairs in the United States and many democracies around the globe.

When words fail to evoke positive change, speaking louder does not help, but slinking away without a word is not the answer either. There is another way; it is the power and equanimity that is brought about by generative silence. Remaining silent on a matter of public import is often seen as "remaining neutral," and at times, it is. But there is nothing neutral about silence when it is tended to in dialectical relationship with speech. There is a tension between the two that must be held for public dialogue to be the bonding relay of opinion and the common good. Allowing one or the other to provide the necessary girth to carry a conversation is like participating in a tug of war in which one group forgets to pick up the rope. Hence, the endurance of the Aramaic proverb "Speech is silver; silence is golden." We need them both.

Silence is the unspoken sister of speech. Allowing her presence in the room and setting a place at the table of conversation is necessary. How to do just that? It takes practice, but first understanding and awareness of her absence. My hope is to learn together what Silence can do. In spite of her venerable powers of nonverbal persuasion, the many misuses *and abuses* of silence come easily to mind. How devasting to friendships and marriages is the silent treatment, which is just one of the numerous ways silence can hurt our relationships instead of help us. Oppressive, unethical silence is a subject worthy of much discussion and lament, and while it will be more formally addressed in the concluding chapter of this book, it is not the main focus of this volume. Rather, this project concerns itself with numerous, positive ways silence can bring about good in the world—*in your world.*

MAINTAINING OUR HUMANNESS

We begin with a bit of tacit knowledge: Rude is not new. Disrespectful language has long been a part of human interaction. Slurs, barbs, and cleverly placed put-downs function as the verbal gear that seems to ameliorate personal discontent through blame, but essentially keeps us from communicating in peaceable, harmonious ways. Expletives, mean-spirited sarcasm, and witty, dehumanizing characterizations of people who speak, look, and believe differently than ourselves reveal more about those who sling them than those on the receiving end. But where does "rude" come from and why is it so easy for even the most educated person to tumble into its cauldron? Mostly, rude behavior is learned. Just as civility is learned communication behavior, so is the impolite.

To be civilized is much more than knowing how to use a fork and knife or excuse ourselves after a belch. Rather, it involves the ability *and willingness* to consider another before a stark judgment or pronouncement is made. It also involves making a reasoned decision. That is, opting to behave in a consistent and intentional way—stepping away from our most basic instincts to wield power over another or attribute blame—and instead, taking the time to consider a response, to argue a case, or give a measured reply. Each of these decisions is a part of the way human beings maintain our humanity. These are not technological solutions, nor are they political; they are human ones. But how do we reel-in and regain what has been eroding for years? Is it possible to restore civility to our culture? Can we not pull away the extraneous and unhelpful discourse the way a dredge vessel collects the sand and pumps it back onto an eroding beach? Beach replenishment is a matter of manpower, materials, and technology. Civility requires something different. Civility is a practice that at the very least reminds us that we are all made of the same matter—the humus, or earth—puts every human in the same category of value. Working toward such a goal does not mean prizing civility so much that we shirk back and capitulate to evil. Robust disagreement is essential to maintain a fully functioning democracy. Being civil is part of the way it functions. Thomas Spath and Cassandra Dahnke, founders of the Institute for Civility in Government, express civility as much more than politeness. Rather it is the claiming "and caring for one's identity, needs and beliefs without degrading someone else's in the process."[2]

To regain a more respectful, civil discourse requires a mentality that desires cultural harmony and commits to it by standing for participation from all members. Perhaps starting with a basic question is the best route. If most agree that public conversation must become more civil, why isn't more attention paid to maintaining civility and cultivating an atmosphere for safe, reasoned speech? Lack of educational emphasis is part. Busyness is more than half the culprit. The other part is that our days are taken up with a much wider circle of influence than once was the case. Introverts and extroverts alike get swallowed up in social media, giving wide swaths of each day to the broad connections we have made in front of a screen. All this rapid-fire connection takes time—and we must face it, it can be fun—but we are using up those precious moments in the cracks and crevices of each day, those "breathing spaces" that once afforded us momentary pause, or a modicum of thoughtful reflection. Further, because screen connection is so much easier and speedier, we can easily and most unconsciously choose to go the route of sound bites, abbreviations, and gut-level reactions rather than responding with the cogent and conscientious better angels of our true selves. We are accomplishing more in less time, but constantly set on our heels to catch up. Sound familiar? The crazy pace is only too common. Sometimes, it can even make a person feel insane. This is not a book about mental health, *per se.* It is underpinned, however, by the well-grounded notion that well-being and mental health are connected to our social selves, and these are completely intertwined with the way we communicate.

There are many reasons to study silence, important reasons to look more deeply at ways it can serve our speech to make way for stronger relationships and help balance our lives with greater equanimity and mental health. Silence is a poor choice when the need to speak up makes itself known, but there are efficacious times for silence, as well. Silence can help us tamp down on the urge to use disrespectful, rude, language when a discussion has passed its usefulness. This is especially so in our age of instant media when the digital landscape is reshaping how we humans make meaning. The first way we might answer the question of "why silence" involves a brief look at the way new media have changed the social landscape. Because every new stage of civilization has come on the heels of technological advancement (Citztrom, 1982; Innis, 1951; McLuhan, 1964; Ong, 1982; Strate et al. 2003), it is important to frame what is happening here in the digital age with an understanding that culture does not remain static; it *cannot*. Change does not automatically mean something is lost, nor is change synonymous with progress. What it does mean is that we are responsible for properly assessing the undulating waves of change, and that it is ours to work together toward its efficacious uses.

Viewing the current era of technological change merely through the lens of our own personal gains and gratifications is antithetical to what we know of as a civil society (Carter, 2019). Exploring the implications of change is necessary in order to move forward with communication best practices. What do these changes in communication mean for the future of families, for the nation, for the human race? Stephen Littlejohn (1992) explains the relevance of technological innovation by using the development and use of the printing press as an example. "The Gutenberg age brought a new sense of ratio into being, in which sight predominated. The rise of print in Western culture forced people into a linear, logical and categorical kind of perception" (p. 326). Today, while people can send messages in the flash of a millisecond, space is not thoroughly conquered. We are still in a predominantly print culture, people attuned to "the word." What does this mean today? It means that text is credible. Writing is still expected. Writing and reading help us think in logical progression. Because of the pervasiveness of literacy, human perception and thought processes are biased toward sight. We still look for the byline and want to know the author. As linguist Walter Ong (1982) notes, in a world of reading, writing, and images, "seeing is believing." Yet, as technological advancements continue, they catapult us into a new kind of "being," a consciousness that typifies something he refers to as "secondary orality" (1982).

Here, in the midst of a rapidly evolving digital culture we are moving in several directions simultaneously: first, to a broader and more complicated sense of self in the midst of new definitions and experiences of community, and secondly, to a more varied and eclectic epistemological understanding of reality itself. The tools we use in communicating today are central to this evolving shift. That is because technological innovation does more than bring new tools to the conversational landscape. It helps to shape not just the way people work, eat, sleep, and study but *the way we think*. Clearly, technologies are not neutral, but are embedded with values (Christians, 2007). The emergence of the printing press placed value on authorship, giving rise to the idea of the expert. The photograph allowed decontextualized stories to emerge, "truth" framed by the borders of an image. Each new technology favors some aspect of human life and degrades others. The power in the spoken word is different from the power of the pen. In turn, as powerful as is the written word, it has for generations been limited to a page, a text, a book, an archive. This is not so anymore. The power of the written word has once again taken flight, soaring around the globe with the touch of a keystroke. And, while the limitations have been lifted, new ones emerge.

THE POWER OF PRESENCE

What happens as email and texts are delivered immediately and enjoyed by friends and family across the globe? The lovely sense of connection is a possibility, much more so than waiting a week or two to receive a postal letter across the continents. Yet, the distance between conversation partners creates a communication environment that is always missing the other's presence. No amount of emojis or other substitutes for human presence can restore the power of the word, spoken and alive. A helpful trope used by Ong depicts the power of the spoken word. Here, Ong used the picture of a hunter and a buffalo to provide insight into the overarching significance of sound. He explained,

> The hunter, remember, can see, touch, smell, and taste a buffalo when the buffalo is inert, even dead. If he hears a buffalo, it's a different matter: the buffalo is doing something. *Sound signals the present use of power* [emphasis mine]. Scholars sometimes say that primitive peoples naively associate words with power. It is such scholars who are naïve: if you think of real words, of sounds, words are always an indication of power-in-use.[3]

Sound is connected to life. The sound of another's voice is an indicator of life. In hearing it we access the other and experience the possibility of accessing a truer understanding of our own identity. "Sound signals the present use of power since sound must be in active production in order to exist at all. Other things one senses may reveal actual present use of power, as when one watches the drive of a piston in an engine" (Ong 1969, 638). Sound is life! Consider the glorious first cry of an infant as she exits the safe womb of her mother. Or the power in the bloom of passion that exists long before a child is conceived, when a man hears his wife say, "I love you," and their bodies meet in beautiful union. There is power in the sound that accompanies such lovemaking. Similar power is experienced in the rippling live wire of sound that underpins the tension one feels when conversation becomes entrenched with ideological stubbornness. It is like a high-speed train barreling across country; once set in motion it is on its course and nearly unstoppable. When one asks a question on social media that is met with derision and attack it is a similar power at work, the power of domination; *power-power-power* pushing, pulsing, making itself known, difficult to readily halt. Unless we understand the dialectical tension between speech and silence and know how to harness and handle the power, our words fall flat or—worse—they are mistaken and twisted beyond recognition, strangled in the grip of unbridled power. Silence can help mitigate the uneven tracks of this runaway train.

Hearing the sound of a friend's greeting is a delight to the ears, and the sound of other voices is nearly as important. "Moreover, voice is for man the paradigm of all sound, and to it all sound tends to be assimilated. We hear the voice of the sea, the voice of thunder, the voice of the wind, and an engine's cough. This means that the dynamism inherent in all sound tends to be assimilated to the dynamism of the human being, an unpredictable and potentially dangerous dynamism because a human being is a free, unpredictable agent."[4] The dynamism is lost if one has damage to the vocal cords or suffered a physical injury to the voice. While that one may write or sign to communicate, the loss of the spoken word is real. Voice is a gift. Without it, conversation is greatly hampered.

The presence and power of voice goes beyond the sound of the spoken word. One's voice is also a corollary of the activation of one's distinctive expression of self. When one's voice is muffled or eliminated from a gathering, the group suffers. Without it, vitality vanishes. The group may still function, but participation and ensuing sense of belonging is lost. It is here that the complex and beautiful process of communication begins to break down. The next level of descent leads to broken relationship. Misunderstanding brews, eventually roiling into a polarized stand-off. The result is often division; sometimes, violence. Unheard conversations need not become the norm, but in order to turn the tide in today's choppy, swirling waters of public discourse we will need to revisit the possibility of true dialogue and ignite a revival in its practice.

There are numerous ways this project might be approached, but since our world has become so saturated in communication technologies, a media ecological vantage point might be the most helpful. Approaching the speech/silence dialectic from the perspective of media ecology is an important move, for as the tools of technology such as the cell phone, camera phone, palm pilots, and various other wireless media increase toward 100 percent penetration, the return to elements of oral culture seem to be emerging and slowly spreading across society (Ong, 1982). Through these digital tools the world delves more fully into using wireless personal mobile media (PMM) and increasingly "virtual" modes of communication behavior become the norm. As a new culture of digital technology emerges it becomes necessary to incorporate a more expansive analysis and methodology into scholarly research. Traditional theoretical perspectives and principles of interpersonal communication, relationship development, and civil discourse still apply, but it becomes increasingly essential to look at more than content in determining the efficacy of this growing culture of digitality. Further, whether communication theory is approached from a social science perspective or that of the humanities, a knowledge of context and history is beneficial in accurately assessing and analyzing the changes in the field.

A second reason to delve more deeply into what silence has to offer us centers on the fact that is typical of any new, major technology: there is a transitional time of adaptation and integration before society at large adopts a new practice (McLuhan, 1964), and as people adopt and make sense of new technologies, they do so in a variety of ways. Speech, in a digitally dominant environment—loud and fervent—does not always work. Rhetorical eloquence practiced by a stellar speaker may continue to persuade, but it can easily backfire when instant media disseminate de-contextualized soundbites that present an unintended meaning or complete misperception. Taking the time to fact check or search out the context is not a regular practice for most. We tend to *jump into* a conversation without waiting to check our own facts. As a result, reactions with fury and fervor prevail over critical thinking and level heads. The immediacy of our digital age simply does not allow enough time to process all the information. The fallout is amply evident. These aspects of digitality are poisoning our public discourse, workplace, and familial relations. The speed and frictionless dissemination with which we are communicating shows no signs of diminishing; an antidote is needed. That antidote is a proper wrangling of silence.

Exactly what part does silence play in the restoration and renewal of a lively, respectful public square? The response to this question is multifarious and is peppered throughout the chapters that follow. That said, it is essential to note that not all silence is helpful. In fact, the numerous types of noxious silence, such as that which attempts to quash the voices of dissent or punish those who dare to speak truth to power, are unfortunately all too common in our world. But this project is not about the oppressive, punishing silences that abuse the beauty and worth of speech. Instead, we focus here on the multi-layered uses of silence that work in favor of harmonious relationships and greater possibilities for social cooperation. The hope is to revive the normalization of civil conversations in the public square and in individual relationships—conversations that heal and carry the potential for reconciliation. This represents one of the foundational pillars of this project.

In addressing silence, we must also consider the way the rhetorical arts are changing, now more deeply submerged in generations of print, and most recently, the digital environment. Alongside the grand tradition of oratory, the digital economy has created new, major platforms for communication that don't involve the voice or the spoken word. In some ways, then, the art of speech is expanding; in other ways, it is shrinking fast. At least since the age of television the world has seen a major shift in the emergence of public opinion through the small screen in everyone's living room. The television greatly expanded the flow of propaganda as well as the rhetoric of popular culture. Literature—along with movies, music, poetry, images, video, and public events—have long be part of what Kenneth Burke has referred to as "equipment for living" (Brummett, 1991; Burke, 1966; Kalendorf, 1999), i.e., in that they become part of the mosaic of visual and multi-sensory rhetoric that helps the wider public integrate these changes into daily life. This has left us saturated in entertainment and newly accustomed to gaining knowledge about a subject via our screens, as opposed to personal experience. Thus, we think we know about a political or familial situation because we have seen it on the screen or watched a clip of it. Discussions that follow are commentary on what *we think we know*, followed by someone commenting on *what they think they know*. Epistemology is upside-down! When a critical mass of the public apprehends what is true based on opinions that are strung together by dramatic—even incendiary—images, discussion becomes unhinged from reality and dialogue becomes impossible. This is one of the roots of the lack of civility that has become so prevalent in our day. There are numerous factors involved in the denigration of the word, but I shall leave in-depth exploration into the economy and government to the political philosophers.

Another of the roots is the change in physical presence. The move from largely face-to-face, proximity-bound communication to distanced, digitally enabled interaction foists us into situations that are unreliable. The mobility factor is enormous. "Bahktin (1981) contends that language is only understood as dialogue."[5] That is, meaning is not found in the language itself, "but in its relational function with the context and convention of social conditions/ historical milieus, ideological motivations, and linguistic environments" (Mancino, 2020,14). Without these elements as part of the communication framework, possibility for dialogue is greatly reduced.

The technical aspect of our media environment creates a situation in which many of our most important conversations are taking place on digital platforms. As they unfold, much of the communication is taking place via text, absent of sound. Many of the predecessors to contemporary communication technologies have become so embedded in daily experience they are no longer visible. The silence these technologies introduce into the semantic environment in some cases reduce sound, while simultaneously adding new and extraneous information to our conscious minds. This is one aspect of silence that I refer to as "phantom silence," that which once had an active presence in the world but today hides in the folds of our culture's dining room drapery or the sandlot of a bankrupt and vacated shopping mall. Silence is there, but only in a whisper heard rarely and indistinctly by those who intentionally set out to search for it. Phantom silence is not true silence. It includes those experiences where messages are shared without the sound of the voice or the confirming layer of credibility that physical presence brings. This type of silence appears to be such but is not generative. It is nothing more than a pale shroud blowing in the wind of an industrial holocaust.

Indeed. Industrial sound has curtailed so much of the silence that has been historically available and thrust us into a technical silence that continues to haunt, one that figures into every aspect of communication whether geographically anchored or in virtual space. It is useful, then, to look at some of the ways the rich history of these technologies has influenced human flourishing and provoked other changes that shape human perception and consciousness. Beginning with the telegraph, at least in the modern age up to (and through) the presence of today's vast Internet, technology's part in creating a media landscape that reshapes our sense of reality is perceivable. It is this aspect of our media that makes silence a ghost, haunting the reality of our everyday lives, detracting from being fully present in the world. Exploring this facet and its ramifications will comprise the greater part of this project. The following chapter, however, leads to a sharp bend in the road, exploring several historic instantiations of intrapersonal silence and communication behavior that exist in contemporary communities of faith. This feature of silence may not be foremost in our larger discussion but is part of the story of silence that may, in fact, be the most significant underpinning of every other communicative use of silence. To this we presently turn.

NOTES

1. Lizette Borreli. "Five Health Benefits of Being Silent for Your Mind and Body." Medical Daily (2016), [May 31, 2019] https://www.medicaldaily.com/5-health-benefits-being-silent-your-mind-and-body-396934.

2. Thomas Spath, and Cassandra Dahnke, "What is Civility."

3. Ong in Altree. *Why Talk?* p. 15. This was recorded in an interview Ong had with Wayne Altree.

4. Walter J. Ong. "World as View and World as Event." p. 638.

5. Susan Mancino. "The Intertwined History of Communication and Philosophy." p. 14.

Chapter 2

Contemplative Silence

During the early months of the coronavirus pandemic when around the globe a critical mass of the population stayed safely sequestered within our homes, a swift, noticeable change began taking place in the natural environment. Birds sang sweetly. Their song increased to levels that many in cities as well as the suburbs had never experienced. With enthusiasm for the beauty of this increased birdsong, word spread across the social media platforms. Many shared images and recordings of the birds and the wonder of the sounds of nature that proliferated as we humans became less active outside. The impact of a quieter environment was blissful. Was it more room and space for the birds to flutter and flourish or did we just notice what was happening in our backyards and balconies with a bit more attentiveness? Some ornithologists have suggested the increased birdsong came as a result of the lockdown. Less noise created a more favorable environment for many species. And so it is for humans; when our surroundings quiet down, our ears detect more. It is not that auditory function necessarily becomes stronger, but that the quiet helps us be more attentive to the sounds and other nonverbal communication cues that are there. This chapter is not precisely about the physical landscape of our world but about increasing our awareness of the wonders that surround us. It is about making room in our days and in our conversations that help us wake up to our world and to each other.

Silence, whether in a mindfulness practice or in the pauses noticed in conversational turn-taking, helps present a backdrop—a necessary foundation—for effective communication. But there is a silence that takes place below the surface. Like a subterranean river it flows steadily beneath the spray of speech and informs our every conversation, our negotiations, and every speech act known. Its strong current provides stability and order to our speech, clearing space, as it were, for reflection and the cognitive processing necessary for meaning-making. The intrapersonal gleaning of silence informs our speech in sundry ways, some so subtle that we are barely aware. And while the interpersonal aspects of silence are primary to this project, there are a number of ways that the balm of silence has yet to be fully explored; one is its place in prayer.

Silence and spirituality have long walked side by side, sauntering along the wooded path of prayer and contemplation. Whether it is framed in religious context and one is inclined toward devotion, or it is used to simply hold space for quiet reflection, contemplative silence allows one to enter a non-conceptual level of reality. When practiced regularly, it assuages the machine-like rhythm of contemporary culture and helps us make sense of what is so often senseless, random, and mundane. Perhaps this is what Pascal was getting when he said that "all of humanity's problems stem from man's inability to sit quietly in a room alone."

Such silence, perhaps, is the most universally recognizable mode of communication, making room for the many existential ponderings that are part of what makes a person a human being. Contemplative silence provides the necessary backdrop upon which one may paint the colors of one's life and find meaning beyond the mundane. It is here, within one's own interior space, that one may probe the parts of oneself without having to capitulate to the principle of utility, and there, perhaps even "pierce the dome," or at least attempt it. Philosophers and religious groups throughout the ages have sought the same through this type of silence because it opens the opportunity for one to walk in a higher level of consciousness. This is so both within one's solitary sense of self, as well as in awareness of the other. Such silence is also requisite in developing a healthy respect for all people groups, revealing a launching pad for civil discourse. This aspect of contemplation, along with providing a countervailing measure to the problem of noise, makes silence a friend, or at the very least, a dependable asset in our communication toolkit.

At first glance, the need for contemplative silence may appear out of touch or unnecessary, counterintuitive at the minimum. This is so for a variety of reasons, primary being the symbolic power associated with speech. Generations have labored in the perfection of rhetoric, honing their skills of persuasion to the utmost. From the school of Athens to contemporary rhetorical studies, speech is *the* empowering skill that allows for governance, democracy, law, and order. And, with the great need for bold, empowered speech to pull down strongholds of oppression, fight falsehood, and advocate for justice, rallying for silence can easily appear to be a counterproductive effort. In fact, opting for silence may immediately seem weak, particularly in the United States where freedom of speech is practiced, proffered, celebrated, *and* often terribly abused. It is much more likely to hear statements such as: "We must learn to speak well and with conviction!" "Be bold, be confident." "Speak your truth,"; as opposed to exhortations concerning the power of silence. These proactive sayings about speech are all self-evident, yet they do not obliterate or deny the calming gift and effective use of silence.

Another counterintuitive factor here is the current widespread use of earbuds and other sound-insulating devices associated with personal mobile media. One might be tempted to think extraneous environmental noise is at last preventable, or at least is less of a problem than it was before noise-diminishing devices. However, the ubiquitous and pervasive presence of these features allow the normative use of digital devices to exacerbate the problem of an already busy mind, as suggested in Postman's thinking about what he called the *info/action ratio* in which mental stress increases as information becomes dislodged from an anchored community. This realm of the intrapersonal and psychological equilibrium is precisely the place positive communicative silence is necessary. But the need for regular quiet intervals in daily life is essential on multiple levels. First, to attend to one's interior landscape requires relative silence; secondly silence creates the centering backdrop for meaningful interpersonal communication. In the pages to follow we explore the ways contemplative silence has been used to address such needs.

The first is monastic silence, an ancient practice that endures in many religious communities today. Along with the Zen Buddhists, Jewish Kabbalists, Hindu Maunists, and other religious sects that draw upon this type of silence, there exists a long tradition of contemplative silence in the Christian faith. This tradition is rich but has been long obscured by focus on the printed word. Typically, this type of silence has been relegated to the monastic orders. This is unfortunate, for instead of integration with the dynamic beauty of the spoken word, silence has been demeaned and cloistered. Mining this rich practice of contemplation uncovers numerous instantiations of silence. For this reason, then, contemplative silence within the Christian tradition will be the focus of this chapter.

THE DESERT FATHERS AND MOTHERS

From the ancient days of the 3rd and 4th centuries, a group known as the *Desert Fathers and Mothers* lived in community in the Egyptian wilderness, making room in their lives to practice silence and simplicity. They refused to conform to the growing bureaucracy and external structure of the relatively new religion called Christianity and embarked upon a move from the city to the desert. There they sought a place of solitude, a respite from the chaos and din of the burgeoning city of Constantinople.[1] Rather than simply trying to escape noise, a closer look at the motivations of these desert-dwelling disciples of Christ reveals that they perceived their radical departure as the only way to authentically know God in the midst of a religion that was quickly collapsing into a Christian-tinged version of paganism.

As Christianity became accepted and normalized through the sanctions of the Emperor Constantine,[2] these early Christians saw that the rules, customs, and structure of the city were blurring the simplicity of the gospel with the constructs of the growing socio-political life there. Their devotion to God was being co-opted by the institutional scaffolding being built up around it. As they perceived, their simple faith was becoming a belief *system*, each day more closely resembling the systems of the world rather than the message of Jesus Christ. This, something they perceived as an unfitting substitute for wholehearted discipleship and devotion to God's leading in their lives, was the primary cause for their departure from the cities to the desert. Rather than submitting to the control of the empire, the Desert Dwellers wanted to maintain their freedom. Escape to the desert not only provided an oasis from the bustling life of the city, but it also provided refuge from the politicization of their faith.

Although their desert experience did not produce a plethora of written texts, some writings have remained. Through these writings the rich heritage of the Desert Fathers and Mothers has been preserved and studied, allowing an interesting perspective to the place of simplicity and solitude in the life of non-monastic silence. Anthony the Great was one such soul whose life in the Egyptian desert did not preclude active interaction with those coming to him for help. He learned how to wade through the choppy, flooded streets of his busy mind to find quiet waters within himself. Anthony has been known to say that the "man who abides in solitude and is quiet, is delivered from fighting three battles: those of hearing, speech, and sight. Then he will have but one battle to fight—the battle of the heart."[3] Many others left to dwell in the desert, as well. Macarius of Egypt, Evagrius, Sarah, and Syncleticato were just a few of the notable members of these communities. They were ascetics and anchorites—literally, rule-breakers—who fled to the desert to form an alternative Christian society where they could step outside of a festering culture of political chaos to live their faith in quiet community.

At first, they set out to meet informally in the deserts of Egypt and Syria, remote and scant places that were far from the bustle of political life.[4] The motivation and entire concept may appear strange, particularly in light of the fact that Constantinian rule brought an end to open and violent persecution of Christ-followers. However, the changes allowing Christians to openly proclaim their faith in Christ without fear of losing their lives did more than just alleviate persecution. Constantine's political appropriation of the Christ message created an entirely new environment, a cultural ethos that put Christians in a privileged class while concurrently (perhaps inadvertently) threatening to quash true devotion by making it politically correct to be a Christ-follower. Those who retired to the Egyptian desert upheld the simplicity and purity of Christ's message of love by choosing to disassociate themselves with the political powers, opting instead for the weak, self-limiting status of solitude and silence.

Some today might consider such a move defeatist, a surrender of one's convictions to follow an escapist route. Yet, choosing the silent life allowed the Desert Dwellers to remain more closely aligned with the counter-cultural message of "the Cross," that which upholds a non-violent, self-sacrificing response to life. Responses to similar misappropriations of the teachings of Jesus Christ in later centuries would sometimes lead to violent ends such as the French and Spanish Inquisition of the 12th–17th centuries or the torturous beheadings of Protestants throughout the 16th and 17th centuries in Europe, but the Desert Fathers and Mothers were among the first who chose action that appeared passive—silence instead of speech—to maintain authentic faith in the midst of politically-charged, cultural insanity.

As the early centuries of Christianity gave way to the Middle Ages, new monastic communities emerged. To grasp the immense import of silence in these communicational settings, we explore the lives of several key figures whose teachings and writings have helped turn the world away from these insanities and return to more civilized conduct. The first, a more recent example of a life definitively shaped by silence is Thomas Merton (1915–1968). This 20th-century Trappist monk whose dialectical use of silence framed his life and teachings lived a radical monastic existence that was shaped by contemplative silence and desire for authentic faith. Yet, as well, silence greatly informed Merton's strongly activist life. Here, in brief, is his story.

THOMAS MERTON

Best known perhaps for the now classic work, *Seeds of Contemplation* (1957), Thomas Merton (1915–1968) wrote more than 50 books and spent much of his time in a hermitage at the Abbey of Gethsemani, a Trappist monastery in Kentucky. His teachings centered on spirituality and involved an aspect of silence that is qualitatively different from the necessary pauses and turn-taking in conversational coherence.[5] This silence is described well by Henri Nouwen (1932–1996) who wrote: "When we are silent we are not giving up on words. We are silent all around the words we speak, out of respect for their truth and power. We are silent because we love words too much to see them abused."[6] Such silence is formative, working inwardly upon the one who chooses to embrace it. This is the opposite direction of the performative use of words in business, media, entertainment, education, and every other sector of society.

Merton's writings on the contemplative life reveal his own spiritual formation and the place of silence within it. He describes himself thusly: " . . . my life is a listening. He [God, *sic*] is speaking. My salvation is to hear and respond. For this, my life must be silent. Hence, my silence is my salvation."[7] In *New Seeds of Contemplation* (2007), Merton describes the interplay between silence and his desire for deeper communion with God:

> This is what it means to seek God perfectly: to withdraw from illusion and pleasure, from worldly anxieties and desires, from the works that God does not want, from a glory that is only human display; to keep my mind free from confusion in order that my liberty may be always at the disposal of this will; to entertain silence in my heart and listen for the voice of God. (pp. 44–45)

Merton's work connects silence and speech in many ways. Intimacy with God is one way; prayer is another. The words of David Runcorn, an evangelical teacher who is ordained in the Church of England, help to bring clarity to this idea in his 1990 book *Center of Quiet*. In it, Runcorn connects speech with the discipline of silence explaining that, "Silence brings us into a new relationship with words and how we are using them. Silence has a way of testing us and restoring truth and life to the words we use. It also exposes the shallowness of our words and the duplicity of the motives behind them."[8] This comes closest to Merton's idea that prayer is the unmasking of illusion.

Indeed, Thomas Merton's appreciation for solitude was profound, but the silence he enjoyed as a monk was not the sum of his personality. A man of contradictions, Merton was also a social activist, speaking boldly against the ill effects of runaway technology and what he called the myth of progress. These concerns were informed (and then tempered by) the deep well of silence and what he perceived as part of his monastic calling—separation from the world. Initially, the choice to pursue silence along with maintaining an active life seems like an anomaly, not at all typical of the common perception of what it means to be a monk. But Merton's unique approach to the monastic life provides insight into the place of intentional silence in a society that has become increasingly technological.

Merton's writing centered primarily on monastic silence—something mysterious and untenable for the average person. This type of silence is not simply the absence of words; it is a spiritual posture that creates a space for deep listening to God, to others, and *to oneself*. He did not pursue a method or particular form of contemplation but associated it more completely with a posture, or an attitude, explaining:

> In meditation we should not look for a method or a "system" but cultivate an attitude, an outlook; faith, openness, attention, reverence, expectation, supplication, trust, joy—All these finally permeate our being with love in so far as our living faith tells us we are in the presence of God, that we live in Christ, that in the Spirit we "see" God our Father without seeing, we know him in

"unknowing." Faith is the bond that unites us to him in the Spirit who gives us light and love.[9]

He argued that although solitude and silence are necessary components to the development of the true self, asceticism was not the solution. Rather, he believed that ignoring the tensions brought on by progress along with all the noise and multiple social challenges associated with advanced technology and industrialism could be harmful and become impediments to the formation of one's true identity.

Merton's more expansive critique of the technological society began in earnest when, after residing in the monastery for a number of years, he observed his fellow monks becoming increasingly restless and distracted. As farm equipment and other noise-magnifying machinery were introduced into their communities, he noticed the peaceful equanimity and collective demeanor that had long marked monastic life was changing. Merton decried this noisy din and blamed advancing industrialism for the erosion of silence. His ensuing agitation among the other monks was evident as he wondered, "What hope is there for cultivating a sense of belonging in a society that is increasingly dominated by a technological mentality?"[10] As Merton's criticisms of technology grew more ardent, he began to observe similar social and ecological dangers in the world beyond his beloved community. His critique was fervent and spanned to several key areas of concern.

First, Merton refuted the secular myth of progress as a panacea for human ills. By what is progress measured, he asked? He observed that progress for the sake of progress does not improve the human condition, and in some cases made it worse. This idea merged with his second refutation—the rejection of the domination of systems based on pursuit of efficiency. Finally, Merton decried the growing alienation of self from self and others, and expressed deep concern that lack of being tethered to anything in the wake of runaway technology was a primary cause in the growing epidemic of loneliness and despair. His antidote to this societal malady was not a rejection of the world, but a deeper commitment and adherence to contemplative silence, which he perceived as one of the most productive ways to address such ills. Merton pursued silence and continued to advocate it while maintaining active engagement with the world.[11]

Like his French contemporary, Jacques Ellul, Thomas Merton contended that technology fosters alienation rather than relationship and argued that silence was the necessary antidote. Similar to Ellul's ideas concerning systemic evil, Merton's overarching concern was with the values associated with efficiency and a loss of purpose or "ends." Because the means and the ends become twisted, well-intended techniques arise in direct opposition to their original inception. Thus, instead of behaviors and consequences associated with freedom and human flourishing, ultimately, our technological tools can produce a destructive effect not only on relational solvency and satisfaction, but on all that it means to be human.[12] We see this today as personal choices may appear to be more expansive in this digital environment, but appearance and truth are not the same. What appears to be true is often a result of information that is communicated through the image; truth, *distinct* from appearances, has a different characteristic. It is transcendent.[13]

Just as speech appears to give away its power to silence, Merton's ideas concerning engagement with the world seem equally counterintuitive. This refers to his concept of *contemptus mundi*, a way of being in the world that greatly informed his unique approach to being a monk. Although the Latin phrase does infer a retreat from society, the separation was not a blanket rejection of the world, but a definitive turning away from its values and transient pleasures. Through application of *contemptus mundi*—Merton invited readers to embrace an interior life of peace and solitude, not by entering a monastery or avoiding external engagement with the world, but through rejection of what was commonly called the rat-race, a mechanistic way of living that is not in touch with the contemplative practices of silent solitude.[14] In this way, his understanding and experience of silence echoes those of the Desert Fathers and Mothers. Early in his writing career he frames silence as part of the desert experience, saying, "The monastic horizon is clearly the horizon of the desert."[15] There, in the silence of one's deepest interior dialogue, one might experience a desert of sorts—a landscape that proves too sparse to build anything but a quiet space for recollection, rest, and self-discovery.

Part of the vocabulary Merton developed to talk about this need for attention to one's interior, he referred to as "true self." To discover the true self, one must pull away from the noisy din and face one's mysterious interior. Though he never framed the inward journey as *intrapersonal communication*, Merton spent much time discussing the inner experience. In this writing, the implicit understanding that inner dialogue and its need for solitude was always there advancing the connection between the inward and outward self. Unlike Erving Goffman whose work in impression management posits a private self and a public self, for Merton, the true self is an essence, the self of one's core values, needs, desires, and sensibilities. This is the self that is not mediated by screen, image, writing, or even speech. And, because a true self implies a false self, this is another aspect of his thinking that forms his thoughts about silence. The false self is essentially that skewed image of oneself appropriated by the words and perception of others, whether those perceptions are correct or not. So, along with the outward exterior one presents to the world, it is also possible that one is blind to his or her own true self. The false self is that which one "puts on," like a jacket. What is under the jacket? The person, or as Merton would say, "the soul." Although not explicitly, the Trappist monk argued that silence could function as an astringent that could reveal a deeper, more inexplicable knowing of one's true self. What are the ways that might help us encounter the soul with clarity? These are the paths of solitude and silence, a duo that has the power to peel away the exterior sense of self to reveal an inward, inexplicable knowing. Merton contended that one's truest identity is largely hidden and needs collaboration with others to emerge.

Embracing contemplative silence does not mean one must take a vow of silence. While most monks in the Christian Tradition live communally within the walls of a monastery, not many sit in silence interminably. And, while there are occasionally those who step outside their monastic communities to make an impact on the wider world, it is rare. For Merton, the dialectical relationship of speech and silence drew him far beyond the borders of Gethsemani. A contemplative indeed, Merton was immersed in monastic community but also active in the world, traveling the globe speaking and teaching about the contemplative life.

Many other names associated with contemplative silence are worthy of mention, mainly those whose expressions of solitude and silence were not of the more traditionally monastic sort. Others, such as John of the Cross, Julian of Norwich, Teresa of Ávila, and Benedict of Nursia—all monastics—embraced lives of deep silence, some, learning to listen in the silence or speaking only when specifically moved "by the Spirit."[16] Each of their writings are uniquely worthy of a careful reading. Their detailed biographies, however, are beyond the scope of this book, but several key figures who lived between the many centuries separating Merton and the Desert Dwellers are most notable. One, perhaps more widely known is Giovanni di Pietro di Bernardone, more commonly recognized simply as St. Francis.

FRANCIS OF ASSISI

When the name "Francis of Assisi" is mentioned, many call up the memory of courtyard statuary depicting harmonious affection between this Italian saint and the animals. Others may recall the ecumenical "prayer of Saint Francis" that begins, "Lord, make me an instrument of thy peace." Still others know him only by what is perhaps the most notable saying attributed to him: "Preach the Gospel at all times; when necessary, use words." Each of these references provide a small portion of the story of this 13th-century man, but none explain the deep reservoir of silence that shaped his life and his teachings.

The impact Francis had on the church as well as so much of western art, poetry, and literature, is well known by many, but his skill as a speaker is not the primary reason. Rather, Francis was quite the opposite; he lived and died in the simplicity of few words, letting his life speak more than his words. The story of this *Poverello*, here in much abbreviated form, tells that of a man who gave up wealth and privilege to become a follower of Jesus Christ with hopes of helping a languishing medieval church return to a state more closely attuned to its mission of love.[17] Francis accomplished much toward this end, though not through the power of eloquence and persuasion but through the unlikeliest aspect of speech—*silence*. His life, neither strictly that of a hermit nor precisely an evangelist, spoke in far greater volumes than his words. While there is no direct record of attribution, this is the man known for the oft-quoted saying to "preach the Gospel at all time and when necessary use words." Francis walked in the tension between these two poles: embodying the message of Christ through a lifestyle of poverty and proclaiming the gospel of God's love up and down the hills of Umbria. In spite of his reticence to form an order or write a formal "rule," his work went on to form the Franciscan Order, and his life made an impact that few have since.

How different the tone and tenor of the church was in the Middle Ages when radio, television, and the Internet did not exist. Yet, a similar confluence with secular culture existed. One of Francis's biographers describes the state of the church as not so terribly different from the excesses in our own times.

> If we had no other source of information but the papal bulls denouncing excesses of every kind, they would be enough to paint a picture of that voluptuous society: Feasts, banquets dissolving in debauchery, lewd parties where minstrels performed their perverse songs, erotic dances and chants that made their way into the churches. The taste for beautiful clothes and precious fabrics led to the most insane expenditures. . . . Masses were said badly, shortened and mumbled.[18]

Historians paint the church of the early 13th century as largely in spiritual deficit. False teaching was prevalent. Heresies abounded. Its sanctioned practices were outlandish, falling far from the ideal faith grounded in the veracity and simplicity of the pure and selfless love modeled by Jesus of Nazareth. Essentially, the church was in dire need of reform. Many of the official clergy lived openly in a debauched state, and the disorder in the monasteries was largely corrupt. No longer did priests involved in common-law marriage or concubinage cause a scandal. "The lust for gold, the incontinence of the monks and nuns had become the laughingstock of the people and the inexhaustible source of licentious tales and satirical songs, whose echoes lingered long after the reforms, had restored the different orders to their early severity."[19] It was into this bizarre and decadent situation that Francis was born and raised. His father, a merchant of purple and other fine cloth, nicknamed him Francesco, ostensibly because his primary business dealings were with the French.

Young Francis was much loved in his community, a rowdy but charming youth, fashionable in style and eloquent in speech. His sweet voice rang out in song through Assisi's streets and his overly generous ways often found him footing the entire bill for feasting with friends. In spite of his reputation for rabble-rousing and too much partying, the villagers loved Francis; everyone was drawn to him. One day in the midst of his revelry, he was struck by the vanity of his rambunctious lifestyle and soon began a transformation from the boisterous boy who loved to lead the youth of Assisi in carousing, to leading the life of a thoughtful contemplative. With no more than the clothes on his back Francis set out, his heart ablaze with passion for God. However, instead of raising a loud cry in the marketplace, his newfound faith sent him traveling the countryside in search of ways to rebuild the wayward church. Eventually, a motley band of disciples followed him into the Umbrian woods where he often retreated to simply be alone with God and his thoughts. It was there that Francis found his strength –strength to surrender his own charismatic power for the ability and authority of God. Although he did, in fact, preach the Gospel from town to town, it was without the fanfare of celebrity status or riches. He walked barefoot, with one frock, begging for food and hoping for an opportunity to speak about the glory and greatness of God. When there were none to listen, he preached to the birds.

Among the many feats and follies for which Francis is known, one aspect of his life stands out in juxtaposition to what is considered holy in American Evangelicalism today. The saint from Assisi found a way to speak persuasively without strategy or manipulation, so much so that others began to follow his lead and model their lives after his own. The key? Francis's speech was informed by silence. He listened more than he spoke, and although he was unafraid to speak directly and boldly—and often did—the practice of silence became a dialectical necessity for the rest of his life. The Franciscan order that his life initiated continues the intertwining blend of contemplation and action, using speech *and* silence to walk in ways that nudge the Church back to its Christo-centric roots.

Although he wrote no books and had minimal education, the "little poor man" is remembered for bringing a necessary salvo to the disordered havoc of Medieval Christianity. He continues to be known for letting the Gospel message speak through silent example more than speech. Approximately 400 years later George Fox (1624–1691) of England was another who drew from the power of silence when he departed from the institutional church to begin a movement which would eventually come to be called Quakerism.

QUAKER WORSHIP: ACTIVISM FLOWING FORTH FROM SILENCE

Officially known as the *Religious Society of Friends*, this small sect of Christianity began in 1653 with George Fox (1624–1691), an Englishman who came to America in hopes of finding freedom to preach a more open, inclusive religion of Jesus. Fox was a dissenter of institutional Christianity and railed against the over-dependence of authoritarian leadership in England. He took great issue with the "many words" that were insincere or spoken frivolously and believed that the truth of the Gospel message could be found through fellowship with God and others, not sacraments, rituals, or heavy-handed leadership. It is here the movement started as a departure from what Fox considered an apostate generation of Christians. Here, he describes the milieu from which his thoughts on silence are informed:

> [. . . .] apostate Christians who inwardly rove from the spirit of God; so are gone from the silence and stillness, and from *waiting upon God*[20] [emphasis mine] to have their strength renewed, and so are dropped into sects, among one another, and so have the words of Christ and the apostles, *but inwardly are ravened from the still life, in which the fellowship is attained to in the spirit of God*, in the power of God, which is the gospel; in which is the fellowship, when there are no words spoken. (Fox, 1976, p. 174)

For Fox, this fellowship could only be faithfully maintained through regular "waiting on God" in the stillness of silent prayer. Herein lies the core of Quaker belief, that is, the existence of an inward life in which the Light of Christ dwells.[21]

Unlike those religious thinkers who practice silence in the quiet of the monastery or hermitage, Quakers apprehend the gift of silence in quite different ways. As leaders in social justice, their attention has long been activated in the work of peace and plight of the oppressed. Quakers were among the first antebellum activists in the eradication of slavery. They continue today to work for prison reform and many other areas where justice is not being served. Their social concerns flow forth from a commitment to the inward way, one that is not quite contemplative but uses silence as a means to stay centered, humbled, and focused on the will and action of God rather than on the temporal fancy of human will. This emphasis is abundantly clear when analyzing Fox's extant writings for they are a "repository of statements which reiterate the confidence that man, if he listens, can hear the voice of Christ."[22] From that "voice of Christ" emanates action. This is particularly so with the Quakers.

Worldwide there are an estimated 300,000 Quakers today living primarily in North America, Mexico, and Kenya. Though their numbers in the U.S. have dwindled to approximately 35,000, their continued preference for silent worship has roots that go deep and branches that have spread lavishly throughout many areas of positive social change.[23] Early American Quakers were tireless activists advocating for women and other oppressed and marginalized groups. The well-known names of Lucretia Mott, Elizabeth Cady Stanton, and Susan B. Anthony –all Quakers –worked at the inception of the abolitionist movement in America. Less known perhaps are the names of John Woolman (1720–1772) and William Penn (1644–1781), whose work in early America had a profound effect in creating awareness of the evils of slavery. Penn, born in England, the more recognizable of the two, founded the Commonwealth of Pennsylvania as a refuge for those fleeing from English persecution. Woolman's "Plea for the Poor" stimulated public conversation that drew attention to unjust and inhumane treatment of African Americans.[24] His early and ardent advocacy against slavery paved the way for awareness and then dialogue that eventually bore fruit in a long-awaited emancipation.

In some ways Fox's ideas were quite in line with earlier instantiations of religious silence, particularly with those who found exile in the desert. While the Desert Fathers and Mothers are primary among such a witness to silence, hundreds of years before their exile, the Hebrew people wandered in the desert for 40 years until God revealed Himself through a Burning Bush and the Decalogue. Quaker scholar Douglas Gwyn concurs and frames it thusly: "Anyone who has been to the desert knows that vast silence of it—almost completely devoid of even natural sounds like the rushing of streams or the rustling of leaves. This is where God first made himself known to His people" (p. 164). It is in this desert of silence that George Fox believed people could stay close to God instead of becoming dependent upon the formalities of religion. Gwyn goes further to explain the symbolism behind silence in worship, saying:

> Waiting upon the Lord, stopping oneself, is the taking up of the cross in worship. The power of the cross breaks the shackles of the world's sense of time, which captivates the mind, and brings one to the beginning—the hearing and obeying relationship with God known in Eden; bereft of their own words, casting off outward knowledge, all are to stand naked and bare and uncovered before the living God. (p. 161)

Much more than simply the absence of words or a practice that seeks to avoid distractions from inward peace, this silence is a spiritual posture that creates a space for deep listening to God, to others, and to oneself. It is a silence that waits to be filled.

Born the son of a weaver, Fox's fiery form of preaching landed him in prison on several occasions. He railed against the oppressive forms of leadership in the church and preached freedom of worship wherever he went. Though he was fiercely persecuted, Fox continued to use his rhetorical skills to inspire many of his countrymen and women to pursue God outside the boundaries of the state-sanctioned church. He taught his followers to appreciate silence and use it to listen closely for the voice of God, instead of being falsely moved or manipulated by the "voice of man." Thus, he perceived silence as helpful in several ways. First, he used silence as a counter-cultural approach to religion, one that did not resort to the violent, bombastic use of language or ostentatious eloquence to persuade others of the truth. Secondly, Fox perceived it as a way that might lead to more informed and influential speech when the time was right to speak. Though he believed strongly in public witness to the Gospel message, he saw the truest witness to God's goodness could only be possible if one's faith was authentic, that is, if the "Divine light" was lit within those who confessed belief in Christ. Thus began Fox's intensely dialectical relationship with silence.

Because he placed a high premium on truth and the authenticity of one's faith, Fox advocated simplicity in all things, but particularly, in use of language. He made this clear in a poetic discussion of the intended outcome of silence in religious meetings when he penned the following:

> The intent of all speaking is to bring into the light, and to walk in, and to possess the same, and to live in and enjoy it, and to feel God's presence, and that is in the silence (not the wandering whirling tempestuous part of man or woman) for there is the flock lying down at noonday, and the feeding of the bread of life, and the drinking of the springs of life, when they do not speak words; for words declared are to bring people to it, and confessing God's goodness and love, as they are moved by the eternal God and his spirit. (p. 174)[25]

Fox's writings are awash in the poetic. Contrasting silence with the "wandering whirling tempestuous part of man," he seems to offer silence almost therapeutically. It is here that the distinction between the outer person and the inward light of "the spirit" comes to the fore. This aspect of silence involves worship; its use in helping discern God's direction for the community. In the Quaker tradition this communal undertaking is referred to as "an inward witness." Believers gather in silent attentiveness or meet for clearness to discern God's will for a particular Friend regarding personal direction.[26]

"Weighty Friends," those whose words are held in the highest regard, are those known for pursuing wisdom in attentive silence before they speak at all. In sum, under the umbrella of worship, Quakers believe that several positive ends could be reached through silence. First, silence evokes inspiration toward the higher good that occurs in the separation or discerning between "flesh and spirit." This is made manifest in gaining direction that emanates from the Divine versus human source. Additionally, as a socially codifying practice, silence helps move the community toward mutuality and the consensus-driven practice of faith and collective social action. Dependence upon God through the Inward Light is what strengthens the community as members collectively discuss whatever guidance emerges out of waiting together in silence. Finally, although the Quaker practice of silence is neither programmed nor formulaic, teaching takes place through modeling proper etiquette. Essentially, the members (Friends) learn from one another. Instead of depending upon one minister to convey wisdom, Quaker youth learn by observing their elders. They learn that silence is not to be feared, but that waiting for the Spirit to stir them into speech is necessary and normal. Sitting in the quiet together, learning to "wait on the Lord," helps the practice of deep, patient listening become a habit that spills over into the wider social sphere. Rather than launching into "many words" that are often reactionary or even incendiary, this practice teaches patience and moral development.

Exploring the nuance of Quaker silent worship may be helpful in ascertaining the place of silence in contemporary communication behavior, for in our busy world of information the need for grounding is increasingly pronounced. Although contemporary communication theorists are quite removed from that of George Fox and early Quaker practices, a closer look into their theology eliminates silence from being an abstraction. Here, silence becomes more than tacit knowledge, but transforms by application into a deeper understanding that listening skills may be taught by becoming more intentional about the practice of silence. Learning the discipline of silence as a foundation to intelligent, civil discourse is warranted and makes much sense, perhaps even for students at the elementary stage of their schooling. The benefits of silence and adjustment in this thinking might translate to new areas of training and emphasis in education, public discourse, and interpersonal relationships.

In some cases, silence goes beyond the interpersonal and becomes the salve that helps the oppressed survive, as in the story of a contemporary of George Fox—Madame Jeanne Marie Bouvier de la Motte Guyon.

JEANNE GUYON

During the same century that George Fox lived in England, a French woman of wealth and nobility learned the benefits of silence through a series of formidable sufferings, leading her to a practice of silence she called "the prayer of the heart." Jeanne Guyon (1648–1717), known in French history simply as Madame Guyon, found herself at the center of a political drama involving King Louis XIV and his efforts to keep Protestant Quietism from bleeding through the walls of the Roman Catholic Church.[27] Although Guyon did not profess Quietism, her experience of silent prayer caused suspicions to rise against her. Ultimately, although many avid supporters (including her cousin, François Fenelon, a high-ranking churchman) vouched for her orthodoxy, Guyon was accused of heresy and sentenced to prison by the King. Eventually, she was transferred to the Bastille and spent seven years there in isolation.

Her lengthy autobiography (1688) records the events of an unusually taxing life; a father who forced her into marriage when she was just fifteen to a man 23 years her senior; a sickly husband who assigned a maid to her every move so as to prevent her from even private moments of reflection and prayer; a church that refused to receive her voice as prophetic and turned her piety against her. Despite the historic drama involved in her story, it is the legacy of her shorter work, *Union with God* (1981), that remains most influential and widely read. The text, edited and revised from her publication in 1685, *A Short and Easy Method of Prayer*, has continued to inspire readers to find rest and peace in solitude and silence, and though relatively obscure, has appeared in various forms and editions over 300 years.

Part of the reason this devout woman's life took such a tumultuous turn is that Europe was still reeling from the rippling effect of the Protestant rebellion against Catholicism. France's King Louis XIV was especially attentive to any hint of Protestant infiltration in his court, and one of the chief bishops—Bossuet—read her work and decided it was treasonous to king and country. What was Guyon's crime? She was purposeful in prayer and advocated practicing prayer in silent communion with God—anywhere and everywhere. That is, one need not be in a cathedral to pray. Guyon never intended to write her method of prayer down. Rather, the books came in direct response to a query for deeper understanding. But her writing was ardent and regaled the freedom to commune with God in the depths of one's soul without the need of priest to mediate. Guyon wrote with passion about this experience and spoke with confidence in the ability to read and study scripture. However, her presuppositions about the simplicity of prayer and real connection with God through Christ were too radical for 18th-century France. Time and again she found herself embroiled in a religious-political upheaval not because she refuted any part of her Roman Catholic faith, but explicitly because she advocated a type of spiritual practice that encouraged others to pray in similar fashion. This "prayer of silence" was central to her experience and teachings.

The antithesis of speech and preaching, silence is surely not all that is necessary for spiritual formation but is a measure that one might pursue to seek a life of devotion and inward peace. It involves surrender and sacrifice, two aspects of spiritual discipline evident in most all world religions.

The road of silent prayer, however, is not to be undertaken lightly for many who have attempted to reckon with even an hour of total, undistracted quiet surely would agree: silence can be an awkward, menacing stalker. For Jeanne Guyon, laying hold of silence as a spiritual practice involves suffering, even a type of death. Certainly, this "death" is not physical, rather a separation of the soul from its own natural tendencies and desires. She explains:

> Everything born of the will of the flesh, everything that comes out of even the good will of man needs to be brought to complete death. When this happens, nothing but the will of God is left. When the old will has been completely extinguished, then God's will begins to take its place.[28]

Both the English translation and Guyon's original language make it difficult to understand that her meaning centers on cultivating a heart of complete devotion and surrender, even the surrender of one's power of speech. Guyon was not a martyr, nor did she express intent toward physical death or self-flagellation. Rather, instead of seeking a God who is out there somewhere, she engaged with the immanence of God and taught that one must be *willing* to suffer, sacrificing one's goals, preferences, dreams, and desires—even perceptions of self—at the altar of God's perfect will. Opting for silence instead of speech quashes the active life of the soul and, according to her simple method of prayer, allows God's work in the believer's life from a posture of quiet surrender.

Essentially, this posture opens one to new realizations and perhaps, even revelation. For this noble French woman, reckoning with the harsh terrain of interior silence was part of an inward journey that led to a state of communion with God to which the contemporary title of her book refers. How does this peace arise? How does one's life become transformed from tumultuous and tormented to one of quiet repose? Silence is the environment that clears space for God to speak. Use of many words to share the Gospel message places the emphasis on human speech and persuasion, but with the prayer of the heart Guyon draws the focus away from human effort and striving toward a Supreme Being who is holy and wholly able to draw open hearts to Himself. Nor is it striving that brings about the transformation of the soul; it is the Lord God who goes after the lost sheep. Here, she describes it further:

> The stages of this pilgrimage which bring the believer toward faith are each characterized by prayer that is an ever-ascending movement toward silence. That is, the powers of the soul gradually become totally quieted. The final stages of faith (prayer) are a complete secession of every tiny effort. (*Union* p. 68)

and

[Through, *sic*] . . . silence, this advanced believer lives in God and lives from God. It is by the silence of the soul that he communicates with God. A soul that is thus dead to its own working and to all provision of itself (that is, dead to its own workings and to all appropriate of the self-nature), to that soul, silence becomes both a wonderful transmission and receiving of Divine communication. (*Union* p. 73)

Here Guyon delves into the possibility of intimacy with God—a living God, one who responds, comforts, and strengthens; one who is the orienting principle or power in her life. This experience, juxtaposed to that of the masses in 17th-century Europe who walked through the rituals of Christianity and believed its tenants, but kept an intellectual distance from a true Presence of God, is implicit in her words. Through this communion, she receives, by extension, deeper, more fulfilling relationships with others.

Guyon's prayer of silence was a way of being in the world that helped her refuse to see herself as a victim or objectify the other. Instead of burying the pain of being oppressed, persecuted, rejected, or simply misunderstood, she endured and welcomed them as God's gift of transformation. Instead of wallowing in the anger of persecution and unjust treatment, she turned the pain of being misunderstood, falsely accused, and imprisoned into an opportunity to sink deeply down into the center of her being—that place that is beyond space and time. Her spirituality, based on what came to be called the "prayer of silence" relates well to our present discussion of the speech-silence dialectic.[29]

Her ideas about this type of prayer relate to the art of listening, and although they emerge from a posture of spirituality they are deeply entwined with the philosophical concept of dwelling. Embedded in the thinking of many theologians, philosophers, and communication theorists such as Martin Heidegger (1889–1976), Martin Buber (1878–1965), and Kenneth Burke (1897–1993), Guyon's focus on union with God underscores the need to develop –or uncover –a deeper sense of being. Like Heidegger whose *Being and Time* (1927) posits that being *is* time, practicing the prayer of the heart allows one to be fully present to the moment, thus fully alive. This is so not only of the self as one who is *present* in time, but of a Supreme Being who exists over and above time. For Guyon, silent prayer holds space for the transcendent. It reaches into time through the historicity of Jesus Christ, making room for God's active presence. The concept is not dissimilar to Buber's thoughts regarding the human longing for relation. His ideas were grounded in a deep belief in God as wholly Other, the primary relation. As he wrote in his classic *I and Thou*, "In the beginning is the relation—as the category of being, as readiness, as a form that reaches out to be filled, as a model of the soul; the *a priori* of relation; the innate You" (*I and Thou* p. 78). Though she lived centuries before the German philosopher, Guyon's experiences were predicated upon understanding that her life was "in relation." In her yearning for a living relationship with God, she grappled with similar themes.

The need to know oneself underpins the desire and need to know others. In this sense, one's inner voice might well be likened to an airplane runway that provides the necessary precursor to flight. Without calling it self-actualization, in acknowledging this interior place of being, Guyon connected with God and therein made peace with herself. Buber echoes the same when he writes: "The busy noise of the hour must no longer drown out the *vox humana*, the essence of the human which has become a voice. This voice must not only be listened to, it must be answered and led out of the lonely monologue into the awakening dialogue."[30] In this way, Guyon's silent practice of dwelling with God might also be construed as a type of intrapersonal communication, the foundation that establishes the necessary ground for the symbolic action in relationship.[31]

Jeanne Guyon's ideas beckon contemporary readers to reconcile her boldness of agency with the exhortation to practice silence. Though her voice was regularly quashed throughout childhood, marriage, and older adulthood, this French woman's words continue to resound today. Her paradoxical experience of steady interior peace and rest stands starkly against the backdrop of abject suffering and oppression, shedding light, as well, on what it means to be a woman whose muffled voice from the early 18th century survived. Out of the silence she speaks.

MEDIA ECOLOGY, DIGITAL CULTURE, AND LISTENING

The time in which Guyon wrote shared some similarities with this present age. Although she lived on the fringes of the early-modern era, it was also a time when the world stood on the precipice of major shifts in communication and culture. Gutenberg's printing press made it possible for ideas to spread rapidly through the dissemination of pamphlets and papers. Where once the rootedness of icon and image provided order and structure to the lives of the faithful, the Protestant use of the press created new ways of worship, upending many traditions. Reformers saturated Europe with all manner of theological pamphlets, biblical instruction, and printed word, calling into question the total dependence on, and once-indisputable need for, clergy.[32] As the printing press continued to take root, literacy advanced and more people began reading the scriptures on their own. The very notion of ecclesial authority was being shaken.[33] Other changes that proved disruptive to traditional cultural practices were also instigated by the new media, but it was the eruption and availability of so much new Gospel-centric information that created a rippling effect of monumental significance.

Today, the digital media environment is having an effect of similar intensity in the way daily life is conducted. Over 6 billion cell phones flicker with artificial light connecting us to each other in such a way that no aspect of culture remains untouched. From friendship, dating, and familial relationships to public policy, education, the church, and every other institution, the open access to information presents a vast terrain of opportunities as well as challenges (Lanier 2010; Ward, 2015). As a result of the growing embeddedness of a culture informed by digital technologies, the ensuing glut of information has also been instrumental in shaping a mode of being in the world that is antagonistic to peace and rest. In fact, since the telegraph and television, the pervasiveness of personal mobile media (PMM) has only expanded the psychological imbalance proposed by Neil Postman's information-action ratio (1985).[34] This tendency is partially due to what has been called "social saturation," a situation in which the average person is no longer able to attend to all the information required to properly manage their relationships (Gergen, 1991).[35] To counteract this glut of internal and external noise, a surge of attention to the physical and emotional benefits of silence is taking place.[36] Aps like "the pause" and "relaxx" are becoming popular because people "are desperate for silence," explains research director of the Global Wellness Institute Beth McGroarty.[37]

More recent studies continue to suggest that the heightened pace of the information age exacerbates the already high stress levels among those living in western cultures.[38] Other similarities exist as well. In some ways, the rich experience of community which once was commonplace in America has given way to what could be called hyper-individualism. Particularly in the West, this way of being in the world normalizes superficial relationships and is rapidly acculturating practices that exacerbate the frayed edges of traditional community, such as sending out flares of birthday and funeral acknowledgments through text-messaging and social media rather than planning a face-to-face gathering. Ironically, as much as the printing press may have helped to create the concept of an individual, PMM seem to be taking us to a new level, one that thrusts us into hyper-individualism and isolation. Noted environmental activist and conservationist Bill McKibben observes the same, saying: "The past five hundred years have elevated us to the status of individuals and reduced us to the status of individuals. At the end of the process, that's what we are—empowered, enabled, isolated, disconnected individuals."[39] This disconnection does not make for peace or rest, nor does it build essential community.

Additional cultural factors emerge as a result of the new media environment and by no means are they restricted to the spiritual or religious aspects of silence, nor do they necessarily warrant a wrangling with contemplative prayer. However, the key figures mentioned in this chapter provide a brief look into the way the speech/silence dialectic might address all manner of social ills and conundrums. For example, the enlarged circle of influence and vast openness made possible by today's rapid advance of technology has created an "always-on" mentality that is growing, creating added stress and busyness to the average American life.[40] This phenomenon requires attention, not just adaptation. Busyness is not going away. It does not appear as though the waters of information will recede. We would be remiss not to ask ourselves, "Is this sustainable?" Perhaps incorporating a rhythm of solitude and silence into our lives will create a measure of protection against the onslaught.

MIT professor Sherry Turkle confronts this very issue with concern about the dangers of losing both a healthy sense of self and close social relationships because of the new value our culture has placed on the ability to multi-task.[41] A part of this problem involves not the occasional busy day, but a switch in mentality. Our new tools create an environment that allows multitasking, and ultimately favors it. Turkle bemoans the change in attitude about multitasking and wonders if we are using our digital media to our own disadvantage: "Subtly, over time, multitasking, once seen as something of a blight, was recast as a virtue. And over time, the conversation about its virtues became extravagant, with young people close to lionized for their ability to do many things at once."[42] No longer do we resist the alluring taunt of always-on media; we seem to have given ourselves over to it as inevitable. What is perhaps even more concerning is that "we bend to the inanimate with new solicitude."[43] Canadian journalist, Michael Harris concurs and has written an entire volume addressing this, particularly the way the pace and busyness of the average person living in America eliminates room for the "absence" of activity. Without a reserve of solitude, important human attributes such as unstructured play, day-dreaming, and personal reflection become superfluous and will fade from experience. Harris explains that "[s]olitude may cause discomfort, but that discomfort is often the healthy and inspiring sort."[44]

The value of silence as a public good is clear as well. Its presence creates breath, gives room for pause and reflection, and supports human flourishing on many levels. When used well and intentionally, a greater possibility exists for human compassion and caring to emerge. Used in this positive sense, silence helps create inner balance which allows for more thoughtful speech. There, out of the center of one's being lies the often-dormant motivation to actualize the good. The inclination to uphold human dignity and work toward a common good becomes a greater possibility. Though these positive motivations are not guaranteed, without this type of generative silence there is little place for meaningful, spirit-infused speech to arise.

The need for such space and time to breathe, and simply *be*, has perhaps never been more evident. The cry for personal space to reflect and rest is growing. Silence gives us a way to apprehend its benefits, letting the dense, low-hanging clouds of information pass by. Through this brief look at the use of silence in religious contexts, the need for silence begins to sharpen. Apprehending silence may take a great deal of intentionality, but as an antidote to the noisy din of our busy, technological age is invaluable and necessary to creating inner equanimity of all persons. As well, without a strong dose of silence the promise of healthy, rigorous dialogue shrinks. Regular intervals of silence support intentional listening, a necessary component to effective communication. Immersed in this age of digitality we would do well to check ourselves: Do our words flow forth from the depths of being, waiting patiently until language, appropriate and meaningful, emerges from a reflective process? This is difficult enough to achieve when community ties are strong and relationships are anchored in respect and the strength of face-to-face communication, but this ideal is even more challenging in an environment where polarized speech and incivility reign.

NOTES

1. Constantine became Emperor in 323 and soon after began to Christianize the pagan temples by outlawing their existence and turning them all into houses of Christian worship. Now, instead of being fed to the lions, burned, and undergoing so many other persecutions for their faith, Christians could worship God freely, without fear of condemnation. On the other hand, because it was politically advantageous to be a Christian, many came to the religion of Christianity without coming to a living faith or sharing in the values and practices of Jesus-followers. These Desert Dwellers wished to avoid this temptation and sought a simpler life of vibrant faith in the barren deserts of Egypt.

2. The credulity of Constantine's faith is contestable to this day. Although there is much evidence that he made a confession of faith, there is equal evidence that he professed his faith to gain favor with the growing population of Christians and overall political clout.

3. Owen Chadwick. *Western Asceticism*. p. 40.

4. While this seems the most credible account, there are conflicting stories about the legitimacy of the Desert Fathers as Christians. Some historians claim that it was only the first group who fled to the desert that were Christian; that those who followed were being persecuted because they did not take on Constantine's political policies and become Christians. There are even those who decry the existence of St. Anthony, the most well known of the Desert Fathers. The Desert Fathers were the inspiration for many groups that followed including the Rule of St. Benedict, the Hesychasm movement (those who sought quiet, tranquility, and stillness), the

Pietists of 17th century who evolved from early Lutheranism, and many other types of Christian mystics.

5. In a small, spiritually oriented discussion of contemplation and silence in the 1957 *The Silent Life*, Merton framed the life of a monk as a completely non-utilitarian, but necessary, presence in a world that is transfixed on efficiency and progress. He acknowledges the lack of resonance most westerners experience when considering the monastic life, explaining, "In a materialistic culture which is fundamentally irreligious the monk is incomprehensible because he 'produces' nothing" (p. 10).

6. See Henri Nouwen. *Genessee Diary*. p. 134.

7. See Thomas Merton. *Thoughts in Solitude*. p. 77.

8. See David Runcorn. *Center of Quiet*. p. 100.

9. See Thomas Merton. *Contemplative Prayer*. p 10.

10. Ibid. *The Silent Life*. p. 12

11. This is one of the things that made Merton such an unusual monk. He was a contemplative, practicing silence readily, but also an activist.

12. Discussed at greater length in chapter 2, *La Technique* is that element of the infrastructure in all institutions that values efficiency more than ethical responsibility. It is there, unseen and at work, and is somewhat akin to a computer's processing system that allows individuals to use the hardware.

13. Jacques Ellul. *Humiliation of the Word*.

14. Thomas Merton, 1957. *The Silent Life*.

15. Thomas Merton. *The Silent Life*.

16. Benedict is known as the Father of Western Monasticism. Born in the late 5th century A.D., his contemplative practices ultimately came to be known as the "Rule of Benedict." Although the Benedictine monks are not required to take a vow of silence, they incorporate silence into their daily rituals. Their communities are shaped by silence.

17. The Italian word for "poor man," a moniker given to Francis by many of his earliest followers and biographers.

18. See Julian Green. *God's Fool*. p. 88.

19. See Julian Green. *God's Fool*. p. 168

20. All italicized words or phrases in the Quaker texts will signify my own emphasis.

21. The importance of the "inward light" to Quaker thought and practice cannot be overemphasized. Essentially, this light reflects the foundation of Quaker belief, pointing to the active presence of God within each believer. For in-depth treatment of the Inward Light, see the 1972 work of Michael Graves. "The Rhetoric of the Inward Light: An Examination of Extant Sermons Delivered by Early Quakers, 1671–1700." Dissertation.

22. See Michael Graves. *Early Quaker Writings*. p. 211.

23. According to the Friends General Conference located in Philadelphia, PA, there are approximately 35,000 active Quakers in the U.S.

24. See Graves. "Plea."

25. This information is based on records from the 1996 NEH Summer Institute, located in the Haverford library. The discussion about Quakers and Ritual took place at Lehigh University and records the way in which George and Margaret (Fell) Fox

traveled to homes and "eldered." Their lack of enthusiasm for traditional modes of religious behavior such as "much speech," pastors, hierarchy, and "outer things" that would distract worshippers did not preclude the Foxes from forming monthly meetings where new believers could be taught the Quaker way of life. In other words, some form and structure was established as normative. Speaking, particularly, in the form of preaching, was equally normative. Silence was used explicitly for seeking divine guidance (or "the Inward Light") and as a means by which the faithful might ultimately speak truth and wisdom when it was time to speak.

26. The Friends General Conference (FGC) is the official, organizing association of governance of the Quakers in America. [July 27, 2020] https://www.fgcquaker.org/resources/clearness-committees-what-they-are-and-what-they-do.

27. Quietism was a movement that posed a threat to late 17th century France and surrounding Roman Catholic countries because those practicing it emphasized interior quiet over outward works of service. The Pope, along with many of the Royals, believed the direct access to God through prayer would minimize their authority with the people.

28. Jeanne Guyon. *Union.* p. 54.

29. Jeanne Guyon, author of *Union with God, Christ Our Revelation, Experiencing the Depths of Jesus Christ*, countless studies of books of the Bible, and her own spiritual biography, *Spiritual Torrents*, was a French noblewoman who lived and wrote at the intersection of the 17th and 18th centuries. Her voice was outwardly suppressed by a much older, oppressive husband who forbade her to pray. Ultimately, this led her to experience a type of solitude that was enriched by silent prayer, a method for which she became known and sought as mentor.

30. Robert Anderson, Kenneth Cissna, and Ronald Arnett. *The Reach of Dialogue.* p. 308.

31. See Kenneth Burke for more complete treatment of this concept. *Language as Symbolic Action.*

32. Jennifer Powell McNutt. "Robust Instruction: John Calvin's Institutes of the Christian Religion." *Christian History* 116 (2015). pp. 28–32.

33. Jennifer McNutt. "Robust Instruction." p. 29.

34. See Neil Postman. *Amusing Ourselves to Death.* "Information Action Ratio." pp. 68–72. Postman developed this idea in reference to the telegraph. It was the first time in history that information glut became a problem. As information became increasingly dislodged from an anchored community, the result was a loss of social potency and a sense of disconnection.

35. Kenneth J. Gergen. *The Saturated Self.* pp. 30–45; Harris, 2014

36. Pew Research Center (January 15, 2015). Internet, Science, and Technology [retrieved: January 2, 2016 http://www.pewinternet.org/2015/01/15/social-media-and-stress/].

37. See Moreen Benoit. March 12, 2021. "Silence Emerges as a Way to Boost Health." [April 24, 2021] https://www.wsj.com/articles/silnce-emerges-as-a-way-to-boost-health-11615478413?st=xfqae7wkytzl&reflink=article_email_share.

38. American Psychological Association [January 2, 2016] http://www.apa.org/news/press/releases/stress/2012/generations.aspx; Washington, DC. 2016.

39. See Bill McKibben. *Enough*. pp. 46–48.

40. In a survey conducted prior to the pandemic of 2020, the American Psychological Association reported that stress was on the increase in every age bracket. Millennials (ages 18 to 33) and genXers (ages 34 to 47) reported the highest levels of stress. Older Americans also report stress levels that are higher than normal. https://www.apa.org/news/press/releases/stress/2012/generations#:~:text=While%20Millennials%20(ages%2018%20to,of%20Americans%2C%20regardless%20of%20age.

41. Sherry Turkle. *Alone Together: Why We Expect More from Technology and Less from Each Other*. New York: Basic Books. 2012. p. xii.

42. Sherry Turkle, *Alone Together.* p. 162.

43. Sherry Turkle, *Alone Together.* p. xii.

44. Michael Harris. *The End of Absence*. p. 48.

Chapter 3

Attentive Silence

Years ago, I read a book called *Listening to Your Life* by the essayist Frederick Buechner. Even before I delved into the book the title struck me powerfully. Listen to *my* life? I could *listen* to my life? What could that mean? The profound impact of the title hit me at the same period in my life that I was beginning to reckon with silence. It was 1990 and a growing anxiety was arising in my life, one in which I questioned the worth of my work as a magazine journalist as well as the wider purposes of my life. I wondered if I was investing my time wisely. Where did the poet in me go? What happened to the songwriter? Would I ever find actual fulfillment writing as a music journalist or was it more important to pursue the less lucrative but more creative aspects of a writer's life? Countless others before me have grappled with thoughts of purpose, art, leisure, and work; that was nothing new. But there I was in the midst of my own inner wrestling match, not realizing that I was headed into a period of transformative silence that would eventually lead me away from journalism into a deeper study of silence and its many facets.

Learning to listen to one's own life is but one of the many-faceted benefits of silence, albeit an extremely important one, and part of the foundational work necessary to move forward into action. Its benefits include separating wisdom from folly. In life choices concerning relationships, one's calling and purpose, and direction—discernment is needed. Where does it come from? It may require putting the pen down for a while, stepping away from public conversation, or taking a break from the platform. Whether it is the small circle of influence in our personal lives or a larger, more public forum, taking a break from the crowd to listen to the internal voice of one's own life is a part of attentive silence. It takes bravery to move from what is often empty, vacuous chatter toward the hope of more meaningful and effective communication with others, and that . . . is just the beginning.

LISTENING AND CULTURAL SANITY

Listening is the heart of communication. It involves attending to what is said and "reading" the other through multiple nonverbal cues. And, if communication is about meaning-making, meaning is hardly possible without the regular assistance of the demure sister of Speech, *Silence*. Silence is the necessary pause in a lively conversation, helping each of the discussion partners to digest and dwell on what was just said. She is a salve to the barrage of words flung in irrational rage and stands heads-above the pelleting of expletives and wild rants of a disordered heart. A cacophonous flurry of words can overtake the most patient among us. When such an outburst happens conversation ceases, and loss of meaning is just the beginning of a downward spiral that has the potential to land in violence. The steady ticking away of unreflective, vacuous words littering a conversational space can drive one to the point of insanity. It is there that non-judgmental silence may prove to be a needed barrier to the demise of rationality.

Without attentive silence, listening is reduced to auditory functionality. Auditory function is necessary, but it is not enough to make meaning or maintain relationship. Allowing one's self to forget the importance of listening is extremely easy. This may be truer today than in perhaps any other era simply because of the glut of information available through Internet search engines and the ease with which we can access it. Unfortunately, the helpful speed and access work against measured words and reasoned thinking. It is easy—all too easy—to lose touch with what is real and right and reasonable.

Sane people are those who are in touch with reality. A life that is grounded in what is real is intricately interwoven with the language used to communicate. However, this surely does not mean human imagination is held at bay. Reckoning with reality does not dismiss the esoteric musings of a harpist contemplating her next heavenly note or the value of being momentarily mesmerized by the particular shade of blue in a late October sky. These examples are very much a part of the necessary and creative imagination of human beings. What I refer to here as reality is the necessity of dealing with life as it unfolds in one's daily doings: cooking, cleaning, personal hygiene, working through conflict in the home, dealing with bad drivers, navigating office politics, and the countless other realities that ensconce each person's life. All of these require a strong grasp of reality. Without language to ascribe meaning, our ability to properly perceive reality and cope with it diminishes. The result is that reason begins to erode. When reason is lost, we risk losing our sanity. Holding on to sanity means being well grounded in reality. Laying hold of the truth that exists between what appears to be real and what is actually real requires regular wrangling with our own perceptions along with a deep willingness to listen to others. As noted ethicist David Gill explains, "We need a balance of quiet and sound, of thinking and conversation, of listening and speaking, of time alone and time with others."[1]

The necessity of reasoned conversation grounded in reality spills easily over from the equilibrium of the individual to the society, for what holds true for the individual holds true for the culture and listening is at the very heart of the issue.

Many bemoan the state of affairs in global and national politics as a time when no one is listening to each other. We are speaking at each other rather than with each other. Referring to the current state of public discourse, a steady refrain of concern and angst echoes throughout the land in increasing volume: "This is *insanity*!" "What's the matter with this world?" "It's a crazy time!" Claims of lunacy, accusations of idiocy, and the regular use of ugly expletives have become widespread, creating hostility instead of an environment friendly to public conversation. Exactly what do those decrying this debased state of affairs mean when spouting such words of woe? Clearly, we humans have long suffered under our own inability to communicate well. Dare we actually call it a type of insanity? The underlying issues that foment such exclamatory language are many, but essentially, the "insanity" of our times is not a referent to the rise in mental health issues. Much more simply, it means that not much makes sense anymore. A nation that was built on reasoned discourse, open debate, and a mutual desire for the common good appears to be in a moment of rapidly devolving discourse. Hope for true dialogue seems hardly possible, and it is, without the first major ingredient –the *will to listen.* Thus, the starting place for dialogue must be in a willingness to listen, to employ all faculties of hearing and attention; but proper auditory function is only the beginning. Ability to listen is rather simple for most, as long as auditory function is stable, but not quite as simple is the willingness to listen. While many rational, reasonable people would consider themselves good listeners, willingness is more than just choosing to let the other speak. Listening *well* is a matter of intention, focus, and perseverance.

FOCUS, PERSEVERANCE, INTENTIONALITY

In an age such as the present one it is most difficult to maintain focus for there are distractions everywhere. We carry our cares in our pockets via smart phones and often accomplish our work while doing three things at once. Perseverance in listening is even more of a challenge. Even some of the most gracious people turn their attention away from someone with whom they disagree without even a start at listening. It is especially difficult to stay open and persevere if listening to the speaker pontificating or drawing conclusions from unsubstantiated facts. It is intentionality though, that makes all the difference in listening and is, perhaps, its most challenging aspect.

Intentionality begins with asking ourselves, "why." Why am I listening? What is the purpose? What is my goal in listening? Assessing the listening goal is important, for differing goals warrant different tools. We must ask ourselves, do I listen empathically to foster relationship, or do I listen to gain information or fodder for a proper retort? Listening as a partner in debate, for example, requires a different ordering of communicational priorities than listening as a conversational partner. The same is true when listening therapeutically. A counselor must listen without judgment to encourage the client to continue speaking. This is quite different from listening enthusiastically to one's favorite jazz playlist.

There are many valid reasons to make listening a priority, but the one that supersedes all listening goals is a simple and genuine respect for the speaker. The misunderstanding that keeps so many of us from hearty, fruitful conversation is the notion that respect for the other is synonymous with respect for their ideas. Respect for the speaker does not infer agreement or respect for the message. Everyone desires to be respected for who they are. It is a natural part of our humanness to want to be heard and understood, yet too often forget that the other wants (*and needs*) the same. In the last chapter we discussed the many distractions that impede our ability to communicate well and meaningfully. Living in a technological society makes it more difficult to listen well, but there are ways to improve our listening skills. To start, we must address the challenges involved with focus, and that means managing both internal and external distractions. External distractions are more obvious than internal distractions, but both must be addressed. While internal distractions may be even more critical to manage, both types are identified as noise. Noise—even if it is welcomed—gets in the way of healthy conversations; each type must somehow be addressed and filtered.

NOISE

There are several elements to include in the definition of internal noise. One involves the individual ability to properly register nonverbal symbols. Misunderstanding easily happens when nonverbal cues are missing and the extra time it takes to interpret meaning becomes internal noise, particularly when using email or the text feature of one's mobile phone. Another involves the presence of audible sounds that arise in our immediate (external) environment. Some may be pleasant, others perhaps not, but each diminish the ability to concentrate on one's internal dialogue and cognition. External sound becomes internal noise when it diminishes one's ability to cogitate, or properly "think something through." The other aspect of internal noise is closely related and involves any internal interference with cognition, such as worry, daydreaming, preoccupation with dinner plans or yesterday's faculty meeting. This is internal noise; it gets in the way of one's ability to process and respond meaningfully in an interpersonal exchange.

In formal studies of interpersonal listening, it is clear that listening is a process involving "attending to" the sound of a voice. Competing noises and sounds hinder the listener from comprehension, reflection, and thoughtful response. In listening studies, focus is a necessary element of the listening process which is very close to the term "mindfulness." Mindfulness takes place when one focuses on what is happening in the present moment. It is part of the overarching communicative process that utilizes reflective listening. This is particularly important to note as increased levels of ambient sound become regular features of interpersonal settings in the digital age. For example, when multiple communicative acts are taking place simultaneously (as is often the case in digital environments), the noise from one conversation easily bleeds into the other. One may be working on a research paper at the computer screen with a dialogue box open to converse with a friend, while also listening to music and checking the auction prices on one of the many online commerce sites. Beeps and bings, pop-up messages, advertisements—even the faint hum and rustle of equipment—register on the brain as noise. Although it has an amazing capacity to filter unwanted information, the human brain must focus in order to fully engage in message-making. Without it, there is confusion instead of coherence. This underscores the need for becoming intentional about finding a quiet location to converse, particularly considering the many previously noted noise distractions associated with PMM.[2]

The sound of another's voice brings something new and fresh into a text-based conversation. This is so for multiple reasons. Walter Ong (1982) suggests that sound has a special relationship to time unlike that of other fields that register in human sensation (p. 31). He explains that "sound only exists when it is going out of existence" (pp. 31–32). If that premise is true, one may wonder how the average person can maintain conversational coherence or adapt at all to a communicational or semantic environment that is "always on"—blinking, buzzing, interrupting, and receiving information, often from multiple sources simultaneously. The tremendous filtering ability of the brain is a key factor in the ongoing success of the survival of humanity, so adapt, we will. Yet, to simply survive extinction is not synonymous with human flourishing and the maintaining of communities of cooperation. Issues of internal and external noise are problematic in that they hinder the quality and ability to listen and maintain healthy, strong, and durable relationships. This is further illustrated by referring to the work of Canadian composer and author R. Murray Schaefer. His seminal project, *The Tuning of the World* (1977), focused on the lo-fi "white noise" brought about by the industrial revolution. White noise is a result of equipment hum, cars, trains, and other external sounds that (often) become subconscious distractions. Similarly, today's multiple media choices and use have become a type of white noise. They are always there. They function in the background. This background exists in addition to the actual sounds of the personal mobile media that distract from focused listening in interpersonal exchanges. Thus, as PMM are increasingly used and the general public continues to filter the many ongoing distractions to listening, the "white noise" does not diminish but only increases as the techno-industrial elements of the current environment advance.

In spite of the fact that general usage of PMM occurs in a variety of ways from infrequently to constantly and that usage is not uniform, it may be said that extraneous "noise" is more prevalent today than in the past. Indications of this trend are found throughout popular culture, journalist's reports, and the work of organizations such as the American Society for Acoustic Ecology. News outlets in the United States and throughout the globe have broadly reported on the social annoyances of too much noise. In one BCC report called "The Right to Silence" by Duncan Walker, Brits are involved in an ongoing public debate concerning people using cell phones inappropriately. Hoping to adopt the French solution of "jamming the signals" in public places, Walker queried the readership, "The infuriating ring of someone else's mobile blights many a night out at the cinema or theatre. France has decided to jam phone signals to allow audiences to enjoy shows in silence—could the UK follow suit?" (Walker, 2004).[3]

Examples of similar frustrations may be found in communication behavior using older media, as well. It is not unusual for many to have in-person conversations with the radio or television blaring. An example that reflects more the current media environment is the common practice of two people driving separate cars while conversing via cell phone or sending a text message, both trying to navigate traffic signals and ambient sounds while simultaneously listening to their car radios or digital playlist. While the distraction factor of multiple media use is not new, the sheer cumulative effect of newer media use in this way may lead, over time, to a kind of thinking and behavior that limits internal silence regardless of how "quiet" the context may be in any given situation.

Surely, there is a necessary equilibrium to be reached in managing the tension between speech and silence, one that is dependent upon many variables, such as individual conversational style, intellect, personality, fluctuating stress level, physical health, and emotional well-being. The dialectical relationship of speech and silence also is only one of the many polarized tensions that must be managed by human beings in relationship with other human beings (Montgomery and Baxter, 1996). However, in the current media environment, it may be much more difficult to manage these variables effectively. Scott (1979) explains that just as "the spirit of light and dark reaches far back in the history of human consciousness," so does the conceptualization and interdependence of speech and silence as communicative functions also affect human consciousness and the way people think about themselves and others (Scott, 1979, p. 108). This point is integral to the rationale for a study of silence, for as these technological changes continue to unfold, the new mediated environment begins to demand its use simply by the disappearance of other options. This trend mandates that a scholarly process of observation, description, analysis, and evaluation be applied to the aspects of everyday conversation occurring in interpersonal settings. There is much interdisciplinary work to be done.

Just as in the past, many today spend hours speaking via phone, both on cell phones, smart phones, and once in while an old-fashioned landline. In any given setting, much of this talk-time is dedicated to developing relationship. In fact, it may be argued that the very portability of personal mobile media has made relationship development and maintenance easier through the availability of instant connections. Whereas in the past the intent or desire to "connect" throughout the day may have been present, today's cell phones and other wireless devices create an ease and convenience that was not there in the past. Ease, however, does not automatically constitute effectiveness. Listening, which has been found to be essential to effective communication, is not enhanced through these media. The ease and convenience of digital devices cannot be denied, but the countervailing problems that present themselves with increased connection also seem evident. Among these are conversations that often are more superficial. Part of the reason for this is the lack of an anchored environment; exchanges occurring via PMM take place in problematic settings (i.e., public places, cars) and often "on the fly." Over time, the strength of communication skills and ensuing relational richness may be compromised, particularly as the mobility factor becomes the default means of conversation. Conversations utilizing these media may or may not lead to deeper relationships; this remains to be seen. However, it is not outside the range of reason to imagine that screen mediated conversations may ultimately do the opposite of what is claimed, that is, they may work against the depth, breadth, and duration of interpersonal relationships. What *is* clear is that the many missing nonverbal communication cues are only part of the denigrating influence of PMM upon quality interpersonal communication. Attentive listening requires more than the constant connection and immediacy that PMM allow.

Without the ability to listen, or if listening is thwarted by any of the above hindrances, the possibility for meaningful interpersonal communication decreases, for without the means to process and interpret what is being said the listener's silent role as co-creator of meaning is denigrated. The growing number of distractions as people increasingly converse on-the-run in all spheres of individuals' lives—work, recreation, etc., particularly in highly mediated cultures like the United States—seem to be taken for granted as essential. Interruptions, broken thought, and fragmented conversations are becoming the norm in communication behavior, particularly for heavy users of PMM. Empirical evidence of this phenomenon is limited but growing.

EMEDIA FAST

In my own 16-year study of student responses to silence, the findings are clear in several areas and still uncertain in many others.[4] I began this study in 2004. As the years have progressed the outcome has revealed interesting results. After asking students to "fast" from digital media for a period of 24 hours, and then write about their experience, this group of equally mixed men and women between the ages of 18 and 25 continue to point out the difficulty in staying "off" their computers and personal mobile media. But, in removing some of these impediments to listening many of the students participating in the study are animated in their response, describing their experiences as life-changing. Both positive and negative, these responses suggest strong association between personal mobile media, well-being, and social identity.

The assignment specifications allowed students to go about their normal business, spending time with others or in solitude. Their only limitation was to intentionally avoid electronic or digital media. One 20-year-old male named John describes his experiment as feeling

> lost in solitude; I spent time reflecting on my insecurities. It was very anxiety-producing. My natural inclination would be to run away from unpleasant thoughts, but today I decided to let them stay. It was difficult. Soft whispers of insecurity became loud. My brain acted as a battleground, a place where positivity and doubt met to brawl it out. I came out victorious with a better understanding of my fears and insecurities. It was mentally and emotionally exhausting, but I am better for the experience. I was able to go to a place I would not be able had I not been in solitude.

Many responses reflected similar feelings and language used to describe the experience of willingly facing silence for the first time.

Increasingly, and particularly over the last 5 years of the experiment, students mention how difficult it is to function without their smart phones and other computing devices. Yet, almost without exception these same students express something that changed once they traversed beyond the first 6–10 hours without their digital devices. This response from a 21-year-old male who was at first "afraid" to go out without his phone is similar to the experience of numerous others. He wrote:

> I've been going with Jane for 2 and a half years. We're super close and plan to get married. She knew I was bummed about spending the day without my cellphone and was kind enough to say she'd keep me company for the day, so we packed a lunch, got our [surf]boards, journals and towels and headed down to the beach. I thought it was going to be a hard day but what ended up happening is that it was one of the best days of my life. We spent the whole afternoon swimming, talking, writing in our journals, sharing some poetry we each had written (I didn't even know she wrote poetry!). I can't believe how much closer we became just spending the time actually *with* each other. It was like we passed through some threshold of closeness that day.

Other responses told a similar tale, while not typically as dramatic. Some focused on what was lost. Others focused on what was gained. This, from 19-year-old Joyce, noticed the silence. She wrote,

> steering clear of media created so much silence, and the silence forced my mind to race. My thoughts seemed to clear, like never before. At the beginning of the day, I found myself lost in the silence, but as the day continued, I used that silence to my benefit. I filled that space journaling, reading . . . doing things that I normally use the excuse of "not having enough time for."

Simon, 22-year-old male, wrote:

> There were times of boredom, where I just wanted to fill myself with some form of entertainment. There were times of great conversation with my girlfriend, where I realized that I haven't really had time to talk in a while without noise. There were times of great reflection, where I prayed;, read, listened, and just thought. I gained a little insight into myself after the fast. I realized that I waste a lot of time.

In each response to "how you spent your time," students most often referred to the presence of silence.

Twenty-year-old Kayla explains:

> The most valuable lesson in this whole experiment is that I really need to take time out for myself. I used to think that going online, listening to my iPod was

time well spend alone, but I was wrong. I need time to think about things I want to change about myself and my life and being consumed by the media has not helped me. When the earbuds are in my ear or the television is on I am distracted from my inner thoughts.

Along with self-awareness, the fresh and unexpected presence of silence allowed the students to increase in their awareness and attentiveness to their environment and other people. Their listening increased and this attentive listening set the tone for a richer experience.

Along with the saturation of these media and exponential increase in distractions, the text-based environment of the Internet in the last two decades has served to foster the "short cut" mentality in speech and writing. This is particularly so in the common mode of communication through cell phones known as text-messaging, or "texting." Use of acronyms, emoticons, and what might be called "Internet language" such as IMHO (in my humble opinion), LOL (laugh out loud), BFN (bye for now), DMM (Direct message me), etc., each represent part of the growing, reductionist trend of language. Truncating language in such ways by using substitutionary signs and symbols for letters, words, and phrases creates even more complexity in the communication process. What's more, attentive listening is further comprised simply by such lack of precise language and missing nonverbal cues.

In terms of conversation itself, many variables impede the flow and salience of it, including distractions. Some of the variables are completely human (personality- or mood-driven), such as lack of interest or one party being pressed for time. As previously mentioned, others are fostered by the technologies themselves, such as the fact of distance. When interlocutors are not communicating in close physical proximity, the burden to make up for missing communication cues and hindrances to listening can grow tiresome, or listening may be perceived as less important.

Where there is desire for meaningful conversation, the distractions may be more subtle or hidden. When interlocutors are engaging in speech with little time or desire for conversation, very often the distractions will not even be noticed. It is in the nature of human beings to adapt to our environment, and there are myriad ways one can adapt to external noise or any other distraction. However, as Rhodes contends, there are specific "behaviors that will prevent understanding from taking place including ceasing communication, responding irrelevantly, responding in a confused manner, or doing just the opposite of what is required—in other words, not listening effectively" (Rhodes, 1993, p. 230). To listen effectively requires desire to listen, willingness to listen, and a general comprehension that listening is a worthy endeavor. Today's media environment, so heavily immersed in mobile communication capabilities, is not conducive to these listening goals. While this does not mean that listening well cannot (or will not) occur, using these media as a regular means to communicate does work against that ideal.

When words are filling our mouth and thoughts swirling in our busy mind, it is easy to forget the importance of listening. Taking a break from others, from our media, from our work, and going to a quiet place is not a radical step, but one that is atypical for most busy people in the West. Unless one is a monk or unusually situated in contemplative practices, it is unlikely that the choice to quiet one's self in intentional solitude will be made, yet these practices have been shown to help in listening. One of the reasons for this is, as mentioned previously, we are living in a world that is saturated with words and images. We are in the information age, and there never seems to be enough time to take it all in. But taking a break from the work-a-day world helps create a space for our listening and will help set a tone for bringing our listening "best practices" to others.

Just as there is a listening that can be defined as "attentive," so there exists an attentive silence. According to Robert Bolton (1990), this type of silence helps foster conversational coherence because through it the listener gives "the speaker time to think about what he is going to say and thus enables him to go deeper into himself. It gives a person space to experience the feelings churning within."[5] In this way, silence plays a key role in the process of listening, one that is far from synonymous with passivity. Silence is a choice, one that supports a decision to become more intentional about listening. Sometimes silence is the most fortuitous element in an intimate conversation, and often a most worthy option when dealing with conflict. When silence isn't an integral part of conversation, open discussion can quickly dissolve into words devoid of reason and laced with irrationality. Bollnow (1982) discusses his perception of silence as "wordless agreement," but goes much further to address the essence of silence by describing it as behavior that "consists in not intervening straight-aways, but of simply standing to one side with a certain understanding smile" (p. 45). What a lovely image. Through it, he explores the need for people to communicate in ways that are deeper than words, suggesting, "Where people understand each other's inmost thoughts no words are necessary, they can sit together in silence and precisely in this mutual silence have the sensation of belonging together" (p. 44).[6] The implication here is that this communicational dynamic is virtually lost in today's media environment, and if it is not lost entirely, it is on the path to becoming a lost art.

Returning to the speech/silence dialectic, Bollnow (1982) infers a deep connection between relational richness and this type of affirming or *knowing* silence, one that is served by conversation, as well. Throughout his work he explores the need for reflection in conversation and discusses the way interpersonal communication gradually becomes more profound as listener and speaker interact to gain clarity and definition. The importance of this type of dialogue cannot be underestimated. It threads throughout marriages, friendships, business relationships, religious communities, and the neighborhood. The need for this form of silence to establish a strong dialogical foundation is clear in Bollnow's thesis.

> Genuine fulfilled silence only sets in after an intensively conducted conversation; for the inwardness that is essential to silence is only achieved through conversation—though admittedly there are other ways of achieving this inwardness, for example though exercises in self-oblivion or quiet mediation, even if this kind of quietness could hardly be called silence. A person when alone is not silent. One can only remain silent in company with another or even though this is more difficult with several others. But it would be wrong to describe this silence as a deficient form of speech, i.e., as a lack of something, whilst genuine silence means a fulfillment that transcends speech. (p. 46)

The frustration many feel in attempts to create space for hearty conversation occurs for a variety of reasons but often because the semantic environment is untethered to space and/or time. Meeting synchronously in a Zoom environment locates all participants at a given point in time, but spatially spread throughout numerous environments. The fluctuation of time and space within each person's perception creates a wobbly ground for conversational coherence. What is happening in the background can be distracting to either or both participants. Is a cat, for instance, creeping across a shelf in the background of a co-worker in Europe while the co-worker in Canada is distracted by their children's voices in another room? To address this spatial instability, one must first understand the depth of change the new media environment brings, and work to be proactive in wrangling the changes toward more solid ground in order to minimize communication breakdown. The media ecology in which conversation is today so deeply embedded was addressed in the last chapter but warrants discussion of several key areas that intersect with relational richness and interpersonal strength. These are: respect, deep listening, and intentionality.

- *Respect* for the other is essential in any conversation, but it is critical when it comes to relationality. Relational listening is connected to silence and the mutual give-and-take in a conversation. It will be addressed more specifically in chapter 6.
- *Deep listening* to the other without preconceived ideas or judgments about what they will say or mean is another way to frame dialogic listening. In chapter 6 we delve more fully into dialogic listening and its ethical implications.

- *Intentionality* involves attitude. It is the "why" of listening. To become more effective communicators we ask ourselves, "What is the goal of listening?" We then can make more intelligent decisions about where our conversations will take place, what channel will be used, and what words are necessary. Intentionality creates a foundational grounding and the necessary commitment to move further up the road toward dialogue. Without the strong intention to maintain this place of mutuality, efforts to conduct conversations that bring insight and healing largely come to naught, and more easily slip through the cracks of civility.

Many more communicational goods are needed to strengthen the cords of civil discourse, but if we are to rise up to higher levels of civility in public conversation, and continue to pursue healthy democracy, these three are the precursors necessary. Without them, meaningful communication is not possible. Social media can be used to help keep family and friends connected on a superficial level, but these platforms are not conducive to true dialogue. In fact, is probably best to exclude social media from the setting for any hopeful dialogue. While there, use language sparingly and economically. By refraining from contributing to a weighty conversation on social media we practice silence and remove the risk of sabotaging an important conversation off-line.[7]

Even when conversations are taking place face-to-face we must recognize that intentionality and the media environment are connected. Planning a conversation in a place that is free from distractions, both external and internal, is a start. Making sure that digital devices and connection to information outside of the conversational setting are turned off is a second step. As well, the goal of dialogue is furthered when the setting for dialogue is free from the "home-base advantage," so that one party is not the most comfortable in their own setting and the other is not. Intentionality involves an attitude of willingness and determined effort to create space for communication. For example, devices that vibrate in one's pocket or sound off in the middle of a meeting (cell phones and beepers) as well as those that enclose personal space and captivate attention (iPods, laptops, camera phones, etc.) each are prone to being used in the most immersive ways, and this may be increasingly wearing down the ability to make sense of the primary conversation.

These phenomena are all subject to the ways in which human beings use them, but once use has become habituated it is difficult to be intentional about curtailing or stopping their use. Observing the contrast between carrying a paperback book around or a smart phone or e-book device may be helpful. Both are types of mobile technologies. Both may capture one's attention, their presence reminding the owner of his or her desire to read. However, a book is not digitally programmed nor does it pulse inside its owner's hands.

It does not come with a "ringer" that compels one to pick it up and check it, nor is it networked within multiple outward strands of connection such as an Outlook calendar, digital appointment service, or wireless "smart" technologies connecting with everything from one's oven, lights, and doorbell.[8] No expectation exists for the book carrier to read his book as he moves about daily activities. In the case of the smart phone, iPad, Apple watch, or other PMM, however, the expectation to respond to devices and the urge to use them are considerable and seem to be intensifying. When asked about their experience, undergraduate students using these technologies between the years 2014 and 2021 expressed anxiety when confronted with an inability to respond immediately, a reaction that did not exist in the early 2000s and before.[9] Smart phone technology, combining the use of telephone, search function, mail service, and camera creates such an immense force pulling on the nervous system of its users that it is nearly impossible to resist. Some have begun to use the word "addiction" when discussing it.

To address the addictive properties of PMM, several organizations have dedicated their efforts to increasing the public's ability to become better listeners. One such organization, the International Listening Association (ICA), has been working since 1979 to increase awareness concerning the importance of listening, which involves managing distractions to the listening process. Their advocacy involves strategies to help people understand the difference between hearing and listening. According to the ICA, listening is essential for many reasons. First, listening lets the speaker know that he or she is being taken seriously. In addition, one of the main precepts of the organization is that listening is linked to learning. As described by the ICA's mission statement, listening is the cognitive tool used to help people understand their environment and culture: "We learn our culture largely through listening; we learn to think by listening; we learn to love by listening; we learn about ourselves by listening."[10] Without a focused intention to listen, sanity plummets into insanity. Reasoned discourse tumbles into incivility. Public discourse suffers.

Social psychologist, Kenneth Gergen (1991) posits another way of conceptualizing the excessive amounts of data contemporary advancements in media and communication technologies have brought about. He suggests that the "self" is under siege because it is essentially over "populated" by the great influx of people and information now available and pressing in upon the average person. The number of names, birthdays, addresses, phone numbers, likes, dislikes, and other myriad bits of information necessary to maintain social relevance and relational coherence has saturated the average person. This "saturated self" is no longer able to function with consistency, and all relationships become "watered down" and superficial. American graphic designer and founder of TED Richard Saul Wurman (1989) presents an alternative way of addressing the idea of message overload and the accompanying stress on individuals in his concept of "information anxiety." He describes this stress as the perceived gap in understanding between information received and its meaning.[11] For Neil Postman, it is a similar dysfunction, one that he framed as the information-action ratio, an imbalance between the intake of information and the inability to act upon it. This ratio skews the human communication process, making it difficult to process information and creating mental stress.

General anxiety is one major area of concern that intersects with the rise of digital media. Loneliness is another. Loneliness is rising in what appears to be epidemic proportions. A recent study found that loneliness affects the well-being and overall physical health of 46 percent of people surveyed throughout the United States.[12] The reasons, however, appear to be mixed. The need and longing for close connection is a commonplace but is evidenced even more so since the isolation and social distancing practices put in place during the coronavirus pandemic. Described as a daily sense of being overwhelmed by isolation and growing social anxiety, the dynamics factoring into these numbers on loneliness are diverse, but often include the heavy use of social media. One study, for example, was conducted in 2018 by University of Pennsylvania researchers and reported a connection between excessive Internet/social media use. The study found "that students who limited their use of Facebook, Instagram, and Snapchat to 30 minutes a day for three weeks had significant reductions in loneliness and depression as compared to a control group that made no changes to their social media diet" (Berger, 2018). It appears, however, that even those who are not socially isolated and do not report high activity texting and in online platforms also experience a deep sense of loneliness.

The spike in loneliness shows up in a 2018 Loneliness Index—a study conducted by Cigna, one of the United States' foremost health insurers, in which among the 20,000 people surveyed, almost half reported feeling lonely sometimes or often. The index separated "very heavy users" of social media from those reporting never using social media. "Respondents defined as 'very heavy users' of social media had an average loneliness score of 43.5—not remarkably different from those who reported never using social media, 41.7" (Cigna Research Study, 2018). It may be that loneliness is simply being reported more accurately in this age of information, but the one steady contributing factor to loneliness appears to be the lessening of face-to-face interaction. Without it, the much-needed confirmation is diminished considerably, or lost. While heavy use of social media may punch holes in a person's confidence level because of conveyed disconfirmation, it is likely that the lack of confirmation is actually more dangerous. Overt negation, bullying, and other disconfirming practices are contributing factors in the rise of loneliness, but according to some scholars, they are not as damaging as the lack of physical touch and face-to-face communication, for as people look to find a sense of community on social media, the paltry "tangential responses" experienced there can have an even great detrimental effect, particularly for the youth who are in the thick of developing a more substantive, steady sense of self. As a person loses their "grounding in direct somatic experience" feelings of disconfirmation and loneliness are apt to rise, as well. This is part of the rippling effect that the lessening of physical proximity puts into motion. It is a chain reaction of sorts that does not lend itself to the commonplaces of civilized behavior, civility being one such societal good. The severity of this situation increases as we find fewer places for silence and solitude.

A growing body of research in this area points to these problems suggesting that the distractive and addictive properties associated with PMM contribute to the objectification (Lanier, 2009; Turkle, 2015; Twenge, 2016; Rushkoff, 2020). The work of earlier communication and interdisciplinary scholars, Martin Buber (1965), Joseph Walther (1995), and Julia Wood (2004) advance this idea. Wood suggests that many obstacles to listening are increasing in the present age particularly because of new media. She lists five primary hindrances to the listening process. They are: message overload, message complexity, noise, technological overload, and preoccupation.[13] Each of these factors work to construct new dynamics in interpersonal communication. Message overload may be the easiest to understand. Our PMM allow us to receive or send a message anywhere. To be constantly ready to accept another message when one is endeavoring to carry on a meaningful conversation with another does not create the atmosphere in which people are prone to self-disclose or discuss of any matter in depth. Wood raises interesting questions in this regard wondering, "Can we really engage others if we have a cell phone handy and will answer it if it rings? Can we listen well to any conversation in person or on a phone—if we are actually or potentially involved in more than one conversation?"[14]

The hindering elements of *message complexity* greatly affect one's ability to listen attentively. Military personnel are accustomed to using the most direct and simple language, especially in command situations for this very reason. The less complex the message, the less chance for misunderstanding. A similar trend in short-cutting language has begun to emerge in texting and tweeting. In emergency situations this may be helpful, but as the use of PMM continues to expand as part of the social environment for relationship development, community action, and public discourse, the truncated, direct language used so often in text-messaging can too easily be misinterpreted. The missing nonverbal communication cues and other variables that hinder conversations taking place via PMM become more pronounced as the message content becomes more complex. A simple "Hi, let's meet at three" is not typically problematic when spoken through a cell phone if those interacting have specified a location to meet and do not experience any of the aforementioned problems associated with the use of digital devices. However, when messages are more complex the distractive elements are exacerbated and communication coherence is at risk. This is compounded by the many different conversational styles individuals bring to the table of communication. Contemporary linguist Deborah Tannen (2006) does research in the area of conversational styles and suggests that one reason so much interpersonal misunderstanding occurs is because people are different in their awareness of turn-taking cues and often don't wait long enough for the other to respond before jumping into the conversation with a response. One may interpret an eager responder as rude while the other may perceive a bit longer pause as apathetic, disinterested, or boring. Attempting to engage in a weighty conversation using a smart phone with either voice or text adds to this turn-taking dynamic thus adding to the complexity of the message, thereby reducing meaning-making and the overall effectiveness of the conversation.

Another of Wood's five hindrances to effective listening is a subject treated earlier in this project, *noise*. As previously noted, noise can be described as external or internal and may include the environmental sounds just mentioned such as the roar of crowds, passing traffic, construction machinery, as well as a multitude of other types of external distractions to one's concentration. The mobility factor is key. Now, instead of being anchored in place and time, one can answer a phone call or respond to a text on the move, using PMM in situations where these external noises are more prevalent or obvious. The problem with extraneous, unwanted sound has escalated and is even generating citizen activism in the way of many new organizations.[15] One organization involved in addressing the problems with noise and technological overload is called the American Society for Acoustic Ecology (ASAE). Founded in 1993, the ASAE's constituency works to disseminate "research results and curriculum, materials, sponsor lectures, conferences and other events and support creative exploration of the soundscape through sound art and installations" (ASAE February, 2022, p. 2). Acoustic ecology is the study, management, and interpretation of natural sound environments. The organization is dedicated to preservation of the "soundscape"[16] and their primary aim is protecting the human-made sound in the biosphere.[17] The ASAE is one of many such groups and organizations that operate through the West both informally and formally to reduce the level of external noise in public places.

It is not surprising that organizations such as the National Hearing Conservation Association have introduced such measures as the Quiet Communities Act of 1997 to the EPA.[18] The Act was introduced in the 105th Congress on February 4, 1997, in order to re-establish the Office of Noise Abatement and Control. The United States Congress moved to adopt this

Act because studies showed the ramifications unchecked noise created in environments for many Americans that proved unsuitable to life, liberty, and the pursuit of happiness. Among the reasons cited for the Quiet Communities Act are two that establish noise as inherently problematic to human beings. The Act reads as follows:

1. For too many Americans, noise from aircraft, vehicular traffic, and a variety of other sources is a constant source of torment. In fact, nearly 20,000,000 Americans are exposed to noise levels that can lead to psychological and physiological damage, and another 40,000,000 people are exposed to noise levels that cause sleep or work disruption.
2. Chronic exposure to noise has been linked to increased risk of cardiovascular problems, strokes, and nervous disorders. Excessive noise also causes sleep deprivation and task interruptions, both of which pose untold costs on society in diminished worker productivity. (Quiet Communities Act of 1997)

Technological overload is another of Wood's hindrances to listening and is worth mentioning. Although similar socio-technological phenomena have occurred in every era since the invention of the wheel, today's technological innovation has filtered through society at exponential speed. Past shifts in cultural norms may have prompted comparable change, but the current transition from the electronic age of information to digital culture has occurred much more quickly, shaking the tectonic plates, as it were, of social norms and propriety. One example is the overload of information stemming from the radio and television revolution of the 20th century. The proliferation and ubiquity of these media created a cascade of interest in personalities that appeared on these outlets, stirring up desire to gain as much information as possible about actors, anchors, and all those involved in the surrounding entertainment industries. Enter the modern celebrity.

Television also helped move the general perception of the world from town, state, and national interests to the global. Today, technological overload continues, but not just in the number of messages we must wrangle with, or their complexity. *Technological* overload involves reckoning with the nearly constant deployment of new devices and apps. The "latest and better" editions of our PMM keep the public adapting to more complicated ways of living daily life. We are so busy adjusting apps and settings, purchasing the latest upgrades, and learning the newest software, it has led to tech-fatigue, most recently known as "screen fatigue." When one considers the rapid growth of wireless technologies, their growing numbers of functions and styles, and their increasingly seamless connectedness to the Internet, it is not difficult to imagine technical overload becoming even more problematic in the future.

Although the sheer number of digital devices used by the general public today suggests correlation to the debasement of listening, it is not enough to establish as singular or deterministic. However, current research suggests the listening process is indeed compromised when using personal mobile media. Data gathered by Deloitte Research and the Cellular Telecommunications and Internet Association (CTIA) research center, point to the number of U.S. subscribers to wireless services which topped 194.5 million early in the century.[19] In 2019 that number had grown to nearly 450 million wireless customers—more cell phones than people! Globally, the number has expanded exponentially with statistics from the telecommunications industry suggesting that the total number of wireless subscribers now exceeds 8 billion.[20] While the presence of these digital devices does not indicate causation, understanding how listening is compromised through multiple distractions suggests a sure correlation. Along with debased relational coherence, the magnitude of the presence of these mediating devices suggests that using them the way we do is addictive and harmful in a variety of ways. This we will address in a later chapter.

MULTI-TASKING

Along with technological overload and other obstructions to listening, an additional impediment is the propensity to multi-task. Some may argue the ability to multi-task is a cultural good, lauding new media development that makes it possible. But multi-tasking does more than inhibit healthy listening skills. It takes up the small moments in a day and packs them full. It also deepens the human propensity toward preoccupation. This might occur in a number of ways, but results are generally the same; we become preoccupied with a task or conversation simultaneous with the task at hand. Preoccupation occurs when those communicating are absorbed in these multiple tasks, such as two conversations happening concurrently. One may be occurring via text on a laptop computer or iPad, the other using voice on the cell phone. Either way those conversing become preoccupied—sometimes absorbed—in a variety of other concerns, thoughts, or activities. While face-to-face encounters are not exempt from preoccupation, the tiny slivers of time spent taking a breath, reflecting on a joyful encounter, or even daydreaming are increasingly truncated and edited out of daily life when multi-tasking with our personal mobile media.

The ability to reason, remember, imagine, and question are inherently human attributes. These are not qualities we should be willing to release to our tools. Throughout history there have been technological distractions that have both enhanced and inhibited this to some extent and/or have had the effect of interfering with listening in the interpersonal communication process. However, in our busy digital media environment filled with easily accessible, increasingly portable media, there seem to be unprecedented opportunities for preoccupation with external distractions, to such a degree that active listening and the overall quality of interpersonal communication are much hindered. As such, along with the benefits and blessings gained by the access and immediacy provided by the wireless technologies comes a virulent curse, a lethal contagion. The ability to shop, game, socialize, and bank simultaneously appear to offer an eager public time-saving measures, but the more we are able to do in a moment's time, the more we will do, even if the doing is scattered and unfocused. Why I dub it a threat is that as we acculturate to this multi-tasking activity it morphs from a way to function in the world to a mindset. Not only does doing more in less time become expected, but the pace and ensuing fragmentation of both the thinking and communicating process can push the average responsible citizen to the edge of sanity.[21] Thus, in the wake of our ability to multi-task, a multi-tasking mindset easily forms. Hence the need for more mindful action presents itself, and *mindfulness* enters into 21st-century vernacular.

Mindfulness is a key component in the listening process. To be mindful it is necessary to "concentrate on what lies between and behind the content in order to understand what another is feeling, thinking, needing, or wanting in conversation."[22] But mindfulness must take place *a priori*. Before one can listen in a focused, intelligent way to others, one must be attentive to one's self, stay grounded, centered, and focused. The need is clear, as well, for leisure –those unfettered moments of dwelling and being, without attention to productivity. These are being reduced to annual vacation. A short poem by William Henry Davies captures this idea.

> What is this life if, full of care,
> We have no time to stand and stare.
> No time to stand beneath the boughs
> And stare as long as sheep or cows.
> No time to see, when woods we pass,
> Where squirrels hid their nuts in grass.
> No time to see, in broad daylight,
> Streams full of stars, like skies at night.
> No time to turn at Beauty's glance
> And watch her feet, how they can dance.
> No time to wait till her mouth can
> Enrich that smile her eyes began.
> A poor life this if, full of care,
> We have no time to stand and stare.[23]

Indeed. Taking time to stare. To dream. To let one's mind wander. The echo of such truth is still discernible, but almost completely counterintuitive in light of the current new media frenzy. To insist on such mindful focus may seem frivolous, but the way we are using our digital devices in this era of technological innovation necessitates such intentionality.

Determining how much focus is needed to concentrate on a matter is not an easy task and relatively subjective from individual to individual. The ability to concentrate also depends upon the geographic space in which one is located while speaking and receiving verbal or written messages. For example, if a cell phone call is made from a busy supermarket or from a car while carrying on conversation with others who are present and with music streaming, it will be increasingly difficult to concentrate. Even when those who are communicating via PMM are accustomed to a higher degree of noise and other distractions, there remains the need to hear (or read), analyze, interpret, and provide feedback. These concerns for interpersonal depth and ensuing human flourishing are not unfounded. It may be difficult in a world increasingly saturated by sound to invite this mindfulness practice, but surely worth the effort.

This concern is part of the subject matter in Tony Schwartz's (1973) book, *The Responsive Chord*. Schwartz, who discusses the persuasive elements of sound that increase the effectiveness of advertising, explores the difference between "sound" and "noise." He demonstrates the importance of using sound, silence, and effects in any persuasive endeavor.[24] One example is a photograph in his book of smokestacks in New York City. At one time, the billows of smoke pointed to the prosperity and progress of the city. In this present age, however, the smokestacks cause an audience to think of pollution. The change in perception is an important element in deciding what types of messages to use that will resonate with a particular audience, which the advertising industry has used to advantage. Another layer of this is the overall expansion of the industry. Advertisements are increasingly directed to individuals (and now, individually tailored to them) via cell phones, smart phones, social media, and e-mail. Increasingly, this new type of "direct mail" advertising has become a large part of an overall strategy to "keep eyeballs on the screen" no matter how large or small. Under the umbrella of "Big Data" major corporations gather information from our digital devices with the intention of selling it. A seemingly helpful and non-intrusive example of this is one of the more significant marketing strategies used by Amazon.com. The company keeps records of the items purchased online and sends "recommendations" or pairings of other books and items in which that customer might be interested. Here again silence can be a faithful sojourner, helping us to pause before sending out photos and personal contact information that can be taken and used in malevolent ways. The momentary (or extended) silence is available to help us focus and think critically about what we make available publicly.

LISTENING AND VISUAL DISTRACTIONS

Another aspect of the challenge of listening is that we are living in a world dominated by sight (Boorstin, 1961; Citztrom, 1982; Ellul, 1985; Isaacs, 1999; Ong, 1985; Postman, 1999, 1985, 1982; Wood, 2004). The increase of visual stimuli has greatly contributed to what we are now experiencing in a dominant and refined form. The surge of the image bombards individuals at all points in the day. We have become a culture of the image. A common example is the presence of television screens in restaurants. These screens' simultaneous broadcasting of images as well as dissemination of sounds can greatly hinder the listening process. In the early days of television, one might find a single TV in a bar, but as the 20th century progressed televisions became regular features in restaurants and pubs. Today, diners looking to converse over a quiet dinner must spend outlandish amounts of money to dine in a restaurant without a TV. This was not so in the recent past. Today, people trying to converse are distracted by the visual display and (often) high volume of the media. These older media coupled with the ever-present smart phone infuse public spaces with external noise and have become poor settings for conversation.

Additionally, acceptance of the image as a means of learning quickly became a part of the American way of knowing (Boorstin, 1961; Postman, 1985). In fact, the nearly instant ability to receive a message through an image, a large part of what Boorstin refers to as the creation of "consumption communities," has occurred, and involves a type of persuasion that is dedicated to encouraging people to become dedicated buyers of anything new that comes on the market (Schultze, 2002, p. 10). This persuasion involves the significant changes in individual (and collective) perception that occur when meaning is established through the image. Particularly, it is the form or structure of one frame (a snapshot), painting, or television video that shapes meaning (Boorstin, pp. 12–15). Using the prominence of the image through the television as an example, Boorstin explained that with the television

> vivid image came to overshadow pale reality. Sound motion pictures in color led a whole generation of pioneering American movie-goers to think of Benjamin Disraeli as an earlier imitation of George Areliss, just as television has led a later generation of television watchers to see the Western cowboy as an inferior replica of John Wayne. The Grand Canyon itself became a disappointing reproduction of the Kodachrome original. (pp. 13–14)

The power of the image to provide candid reports, close-up shots, and vividness helped to establish the expectancy of reality, in many cases, an expectation that exceeded the actual event or experience. "Readers and viewers would soon prefer the vividness of the account, the 'candidness' of the photograph, to the spontaneity of what was recounted" (Boorstin, p. 14). In some ways this is what has emerged today as many appear to prefer social media and text messages to the risks, vulnerabilities, and inconveniences associated with meeting face-to-face.

As the power and persuasion of "the image" morphs from the movie theaters and televisions to our personal mobile media, it is becoming increasingly clear that the number of individual images and components of an image increasingly will play a part in aiding and/or inhibiting the process of interpersonal communication. The effect these images will have in this context promise to be an important and fruitful avenue for scholarly investigation.

ISOLATION

Electronic games, music files, I-Ms, text messages, and cell phone ringers are all available through PMM today; walking around with all of these options may easily create information and entertainment noise that will lure their individual attention, require users to engage in complex time management, or cause them to immerse themselves in PMM devices in an isolated way. The effect on many may be to complicate their everyday interpersonal communication rather than simplify it. As users of PMM and other media in our current environment try to navigate the challenges of working and living in a culture dominated by immersive media, the previously described kind of listening required for interpersonal communication to be considered relational may be jeopardized.

As "everyday talk" increasingly occurs in the virtual sphere, relationships are played out on the streets and sidewalks via mediating devices. Business, familial, and romantic relationships are negotiated at great distances where time and space are increasingly collapsed into shaky fold-a-way ladders of abstraction. These conversations are often muddled and confusing, lapsing into what Postman calls "crazy talk," a type of language usage that regularly misses communication cues, does not really listen to the other, or deals with reality in rational ways. Many problems arise because of this "crazy talk." Instead of intimacy—or even coherence—relational goals are easily thwarted. Instead of meaning-making, business partners, family, friends are thrown into torrents of conflict and misunderstanding. How may this be rectified? A closer look at Postman's ideas about communication-as-process helps to clarify. Returning to the garden metaphor, he writes: "If there is no sun or water, there is nothing much the plant can do about growing. And if there is no semantic environment, there is nothing much we can do about communicating" (p. 9). The first step then, is to recognize the semantic environment, today's being the massive media landscape within which we all function. To navigate the major changes in semantic environment we must reckon with a more informed and sentient appropriation of what we are dealing with, taking care not to exempt ourselves because we are *so evolved*. Postman continues, "If communication is to happen, we require not merely messages, but an ordered situation in which messages can assume meaning . . . [and remember that, *sic*] a semantic environment includes, first of all people; second, their purposes; third, the general rules of discourse by which such purposes are usually achieved; and fourth, the particular talk actually being used in the situation" (p. 9). The rules of discourse have been turned upside down since the 1960s, and with the emergence of personal computing coming to the fore in the early 1990s the rules have all but been obliterated. New rules will appear, and as the social protocols fall into place our world will see even more change in the semantic environment. Hopefully, human communication will steadfastly be preferred and used with increasing intention. Another type of destructive use of language is a very particular type of damage to human communication and is what Postman calls "stupid talk."

Described as "talk that defeats legitimate purposes," both "crazy" and "stupid" talk are decried by Postman as poor usages of language and sources of "trouble" in human affairs. Both are ineffective in any attempt to achieve purposes that could be construed as "good" (p. 74). This was evident to the New York University professor as he observed everyday discourse of the mid-twentieth century. Now, with even more devices and platforms for communication made possible through the use of digital media, each becomes a new context or *situation*. Thus, before we can even start the process of moving toward dialogic communication, the "thing we need to recognize is that in thinking about talk, we are dealing with a multifaceted social situation" (1976, p. 10). A common mistake is in thinking that communication deals strictly with words isolated from relation or situation. Today, with the greatly expanded options for social interaction, the promise of meaningful, articulate communication appears to be falling flat as the short, truncated exchanges via text or online substitute poorly for the art of conversation. This is because conversations via cell phones, social networks, discussion lists, blogs, various other Internet platforms, along with the ever-expanding means of digital messaging in today's media environment increasingly "connect" us, but do not overridingly improve our ability to communicate. The questions surrounding this phenomenon are important ones, for when we depend on these devices for daily connection points it is easy to collapse the process of communication into a mere sender-receiver interaction and believe we are "close" with those we relate to simply because we are connecting with greater regularity.

Delving a bit further, another key component of crazy talk is that it "cannot be verified or refuted by facts."[25] By this definition, much political rhetoric tends to fall into the category in that crazy talk usually "puts forward a point of view that is considered virtuous and progressive. Its assumptions, metaphors, and conclusions are therefore taken for granted and that, in the end, is what makes it crazy" (p. 86). The clearest example of this lingual dysfunction may be the most recent one as seen in the political rhetoric in the U.S. during the 2016 and 2020 presidential elections, but it occurs continually throughout the world. Meaning unravels when crazy talk dominates a culture. This unraveling may be easier to perceive when a friendship or marriage dissolves for the problem of crazy talk "is not in what it does *for* you but in what it does *to* you. Crazy talk, even in its milder forms, requires that we be mystified, suspend critical judgment, accept premises without question, and (frequently) abandon entirely the idea that language ought to be connected with reality."[26] No matter how much two people have bonded relationally, when crazy or stupid talk prevails, meaningful conversation fades and people part company. Broken friendships, divorce, and political rivalry are nothing new, but they continue to cause pain and imbalance, sometimes violence. When similar communication breakdown and loss of meaning bleed into a large people group, a type of insanity encroaches on a culture. Certainly, the "insanity" mentioned here is not one associated with a psychological disorder or mental illness. Rather, it is a way of being in the world that exchanges sense-making for false premises and illusions and is directly linked to inattentiveness.

The inability to deeply listen to another is where the problem begins. Listening is more than what is being said. It is one way that we defeat ourselves, first through allowing poor listening to become a norm in our lives and then letting it spill over into ambiguous language. Numerous examples of this "crazy talk" occur daily whether they occur in face-to-face settings or online. If, as Postman maintains, we defeat ourselves by the way we talk, what does it mean for the possibility of dialogue and ensuing cultural goods necessary for a civil society?

Revisiting Postman in this century reminds us to take seriously his adage that new technologies do not just add something new to our world; they change everything. As the digital devices and computer programs used to support this process become more commonplace, it will be necessary to look more seriously at the semantic environments they help create and to ask ourselves: Will we allow the expedience and utility of PMM to be sufficient reason for allowing crazy talk and stupid talk to prosper? Or, will we get out our spades, turn over the few clods of soil, work up a sweat, and pull out the weeds that clutter the landscape upon which all human relationship is born?

Will we savor our speech, use it to create a more civil society, strengthen our relationships, and build communities that defy the demon of denigration of language? It is not up to a device—digital or otherwise—to decide. Only *human* beings can make the decision to rise above crazy, stupid talk. And the decision is one we each must make daily.

Some may say that listening is merely a function of communication, a means of interpreting sounds and making sense of what is being heard—an auditory function—and that meaning is located in the words themselves. My argument is that listening is much more significant to the art of communication. Listening is an essential but first step to the process. True listening requires a deeper commitment to conversation and to the needs of others. It is here that silence becomes quite an important feature. In the following chapter, the discussion evolves to incorporate the place of silence as integral to a philosophy of communication that is workable for this new age of immersive and ubiquitous media. We move from treating silence as an artful but pragmatic necessity of communication effectiveness to understanding its part as an overarching element in the way we think about communication, relationship, and personhood itself.

NOTES

1. David Gill. *Doing Right*. p. 293.
2. This aspect of "disappearing silence" is part of the focus of environmental groups who are often politically active to help maintain open spaces, parks and wooded areas, and an acoustic environment that is friendly toward birds, animals, trees, and humans. The work of the acoustic ecology association is helpful in this area of focus.
3. In the States, organizations such as New Jersey's HORN (Halt Outrageous Railroad Noise), the NJCAAN (New Jersey Coalition against Aircraft Noise), and a multitude of other global noise control organizations exist and lobby for the express purpose of protecting quiet spaces. The Noise Control Clearinghouse lists numerous organizations on their "QuietNet" website. Their slogan is simple: "Good neighbors keep their noise to themselves."
4. eMedia Fast conducted from 2004 to 2021.
5. Robert Bolton, in *Bridges not Walls*, ed. John Stewart. p. 118.
6. Silence of this sort may be functional as well as dysfunctional; however, my reference to it assumes there is a well-established base of relational credulity and healthy evidence of communication behavior that is verbal as well.
7. Notorious for rants, rage, inciting speech, celebrity "Twitter wars" are common but more likely part of the star-making machinery stirred up by their publicists and surrogates. In what proponents of the platform frame as the ability to speak truth to power, many of these online "wars" begin with non-celebrity citizens commenting

on sports, government, or the news, in general. Few are civil, fewer still evoke any positive conversation.

8. Smart technologies are not limited to connection between devices. They also include use of stand-alone devices such as a Kindle or other type of eReader. Increasingly, digital books are available "in the cloud" and accessible through mobile apps.

9. My own ongoing research in this area points to a distinct change in anxiety level among college-aged students once the iPhone plus models came to the market in 2014. That year, a University of Florida study revealed 86 percent of college students were heavily using the iPhone. The continued pervasive used of the iPhone appears to have added to the "need" to respond immediately to texts.

10. The ILA is an interdisciplinary and professional organization that publishes the *International Journal of Listening*, as well as a quarterly newsletter called the *Listening Post*. The quote is part of the association's precepts and attributed to Robinson.

11. Much of Wurman's work helps to formulate the different types of information entering an individual's field of view. His "Five Rings of Information Immediacy" present some correlation with the work of other scholars in various disciplines and include the following types of anxiety-producing overloads: cultural, news, reference, conversational, and internal information. For a closer look at his theories, see Information Anxiety in references.

12. Alexa Lardieri. "Study: Many Americans Report Feeling Lonely." *U.S. News & World Report*. [November 17, 2021] https://www.usnews.com/news/health-care-news/articles/2018-05-01/study-many-americans-report-feeling-lonely-younger-generations-more-so. May 1, 2018.

13. Julia Wood. *Communication Theories in Action*. pp. 161–164.

14. Ibid. p. 162.

15. Social media such as blogs, podcasts, YouTube videos, etc., seem to have sparked an increased level of consumer and citizen activism, but the very usefulness of these media feeds into an excess of noise and information that prompts further use of the new media. This self-perpetuating cycle keeps people generally busier in using the media, not necessarily actual activistic action. The trend is something to look at closely when considering the dialectic nature of speech and silence as it plays out through our communication technologies.

16. Acoustic ecologists such as R. M. Schafer study the relationships between sound, the listener, and the environment. The way acoustic ecologists approach the presence and absence of various natural sounds is quite different from that of a media ecologist. A related vein of study is the science of sound cognition (psychoacoustics), which looks at the way various sounds influence the thought process. See: R. M. Schafer. *The Tuning of the World*. New York: Knopf, 1977.

17. The ASAE and other like-minded organizations, such as the World Forum for Acoustic Ecology, seek to reduce the amount of noise that is generated by machines, technology, and other influences that pose either significant health risks (as in hearing loss) or those that denigrate the need and desire for quiet, in general.

18. The NHCA is an organization dedicated to conversing about the "quiet" necessary to insure good health. The organization monitors noise reduction ratings, EPA findings from the Office of Noise Abatement and Control (ONAC), and are advocates for occupational safety and noise protection. They are among several active organizations working to improve regulations, disseminating information and increasing awareness of the hazards of too much noise in the environment.

19. This number was accurate in October 2005 and is continuing to increase.

20. Statista. 2021. [October 15, 2021] https://www.statista.com/statistics/262950/global-mobile-subscriptions-since-1993/.

21. University of Michigan studies in neuroscience point to brain functioning that pauses to collect data when attempting to process more than one piece of information at a time. See NPR report for further details. https://www.npr.org/templates/story/story.php?storyId=95256794.

22. See Julia Wood. *Communication Theories in Action*. p. 173.

23. This poem is in the public domain, written by Welsh poet William Henry Davies [1871–1940].

24. *The Responsive Chord* (1973) discusses the sound environment and human response to it. Schwartz is best known as an inspired "sound gatherer" who has collected and recorded thousands of natural and socially constructed sounds since 1945. Reviewers have called it a map of the changes brought about by radio and TV, and the *New York Times* called him the "king of sound." See Tony Schwartz. *The Responsive Chord* [retrieved on February 26, 2006] from http://www.tonyschwartz.org/responsive-chord.html.

25. Neil Postman. *Crazy Talk, Stupid Talk*. p. 90.

26. Ibid., p. 85.

Chapter 4

Ontological Silence

His imagination lit up the lives of thousands of children for almost 40 years. The Neighborhood of Make-Believe was a special place created by children's television pioneer Fred Rogers (1928–2003), one that allowed young viewers to make sense of life's quandaries in a way that respected their childlike fears and emotions. King Friday, Lady Elaine Fairchild, and Daniel Tiger became more than puppets to the many children whose rapt attention he held from the time the show aired in the U.S. in 1968 to 2001. Rogers used language and conversation creatively to build a sense of safety and a sense of home for his young viewers, one that helped shape the very sense of their being in the world. More than marketing trends and passing commercial fads, his approach to children's television was rooted in the biblical axiom "love thy neighbor." Though not directly espoused, his philosophy seemed to be informed by Heidegger, who famously said: "Language is the dwelling place of being. In its housing man is home." *Home*, in the heart of a neighborhood where mundane arguments and annoyances are frequent, but people listen to each other and find their place of belonging therein.

At the time of its airing, the work of Fred Rogers was seen as quirky by many adults. Bemused at the raw simplicity of his mannerisms, tone, and commonplace themes, Rogers even became the punchline in late-night comedy. But children—the young and the innocent—could not turn away. Their eyes fixated on his face and their bodies leaned into the screen to absorb every word of the American television icon; children couldn't stop watching him.[1] What did Fred Rogers offer? Was it just the slower pace or the simpler time? Surely, not. Some background is necessary.

The 1960s were extremely volatile. Wars, movements, uprisings and strikes took place all around the world, and in the West, 1968 was perhaps the most explosive. In the U.S., two major political figures were assassinated. Both Robert J. Kennedy, a presidential candidate, and Martin Luther King, Jr., unofficial leader of the Civil Rights Movement, were gunned down in cold blood. Just a few years before, the U.S. president, John Fitzgerald

Kennedy was also assassinated. Voices of unrest and protracted dissent rang all around the world. Mao Zedong's *Little Red Book* thrust the Chinese people into a revolution resulting in hundreds of thousands of deaths. The Cold War raged with a constant threat of nuclear annihilation lurking in the background of daily life. Along with all the social turbulence, popular culture came to full flower in the '60s. Radio, film, television, and the "British Invasion" of England's top music group, The Beatles, toured around the world to audiences of screaming teenagers. Although its roots began much earlier, the pop culture of the '60s was transformational in what was then simply called "show business." The serious dealings of news and politics began to blur with the creative endeavors associated with music and film, and fashion. Enchantment with modern entertainment was born.

In all its glitter, glam and speed, the entertainment industry was in full throttle when Fred Rogers began his unlikely success at station WQED in Pittsburgh, Pennsylvania. His approach was more than counter-cultural; it was revolutionary. Grounded in the study of childhood education, Fred Rogers believed that the routine of beginning each show in exactly the same way with the same music and greeting of "Hi Neighbor," was part of the foundation of creating a safe neighborhood for his young audience.[2] Trust being key to his approach, Rogers was intent on building relationship, which is one of the reasons he always referred to the program as a visit rather than a show. Each of the "visits" combined a bit of puppet fun with a lesson in empathy, that characteristic that allows human beings to understand and care about what happens to one another. James K. A. Smith, a contemporary philosopher, pairs empathy with imagination. "Empathy is ultimately a feat of the imagination, and arguments are no therapy for a failed shriveled imagination."[3] Empathy is where ethics and communication meet.

Understanding another's pain does not come naturally but must be learned. This was Fred Rogers's philosophy and the way he scripted and produced the nearly 900 episodes of *Mr. Rogers' Neighborhood*. Allowing his young audience the space and time to process what they were seeing was part of his brilliance.[4] This generative silence is what Fred Rogers brought into children's programming as much (or more) than a new type of children's show. He brought young ones a way of being in the world, one that was more deeply rooted in personhood than technology. Rogers gave children a way they might understand their own personhood and learn to respect the personhood of others. In Mr. Rogers' company, children were learning what it means "to be." Without understanding the word, it was for many of these little ones their first lesson in Greek philosophy.

PHILOSOPHY AND INTERPERSONAL COMMUNICATION

Rhetoric and Dialogue, Aristotle and Socrates—since the days of ancient Greece, these subjects have been inexorably linked. The study of communication and the study of philosophy have grown up together, taking twists and turns along the broad branches of the tree of knowledge. Then, the ability to speak well revolved around the polis, a properly functioning government, and order in the streets. From Socrates, Plato, and Aristotle to Augustine, Aquinas, and the moderns, the association between language and being, reality and truth, justice and order have remained key components in the Great Conversation. Today, that conversation continues, and while so much of its current instantiation centers around technological change, the key to understanding what is at stake is to grasp the fundamental importance of the communication process to all that it means to be human. This process is intricately woven into every human being. It is more than significant. It is connected to our purpose and our personhood. Speech is where we dwell.

Some of the more contemporary discussions surrounding these connections emerged in the research of Walter J. Ong (1912–2003) and his framing of the psychodynamics of human consciousness. His project focused on the changes that occur in human development as individuals and people groups switch from primary oral cultures to those that are literate. His work is situated in the well-established fact of humans as symbol users, shaping culture through our use of language (1982). Ong's contribution to the conversation was immense. Throughout his corpus, Ong emphasizes the cultural and ontological importance of language, noting that in the spoken word there is a greater power—a more present, active power—than there is in the written word (Ong, 1982, 1953).

If the spoken word of *Homo loquax* is inextricably linked with understanding our humanness or sense of being, our smart phones and other mobile devices require a more critical look into how they shape our being and how we use them. Whereas print and image technologies may have served to isolate human beings into more individuated worlds of knowledge, the most recent and emerging technologies (particularly the smart phone), serve to connect people through the spoken word and open up the possibility of greater conversation. Although much remains to be seen in this respect, the flourishing of dialogue and quality of speech as they relate to the use of personal mobile media are highly relevant. It is unfortunate, however, that as these media and their uses evolve and claim more and more conversational space, the prospect of dialogue dims.

Co-presence, or that type of interaction that allows synchronous communication while not in physical proximity, is becoming the norm. As wireless technologies quickly advance, communicating this way becomes more fluid and engaging. It is far more enjoyable to experience interpersonal connections on our digital devices that don't pixelate or add extraneous white noise, but the growing pervasiveness of such progress encroaches upon expectations associated with physical presence. Ultimately, the normalizing of co-presence creates an environment that stands to denigrate the importance of physical presence. The need for presence in effectuating true dialogue also influences our understanding of what it means *to be* in the world. Presence must not be minimized.

When undertaking a discussion of the philosophical underpinnings of what it means *to be*, the discussion may be approached from numerous stances. Here, we undertake an approach that focuses on two primary areas of being, human presence and purpose. First, we turn to purpose. *Telos* is the ancient word signifying purpose, ultimate goals, or desired end, and while it is not much discussed in everyday vernacular, everyone has a teleological bent. For some, the predilection to reflect upon purpose is so deeply masked beneath the externalities of daily survival that it might be missed. In fact, it often is deeply buried.[5] Others understand *telos* only as a mirror that reflects lack of purpose. The missing sense of one's purpose may be something felt but is kept in a quiet little corner of the subconscious, peering out into conscious perception only in dire or life-threatening situations. The desire for purpose may be evidenced by a state of nameless ennui, a random malaise that returns as an unwelcome guest without permission or warning, its hapless appearance noted by world-weary tedium or general dissatisfaction with life. *Telos* is that aspect of our humanness that propels us to find meaning and purpose and is the veritable key to happiness and fulfillment.

The connection between one's ability to communicate effectively and a personal sense of purpose is strong, speech providing a major part of how purpose is discovered. The ability to acquire speech is built into our DNA, but the art of communication is a skill, and as such, takes practice. To speak gives us the opportunity to make meaning together, to co-create culture, and advance the human race.[6] As noted communication scholar Quentin Schultze reminds us, "Through communication, we acquire shared values, beliefs, and attitudes; [. . .] we learn a common language, culture, and faith."[7] In spite of the magnitude of the worth of the word to accomplish these things, the word communication has become a bit nebulous. To some communication is "everything!" Others use it without a second thought to refer to a wireless network "communicating" with another network.

Receiving a peripheral message out of the corner of one's eye from a looming highway billboard certainly constitutes message transmission, but the level of subliminality that exists and the reception with which said message is received along with the intent upon which the board was erected, each are components of the process of communication. These, however, are not examples of interpersonal communication. Whereas there is indeed rich rhetorical significance in the images so preeminent in Western culture, and intentionality to transmit a message, these visual stimuli do not qualify as communication *per se*, that is, in the sense in which we are using the word in this project. This narrower view of communication is human-centered and undoubtedly contested in both academe and the wider culture. These examples of transmission of information are not between subjects who seek to make meaning on the road to finding purpose but are transactional.

In 1909, Charles Horton Cooley wrote, "By communication is here meant the mechanism through which human relationships develop—all the symbols of the mind, together with the means of conveying them through space and preserving them in time" (Durham-Peters, 1999, p. 9). An excellent and apt understanding of human communication, but perhaps an even simpler and narrower definition of communication is possible. Communication is the mutual exchange of intended messages within and between human beings, persons seeking to make meaning together. This definition surely includes the verbal and nonverbal aspect of message exchange. It may include motivation to persuade or be simply informational; either way it involves relating.

Like Cooley and many other scholars of repute (Arnett, 1986; Brummett, 1991; Buber, 1970; Durham-Peters 1999; Postman, 1999, 1976; Rogers, 1980; Stewart, 2006), to make progress in any worthy endeavor requires that we understand the concept of communication as something that involves every aspect of our humanness, rather than as a formula or model of sender-receiver and message transmission. This is where an ontological view of silence begins.

Communication and philosophy have long held intertwining threads in the rich tapestry of academic discussion.[8] The more carefully one explores communication and the function of silence as part of meaning-making, the more philosophical the discussion becomes. In the last chapter, listening and digital media took center stage, and as we moved through our exploration of silence, we left off on the precipice of what it means "to be." *Being*—or the groundedness of one's sense of self—is intricately woven into the fabric of communication and is part of the dialogic necessity of silence. Without ontological grounding, words too easily become gibberish, offered on the flimsy ground of definition, and too easily devolve into a type of insanity. We see this in our current communication landscape as words shoot across time and space via social media. The resultant upset in our collective sense of time and space too easily spawns senseless idle talk, or a type of speech that is confused, inarticulate, or unreasonable, that which is noted in the previous chapter as "crazy talk."[9] Understanding the deep connection between language and being may help us rein in the empty chatter and curtail meaningless verbiage.

To communicate is to participate in an action that is primal. It is symbolic action, that which gives us the power to co-create culture, constructing and shaping the reality of everyday life. "When we communicate, we create, maintain, and change shared ways of life. Communication enables us to cultivate education, engineering, business, the media, and every other aspect of human culture."[10] Indeed, communicative action grounds culture. It is deeper than the interpersonal. It trowels the rich humus of ancestral sensibilities and provides us with entrée into the intrapersonal, to dig deeply into those unconscious areas involving awareness of self and the other. In fact, true communication plunges deeper still, to that inexplicable place of spirit, where we reckon with existence itself. It propels us into meaning. Pieper describes it succinctly: "Word and language form the medium that sustains the common existence of the human spirit."[11] The inexplicability cannot deny its power.

To communicate most effectively one must understand the connection between self-conscious awareness and awareness of the other. Simple awareness of the other moves beyond understanding of his or her presence in the world or in the room but involves seeing the other *as subject* rather than a fantasized or projected other. Silence is necessary for the cognitive processing of the other as a true subject. This is where ontological silence finds its place in the discussion of dialogue and meaning-making. Speech and Silence are intertwined, not twins, but close sisters of the word.

Philosophers have long noted the necessity of silence as an integral part of speech. Some, such as Max Picard (1952), frame the dialectical tension of the spoken word and silence as a metaphor of life and death, correlating the notion of silence to darkness or to death, itself.[12]

Picard suggests that "language sinks down again into the silence."[13] His words are poetic and philosophically aligned with that of German idealism. This is evident throughout his work, an example of which is evident here:

> Man lives between the world of silence from which he comes and the world of the other side to which he goes—the world of death. Human language also lives between these two worlds of silence and is upheld by them. That is why language has a double echo: from the place when it came, and the place of death. (p. 25)

Picard, a mid-20th century philosopher in the existential vein of Gabriel Marcel, placed a high premium on the interconnectedness of silence and speech as a building block of personal identity and relationship development.[14] He explains that "speech must remain in relationship with the silence from which it raised itself up. It belongs to human nature that speech should turn back to silence, for it belongs to human nature to return to the place whence it has come" (p. 21). This philosopher's deep, ontological sensibilities provide a foundation to further our current discussion, underpinning the notion of speech as part of the human imperative. Picard's thoughts are either obsolete and no longer contain any significance or they remain an unswerving part of the long debate surrounding truth and human nature and must be reckoned with in order to make sense of life in the digital age.

Contending that "silence is present in language . . . even after language has arisen out of silence" (p. 22), Picard further associates personal security and strength of human relationship with an awareness of silence, suggesting that

> the world of language is built over and above the world of silence. Language can only enjoy security as it moves about freely in words and ideas in so far as the broad world of silence is stretched out below. From the breadth of silence language learns to achieve its own breadth; silence is for language what the net stretched out taut below him is for the tightrope walker. (p. 22)

These eloquent words exemplify the kind of creativity Picard is concerned about losing. His stance on the detriment of noise to the communication process is evident throughout his writings but is not due to a romantic desire to go back to nature. Nor is his project built on nostalgic wistfulness. What Picard termed the "substance" of silence is a prerequisite for the action that must emerge from words that are uttered. As he explains, "There is no silent substance in the world today. All things are present all the time in an atmosphere of noisy rebelliousness, and man, who has lost the silence in which to sink the all-too-many, all-too-present multitude of things, allows them to evaporate and vanish in the all-consuming emptiness of language" (p. 56). Here it is possible to construe the notion that there is a connection between the growing absence of silence in the media environment and the degradation of civility that is apparent in the present age. If the technological milieu continues to expand with the sort of exponential increase seen throughout the first twenty years of this century, there is little doubt that it will not remain on a similar trajectory.

Although there is no intention to infer causal correlations between the lack of silence and the intractable social ills of divorce, crime, depression, fragmentation, and other socio-psychological epidemics of late modern society, there are enough parallel chords to suggest what might be considered an association; at least, perhaps, there may be some attributable dynamics. These and so many other correlating aspects of Western industrialism are a worthy subject of research, but are, however, beyond the purview of this project.[15] It is a commonplace, however, to note that the presence of these social ills has increased as the Age of Industry has given way to a digital economy. Whereas a bank robbery was once a singular event that (if successful) could do great damage to a local bank, today the infiltrating disease of cyber-crime spreads its tendrils throughout the globe with far-reaching effect. The same virus has infected most all areas of societal function: Education, Religion, the Arts and Sciences, Industry, and Government. The soundness of these institutions stands or falls on the ground of rhetorical legitimacy, but our technological tools are re-shaping and redefining *what is* more quickly than we can adjust. To explore this notion with a more granular look into the place of language we turn from generalized institutional ramifications to the microcosm of interpersonal relationships.

The dynamics of interpersonal relationships are changing. What it means *to be in* relationship looks vastly different today than it did even fifty years ago. Especially in the West, romantic relations, business partnerships—even the notion of friendship—has taken on a patina of the impersonal rather than interpersonal richness. Although great attention appears to be employed in presenting a thriving relationship to the public, the depth of relationship is sliding the downward slope of devaluation and diminishment. Consider the most recent statistics on familial stability, crime associated with broken family ties, the increase in juvenile crime, and spousal abuse.[16] Is there a correlation between these sad social trends and the increased distractions and lack of silence that this post-industrial society inspires? Once again, Picard (1952) makes this clear in his assessment of the power of language and its ability to motivate human action. Instead of sweetening human relations and creating refreshment and meaning, language has become "hard and obstinate," laden with emptiness rather than life (p. 27). This, he explains is because speech has become detached from silence. And what happens when this detachment becomes stubbornly ingrained into the daily doings of a culture? Picard explains,

> When language is no longer related to silence it loses its source of refreshment and renewal and therefore something of its substance. Language today seems to talk automatically, out of its own strength, and emptying and scattering itself, it seems to be hastening to an end. (p. 26)

Such detachment from silence denigrates contemporary conversation further, for as we appear to be communicating more, the quality of our conversations is demeaned by truncated, acronymic short-cuts, a tendency Picard describes here long before the appearance of digital communication devices. "There is something hard and obstinate in language today, as though it were making a great effort to remain alive in spite of its emptiness. There is also something desperate in it, as though it were expecting its emptiness to lead it to a relentless end, and it is this alternation of obstinacy and despair which makes it so restless" (p. 26).

Certainly, conversational quality is not universally debased. The hushed tones of sexual intimacy or the whispered moments of friends sharing secrets have not died, but there is something that rings true in this 20th century philosopher's words. After only approximately a quarter of a century conversational norms have changed monumentally. Tolerance for lengthy conversation, as well as the ability to fruitfully engage in one at all, is becoming more difficult. Where there is generally a natural ebb and flow of speech and silence in healthy and effective face-to-face conversations, use of a cell phone often makes them stilted and fragmented. The constant presence of the cell phone in our hands and the growing observation of the addictive ways we use it connects to Picard's assessment that without silence "all things are present all the time in an atmosphere of noisy rebelliousness" (p. 56). Without an appreciation and practice of silence there is little order or structure to what is being communicated. Although the dynamics are different, the same is true for e-mail and text-messaging. Text-based interpersonal exchanges are often characterized by their choppy, abbreviated, edited, and typically truncated structure, elements that wreak havoc in interpersonal relationships.

Despite the relative sparseness of communication research on silence, Picard is not alone in his emphases on the ontological and relational ramifications. Scholars advancing the interconnection of communication, silence, and being often find themselves at the edge of a practice known as *dialogue*, that type of communication which emerges from the solid ground of being, where meaning and substance return to the communicational foreground. To hope for an advance toward dialogue, one must be willing to listen with an openness that is ready to receive the other without having to persuade. For this hope to truly inspire toward change it is important to understand what the work of these philosophers implies. To communicate involves a process that allows people access to one another—a process that provides a way to engage in meaningful discourse and a way to gain greater ability to share space harmoniously. It is this aspect of the symbolic exchange that provides equipment for living, enabling people of diverse backgrounds or differing ideologies to walk together using civil, sane, meaningful speech.[17] To engage in dialogue both parties must be open to it. As it does not come naturally to engage in dialogue, we must teach, remember, and insist that our conversation not be relegated to bits and bytes, recalling regularly that communication is not simply a matter of sending and receiving messages, but a complex process that requires intentionality. The reach of dialogue is deeper; it requires both intentionality and desire.

Communication includes not only the subject itself, but the entire environment in which the subject exists. This environment is often invisible, but includes the people themselves, the particular purposes of their conversation, the principles underpinning the interaction and the overall performance. This idea gains further clarity in the work of many communication theorists, philosophers, and social scientists. One, in particular is Martin Buber (1878–1965), another 20th century philosopher who perceived silence as one of the necessary components to "living speech," that is, a type of communication "which towers above the spirit of knowledge and the spirit of art because here evanescent, corporeal man need not banish himself into the enduring matter but outlasts it and rises, himself an image, on the starry sky of the spirit, as the music of his living speech roars around him—pure action—the act that is not arbitrary."[18]

For Buber (1970), living speech is essential for it is in these encounters that individuals may find meaning and truth. He explains that it is only in "silence toward the You, the silence of all tongues, [that, *sic*] the taciturn waiting in the unformed, undifferentiated, pre-linguistic word leaves the You free and stands together with it in reserve where the spirit does not manifest itself but is" (p. 89). In other words, for *conversation* to be dialogic there must be a measure of silence. Certainly, complete silence is problematic; Buber does not advocate this. Rather, I believe, he positions silence and speech as working together dialectically in an ebb and flow, a give and take. The tidal metaphor provides another way to picture the beauty brought about through this intersection of silence and speech. They must be intermingled. The well-spoken word rising from the groundedness of silence, a receptive silence—one that is open to hearing something deeper than the words that are expressed. Both are necessary for meaning to emerge. Especially in mediated conversations, the dialectic of silence and speech is vital.

SPIRIT

Another aspect of Buber's project that intersects with the emphasis on presence is his concept of *spirit*. The livingness of encounter refers to the uniquely human element as "spirit." For Buber, the need for this is posited as the most basic need of human beings (pp. 88–89). Spirit, he explains, is part of the mystery to which people are drawn because it is the place from whence we come. He describes it simply, if not esoterically: "Spirit in its human manifestation is man's response to his You," that is, his or her truest, most authentic self (p. 89). Fulfillment of this authentic sense of being involves the capacity to relate—that "power which alone can enable man to live in the spirit" (p. 89). Essentially, then, Buber perceives *being* as non-individualistic, but "in relation." His concept of "spirit" is that which provides meaning, that is, spirit *is* meaning. His implicit critique of technology emerges from the dearth of spirit, the lack of relation, as he explains,

> modern developments have expunged almost every trace of a life in which human beings confront each other and have meaningful relationships. It would be absurd to try to reverse this development; and if one could bring off this absurdity, the tremendous precision instrument of this civilization would be destroyed at the same time, although this alone makes life possible for the tremendously increased numbers of humanity. (p. 97)

The dialectic of speech and silence is apparent in his above statement, and that, combined with the ability to engage in true encounter, is key to understanding the ontological aspects of silence. Our lives are not lived with the precision of machines. We need the ebb and flow of silence and speech to live in relation to one another. It is an organic function, yet our tools acculturate us to form and preciseness, aligning well-being and success with effectiveness and efficiency. This presents a problem, for refurbishing or renewing the place of silence in our lives is similar to asking our ancestral hunters and gatherers to "go on a diet" or "work out to stay in shape." Strong, healthy bodies did not need a gym membership. Their muscles retained strength by virtue of daily life. For dialogue to flourish, this must be addressed. Dialogic speech must retain (and in many ways regain) its place of significance in this highly technological world and thus renew a commitment toward the common good, moving forward with a new respect for civil discourse. What this requires is no less than practice, discipline, and much intentionality.

Understanding that communication is not simply a matter of sending and receiving messages, but rather a process that involves the totality of the relationship in which language is used well and, respectfully, is the first step in moving toward these goals. Ultimately, it takes remembering that "communication is not stuff or bits or messages. In a way, it is not even something that people do. Communication is a situation in which people participate, rather like the way a plant participates in what we call its growth" (Postman, 1976, p. 8). The silence of the seed as it waits in anticipation of growth is an apt picture. In darkness it waits until the sun woos it upward, and breaking through the firm soil it rises, ready to bloom. Postman's metaphor continues as he explains this feature in the process of communication. "A plant does not exactly grow because it does something. Growth is a consequence of complex transactions among the plant, the soil, the air, the sun, and water. All in the proper proportions, at the proper time, according to the proper rules" (Postman, 1976, p. 8). But proper rules are not always in place. Most conversation does not operate with the formal rules of a courtroom. The informality of our social relations allows for variations just as the "rules" requiring sun and soil for the plant do not specify the exact location of the garden or the precise amount of rain. Neither are there such formal rules in most interpersonal situations. This is part of the complexity and ineffable beauty of communication. Words are more than the symbols they represent. Neither are words rootless when grounded ontologically. Grounded ontologically there is no such thing as empty rhetoric.

INTERIORITY

Offered from a basic sense of self and confidence that is in touch with the silence from whence they emerged, words mediate our interiority, making known—albeit fleetingly –the reality of beingness. The sound of our words emerges from within, illuminating some of the mystery that resides in (not) knowing the other, creating an organic platform through which intimate knowledge of the other may grow. As Ong explains, "Sound . . . reveals the interior without the necessity of physical invasion. Thus, we tap a wall to discover where it is hollow inside or we ring a silver-colored coin to discover whether it is perhaps lead instead. To discover such things by sight, we should have to open what we examine, making the inside the outside, destroying its interiority as such" (1969, p. 637). Ong helps clarify this richly revelatory aspect of sound with a musical example: "The sound of a violin is determined by the interior structure of its strings, of its bridge, and of the wood in its soundboard, by the shape of the interior cavity in the body of the violin, and other interior conditions. Filled with concrete or water, the violin would sound different" (p. 637). Without the grounding of ontological silence our grasp of reality begins to loosen, not only in our relationship with self and others, but with what is actual in the world around us. The strong rope of rationality to which we hold steady begins to fray. Becoming awake and alive to the language of being is the starting point of speech and the place silence enters to help ground the process.

Among the many others who weigh in regarding the language of being is Kenneth Burke (1897–1993), the logician, philosopher, critical theorist, teacher, poet, and linguist. Burke developed ideas and theories about the relationship between language, meaning, and cognition, one of which places speech at the center of what it means to be human, that which separates us from other creatures. Burke's view of language is something he called symbolic action, framing speech as the ability to use symbols as what one might call a grammar of being. For Burke, the human being is the "symbol using, symbol-making, symbol mis-using animal"; the use of symbols (which extends beyond the limitations of language) is the defining element (Burke, 1961).[19] His dramatistic framework emphasizes reality as something that is appropriated in culturally bound symbol systems and is one method of explaining the way human beings experience reality, their sense of self, and sociality.

The fact of symbolization in human beings is something of a miracle. We enter the world with the ability to make and understand symbols, but this ability must be actualized. Linguistic scholars have never stop puzzling about this. This mystery always comes back to the difference between one's interiority and one's action. Language is a behavior. It is a behavior undertaken by all human beings everywhere.[20] As Plato might construe it, the speaking person is the true form of each human. Burkean scholar Ed Appel (2003) argues that Burke's approach places human beings in the unique position of being driven toward perfection or "ultimate" purposes. One element of this involves the motivation (or propensity) to speak (p. 7).

Burke claimed the inherent tension that exists within each human being stems from the fact that we are finite, limited, "vulnerable beings, situated, on the one hand, in an animal's body, with nary a chance of being, in all respects, 'perfect.' Yet we are, on the other hand, infinitely untethered and far-seeing in the gifts of thought and understanding language bestows on us" (Appel, p. 7). These inherent limitations carry over into speech and an ongoing propensity to abuse these gifts. Examples run the gamut of human behavior from lying, to manipulation, gossip, and deep deception. We fail endlessly in the attempt to use speech well. Discussing the private lives of others is far from a contemporary problem, but today news streaks across the world with a single click whether it is substantiated or not. Whether it is the falsified videos known as "deep fakes" or the algorithmic confirmation bias that sweeps through the many platforms of social media, we are a people who tend to take personal advantage of whatever media are available to us, despite the pain caused to others. The speed and access to the ears of others has never been greater, but despite the benefits of such immediacy, the reciprocal losses are piling up.

According to Burke, this symbolic drive is so much a part of the human condition that it will "likely dupe symbol users into thinking they have hit upon the whole truth of the matter as they construct their limited universes of meaning with the block-like terminologies they employ, pulling bits of reality apart and treating them as wholes" (Appel, 2003, p. 1). With this tension ever present, it is not surprising that many are lured by the communicational opportunities that PMM provide, unaware of the caution they must bring to the experience. This is particularly challenging in that the time and space constrictions that these media reduce open up doors for understanding oneself, providing new opportunities "to be." Additionally, the hope to "reinvent oneself" is broader in the world of online communications for there is always another platform to explore. Small-town gossip and the shame associated with it is an experience one can rather easily put in the past because the

Internet has made the world our home. Thus, life on the screen has become more than an alternative way to spend one's time. Less and less do we see time spent on (and with) our PMM as separate from "real life." This may be part of the reason silence has not been seen as integral to the interpersonal situations of PMM. When one shuts down their screen, silence ensues. They no longer exist. The notion of *being* is shaken.

Since speaking seems to instantiate power, *not speaking* may be perceived as fostering the opposite. Yet, there are increasingly numerous times when silence *is* the appropriate response but it is bypassed because of a seemingly inherent belief that all speech is proper, good, and better than saying nothing at all. Joseph Capizzi, professor of moral theology at Catholic University of America, calls upon Augustine in his polemic piece bemoaning the reckless arrogance of so many loud voices in the public square. Enjoining the reader to listen for the transcendent Voice, Capizzi writes:

> The noise of the surety of our colleagues and friends, of sudden expertise, is pummeling our ears, drowning out the silence that we need to hear the word of God. Silence is a space, and silence can be fertile. Without the patience to allow that seed of the Word to grow, our thinking becomes barren. Today, I wonder if perhaps the greatest gift of many of us might be to answer Augustine's question with this: "For now, I do not know."[21]

How many instances of civil unrest or untenable social disorder could be avoided if more of us could simply say, "I don't know." Capizzi's candor concerning his own faith in God will not match that of all readers, but his point concerning the humility of Augustine is well worth taking.

Like Burke, Martin Heidegger (1889–1976) addresses the need to understand being through language in sharply definitive terms when he asks the question, "Is it a coincidence that the Greeks defined the nature of a man as . . . animal rationale? The living being endowed with reason is not wrong but it hides the phenomenal soil from which this definition of existence is taken. 'Man reveals himself as the being that speaks'" (p. 13). For both Heidegger and Burke, it appears that *Homo loquax* supersedes the notion of *Homo sapiens*, for although both scholars recognize rationality and thinking as intrinsic to human beings, the ability and propensity to speak is even more primal.[22]

Although Burke's definition of man incorporates a complex understanding of what it means to be human, the most essential aspect as related to the present discussion involves the use and *abuse* of symbols. Many situations arise both for individuals and within institutions in which instead of using our symbols wisely, we allow ourselves to be used by them. This becomes highly problematic. Clear examples of this are evident in the computer hacking, identity theft, online bullying, and privacy breaches as language is used in virtual space, but this abuse or misuse of symbols may be seen in every era, no matter the technologies used to communicate. Disingenuous language has long been evident in both the recent past and present age, operating in numerous ways, one being through the world of advertising and mass media. For example, while people have largely perceived television and its ubiquitous popularity as a provider of entertainment, information, and news, programming is actually (and primarily) a vehicle for mass dissemination of advertisements. Developed by Philo Farnsworth in 1927, the television spawned an industry that functions as a tool for advertisement, its goal to capture attention and sell products and services. The same is so for the newer media such as cell phones, the wireless Internet, and other mobile communication devices.

While these media serve a purpose in connecting people one to another, they are market-driven with market-centric goals; they are consumer mechanisms. The mobile phone, for example, does not exist so that individuals may make an emergency call from the highway if a car breaks down. While we use it for that along with many other relevant purposes, among them entertainment, education, banking, conversation, etc., the mobile phone primarily exists so that the developers can create revenue. This is not to say that commercial interests do not have a place in the world economy, nor is it meant to infer that humanity return to a more pastoral life. However, understanding the commercial purposes of these devices further underscores the need to choose our PMM and other media carefully, with a critical eye as to their relational salience and potential effect on quality of life. The occasional, emergency use of these devices will not have the grave effect that unfettered, habitual use may, but just as eating one donut once is not a threat to our health, we surely cannot function well on a daily diet of sugar-laden foods.

As our discussion of the interplay between ontology and silence continues, we move to what some philosophers speak of called the *mystery* of Being. Like Burke and Buber, Jacques Ellul (1912–1994) acknowledges the tie to mystery and embraces the very ambiguity of language as integral to all that it means to be human (1994). He expands on this symbolic significance of language, saying:

> We are in the presence of an infinitely and unexpectedly rich tool, so that the tiniest phrase unleashes an entire polyphonic gamut of meaning. The ambiguity of language and even its ambivalence and its contradiction between the moment it is spoken and the moment it is received—produce extremely intense activities. Without such activities we would be ants or bees, and our drama and tragedy would quickly be dried up and empty. (p. 123)

Here, depicting the high drama of life, it is clear that without communication there would be little activity. Drama, however, cannot be had without the dialectic of silence infusing itself within every bit of dialogue. The tension is what "makes" the story, keeps the audience on the edge of its seat, and evokes a response of unbridled applause when the scene is ended. In the drama of interpersonal relationships, the same tension is necessary; otherwise, the actions become mechanical, boring, and better left than embraced.[23] Ellul addresses this indirectly in his thoughts about the importance of recognizing the mystery and complexity of the route to meaning, and explains:

> Meaning is uncertain; therefore I must constantly fine-tune my language and work at reinterpreting the words I hear. I try to understand what the other person says to me. All language is more or less a riddle to be figured out; it is like interpreting a text that has many possible meanings. In my effort at understanding and interpretation, I establish definitions, and finally, a meaning. The thick haze of discourse produces meaning.[24]

This "thick haze" is not to imply that there is virtue in favoring mystery or seeking it, but simply to understand that mystery is part of the process of speech. "Language itself is not rooted in precision, but carries meaning across from mystery by means of metaphor."[25] Understanding this is a step that usually goes unnoticed or ignored. To denigrate the complexity of human communication by reducing it to something mathematical, scientific, or strictly utilitarian is to undermine the beauty and intrinsic worth—even necessity—of language as a means to comprehend our humanness.

The mysteries of human anatomy, for example, are uncovered as scientists seek, experiment, and observe the complexities of what was once the utterly unknown world of genes, cells, all of the body's many intertwined systems. The lack of knowing stirs up a desire to explore and an intellectual curiosity that ultimately helps us deal with death, dying, and the entire condition of our humanness. Mystery intersects with our discussion of dialogue in numerous ways. First, it is not to be despised or something from which we flee, for mystery is a catalyst for discovery. Scientists hypothesize and experiment as they come up against a wall of unknowing, a wall of mystery. Acknowledging the unknown is an essential piece to their future discovery. Thus, acknowledging the mystery of the other as other is essential as a first step toward dialogue. Being aware and awake to our own lack of knowledge provides the impulse to know the other, to listen, to observe, to understand. Mystery is also important in that it mitigates certainty and thus has the potential to stem the sort of arrogance that inhibits dialogue. Embraced, mystery can keep us humble, that ingredient so essential but often overlooked in effective communication. What is unknown bears investigation and curiosity.

The deep complexity of language is an unquenchable well, and when it is understood as a part of what it means *to be*, we are better able to recognize the yearning for the same in each other. This reveals another way to clear the road toward dialogue and civility; it is yet one more of the reasons reckoning with silence is so important. Without silence we are more apt to ramble through a conversation completely ignoring the integrity and dignity of the other, misconstruing what is being said from the start. The notion of mystery in connection with communication is very much embedded in a philosophical approach to language, which is, perhaps, part of the reason the intersecting subjects of silence and personal mobile media have yet to be at the forefront in communication research trends.

Buber's thoughts on "spirit" have value here, particularly since he views spirit symbolically, *vis-à-vis*, the life force. Spirit is the mysterious unseen essence of a human being that transcends flesh and blood, that which is in the breath of each human. This idea brings us again to Max Picard in whose thinking this idea appears implicitly. The philosopher depicts silence as necessary to the work of ordering oneself in the world of work and commerce. Here, he describes silence as containing nearly salvific qualities. He writes:

> To save man from this invasion and congestion of the too-many objects that are beyond his powers of assimilation, he must be brought into relationship again with the world of silence, in which the many objects find their true order automatically in this world of silence where they spread themselves out into a balanced unity. (1952, p. 57)

"Invasion and congestion" are words Picard used to describe the state of being in the mid-20th century, prior to digital media. In this sense it is as if silence functions as a great washing of the busy word, a cleansing to renew and restore equilibrium. Picard's explication of the world of silence and its place in organizing human thought strikes a chord as we consider the ongoing discussion regarding distraction, extraneous noise, and the information glut that pulls our focus away from attentive listening. And, as previously discussed, today's personal mobile media affect one's perception of being by eliminating many of the time-binding constraints in communication. When our language and communication (in general) become detached from time, a new world of possibilities opens us for people all over the world (e.g., globalism). Simultaneous with the possibilities are new challenges. Intercultural communication issues become more pronounced, and the management of day-to-day relationships may become more complicated.

Time and space are two of the ways in which the mind structures reality. Using our PMM to communicate plunges us into perceiving and utilizing time and space in new ways. No longer does one have to wait to see a best friend to share the latest life events. Our digital devices provide immediate access even if the conversational partners are situated in different countries and time zones. Since the limitations of time and distance no longer bind us to their strict limitations of physicality, it is important to note the several ways these changes affect perception. The detachment from time and space has an effect not only on individual perception but on the perception of relationship to others. As Ong explained, "Words are inescapably tied to time. This is why they are alive, why they are strong, why they are powerful: they are actions" (Altree, 1973, p. 15). This leads us to many questions regarding relational stability and the notion of the anchored self.

In his classic work, *I and Thou*, Buber (1970) brought to bear a concept of self as "anchored"; this he termed the "authentic self" or the self that is a paired entity.[26] This "self" cannot exist independently from others or outside of a particular "time" or "space." In Buber's schema, as we have previously seen, when the "I" is not focused on the other as subject, it objectifies the other and creates little room for relationship. Conducting an interpersonal exchange without an anchored self and outside a reliable perception of time and space complicates the situation even more. Further in line with Buber's (1970) concept of the authentic self and "the other," there is a necessary (but not always apparent) dynamic that "marks" the exchange as being truly human. This is one of Buber's more complex concepts, because this interchange between the self and other involves several concurrent elements. Along with the need for taking *time* to communicate dialogically, an ontological element is involved that pushes the symbolic action of the word toward encounter—that which is beyond mere conversational coherence toward the presence of living speech. For Buber, only individuals who have become "single ones"—that is, independent, autonomous selves—are capable of turning toward the other; only these are capable of bringing a dialogic response to the other. He explains, "In order to be able to go out to the other you must have a starting place; you must be 'with yourself'" (p. 21).

Communication ethicist Clifford Christians brings this point to precision when he explains the depth of our human ability to use symbols. Symbolic action and interpretation are intricately entwined and influence our entire way of being. He writes: "Symbols cannot be isolated in our cranium. Our interpretive dimension forms an organic whole with our deepest humanness, and its vitality or oppression inevitably conditions our well-being" (1998, p. 4). And, as is strongly inferred in Buber's project as well, encounter with the other creates the necessary "space" or environment for the uniqueness of what is fully human to emerge from the individual.

Buber, whose thinking on communication is always constituted in the midst of "relation," broadens the definition of communication to provide the deep ontological underpinnings that are found in the intrapersonal realm, for it is there, and only there that we can begin to see (and know) the other, as true subject. It is only there we receive "the revelation of otherness, or the breaking of the shells that encase the self, not about the sharing of private mental property" (Durham-Peters, pp. 16–17). Here again we are reminded that communication is much more about what evolves from the outcome of a dialogic exchange—that is, the encounter and ensuing sense of commonality, rather than about self-disclosure or instrumental speech. This thinking is in complete opposition to the mechanical, cybernetic theory of information exchange. While not expressly dialogue, its dialogic undertones help to move us toward more respectful interpersonal exchanges.

Symbolic action occurs on many levels, but dialogue is distinctive in that while it is not necessary for both parties to agree on a subject, a desire to meet on the ground of common humanness is essential. Each must stand together on a mound called Willingness to approach each other as subjects, ready to work with the tools of mutuality and respect. For Buber (1970), true dialogue touches the realm of the supra-rational; it is the place where mystery and meaning conflate to provide a means of escape from the codifying and objectifying tendency of human beings to treat others as something less than subjects. It also involves the uniquely human functions of interpretation and judgment, both of which are highly subjective and cannot be apprehended by pushing buttons, programming information, or increasing interaction via satellite signals. For such, silence is required.

A true, ontological silence that reminds one of his or her teleological presence in the world must be attended to as part of the mystery of being and is necessary for the most effective, healthy communication with self and others.[27] It is a receptive silence, open to receiving greater understanding of oneself and of the other. This silence is freeing. It is open. It helps release the fear of unknowing, urging us along to apprehend deeper, more meaningful relationship in all of life. The magnitude of the word's worth in the process of being and becoming cannot be overstated, but this can be a formidable task. Words are so packed with power that they easily become idols; we bow to their potency, neglecting to realize that they must maintain a foundation. Silence is the dynamic platform on which our words, pregnant with life, can rise from their quiet womb and bring wisdom. Just as Picard (1952) refers to silence as the friendly sister of the word and explained its intimate connection with the fullness of speech, we note an inherent need for solitude and quiet to be present at the foundational level of the communication process. Picard suggests this is so, particularly as an individual is forming identity and a response to another human being. He writes, "When man is silent, he finds himself, not subjectively, but phenomenologically in the state that precedes the creation of language" (p. 33).

Silence, or the lack of symbolic action, may appear awkward, backward, and inefficient, but it is a necessary phenomenological step toward the thoughtful outworking of meaning. Ong (1969) emphasizes a similar significance and writes, "Language is a search for meaning and meaning is a particularly human kind of search" (p. 5). These ideas line up with Buber's perception of the mystery involved in human relations.

While the Buberian frame is far more qualitative, contextually perceived, and broad than the verbal exchange itself, it is clear that his contribution to the conversation goes far beyond the interpersonal implications. His ideas carry much weight and prescience in the present discussion of quality, meaning, and the teleological dynamics interwoven into speech. If the only idea Buber offered us was that of apprehension of "the other" as other, his project would remain worthwhile, for the ensuing sense of safety that is discovered in true, dialogic encounter is a balm, of sorts, that provides a backdrop for individuals to discover a sense of acceptance and belonging, a place *in relation*, such as needed to thrive as a whole and stable self. This begins with the first babblings of a baby's speech, grows with speech acquisition, and continues with life in the speech community, all of which begins with silence.

This brings our discussion full circle to the livingness of speech and primacy of language as a necessary part of the human experience. What does "living speech" mean in the day-to-day world? How is it translated in the average social situations of people communicating using personal mobile media in an environment that is increasingly enmeshed with said media?

Viewing the complexity of the communication process through the perspective of a media ecologist suggests that the choice of channel is a primary variable. This choice changes the conversational or "semantic environment" (Postman, 1976, pp. 2–20). That is, much meaning may be inferred and predicated upon the types of tools used to have a conversation. For example, using a text message to communicate a marriage proposal is apt to create a widely different meaning than when one asks this important question face-to-face. In other cases, the same tools may be used explicitly to avoid conversation altogether. In a workplace trend reported recently by the *Chicago Tribune* (Rose, 2006), business leaders found that workplace behaviors were changing because of digital devices such as the cell phone and iPod. Office workers wearing earbuds or headphones put themselves in what Cornell University professor Franklin Becker (Rose, 2006) calls an "auditory cave," isolating themselves from the collaborative efforts of colleagues (p. 2). Consequently, learning that takes place from observing what others are doing or by overhearing conversations was being missed, primarily because of the isolating influence of these devices. These and other social ramifications of these devices pose problems for some managers who, explained *Tribune* writer Barbara Rose (2006), "consider the devices unprofessional and disruptive"

(p. 2). In general, she reported, "companies are struggling with all kinds of personal technology. A lot of employers just do not want to have a personal playground atmosphere in the workplace" (p. 2).[28] The fact that not everyone is overtly (or consciously) disturbed by use of these PMM does not negate their potentially distracting and often isolating effects.

Others, more hopeful about using PMM in the workplace, report opposing views. A Chicago-based communications firm, Closerlook, Inc., invites the changes that technology is ushering into the workplace. David Ormesher is the firm's CEO and founder and contended that rather than isolating workers, iPods offer common ground and a sense of camaraderie. He wrote, "They share play lists on the office network and everyone winds up playing each other's music—jazz, classical, hip-hop, world music. You learn a lot about each other just by checking out playlists" (Rose, 2006, p. 2). These developments may be useful in building morale or in creating an organizational culture, unless, of course, the environment becomes so informed by "play" that the presence of PMM distracts workers and undermines productivity.

Some of these new social practices may be perceived as positive, others, as negative. This may depend somewhat on the amount of acculturation that has taken place in regard to the use of PMM (e.g., has the individual or organization been operating in a highly mediated environment with much visual/aural stimulation), as well as a high number of other variables such as individual level of education, general intelligence, physical barriers/limitations such as Attention Deficit Syndrome, type of workplace, etc. Another variable involves the demographics of the office. A workplace made up of employees who are mostly under 30 is likely to function quite differently than a mixed demographic or a company made up of mostly middle-aged and older workers. Generally speaking, whether in business, family, or the public square, the ability to listen effectively is an established element of the communication process. The isolating dynamics of our digital devices demean this process and though the outstanding ability to adapt to new environments is part of the human story of success, adaptation and survival are not always synonymous with the ability to flourish. Analysis of the repercussions induced in part by the current media landscape—particularly PMM –is of prime importance.

FROM INTERPERSONAL TO DIALOGUE

Scholarly work being done to examine and analyze current social protocols in this age of digital dominance is underway, and it is in ethics scholarship that we see some of these factors being addressed in the most practical ways. As personal mobile media become increasingly ubiquitous, the individualistic impulse carried over from the age of print is morphing from the creative use of the word into a hyper-individualism that is tugging at the edges of our social contract. Personal privacy is at stake. Freedom of speech is always fragile. We need fresh eyes to see and perceive what is at stake and how to address it. A sturdy philosophy of communication can do this. As Clifford G. Christians notes, the primordial roots of "freedom of expression in Western political theory depends on the dualism of individual and society, with rational individuated choice accountable to the rules of social contract. The philosophy of language is the opposite. It defines humans as dialogic beings. Instead of solitary subjectivism, the philosophy of language establishes a new framework" (Christians, 2014, p. 272). This perspective, wrapped around a use of language and action that celebrates the sacredness of life, does not deny or ignore the individual but looks to make meaning from a communitarian sensibility. "Language belongs to the community where its meanings are nurtured in the neighborhood, home, and school. Language is not an agent of private meanings that individuals interpret esoterically" (p. 272). Without appreciation for the communal characteristics of language and the reality-shaping distinctions that the word inheres, we are reduced to a sparse and paltry vision of society. Commitment to communities of interpretation in which voices from the margins are welcomed is one way to support the continued flourishing of our mutual humanity. This returns our discussion to silence and Picard, who depicts the problem of objectification as a phenomenon from which humans must be saved. He explains it thusly: "To save man from this invasion and congestion of the too-many objects that are beyond his powers of assimilation, he must be brought into relationship again with the world of silence in which the many objects find their true order automatically, in this world of silence where they spread themselves out in balanced unity" (p. 57). *To be brought into relationship*; this provides an instructive picture. One may imagine Silence personified as agent of reconciliation, working as a balm to address wounds, create space to untangle misunderstandings, and in general, provide a solid ground for knowing and being known. Herein, we begin to perceive the rich layers of silence and return to that aspect of it that allows for reflection but also provides the astringent to clear the mind and move into action with greater clarity. If we let her, Silence can help us mind our inner world, washing over the muddy tentacles of multi-tasking and over-busyness, releasing us from their menacing grip. This basic and necessary element of reflection is something that helps human beings maintain our connection to humanness. As such, it is the pre-condition of speech that receives, observes, ponders, and listens, without immediately engendering action. This leads us to empathy.

Empathy comes from feeling one's own frailty and recognizing it in another. Empathy is something that does not come easily to the healthy, strong, and young. It must be taught. It requires thoughtful reflection. Enter, silence. The connection between empathy, personhood, and personal mobile media is strong. When personhood is denigrated, empathic responses are apt to decline, and now, perhaps more than any other time in human history, the notion of personhood is at risk. The vast breadth of technological advances tempts us daily to believe that humans are programmable. This message may not be explicit, but the very fact of a burgeoning cultural landscape teeming with extraordinary systems of computation that allow us to use it without understanding it subtly forms and re-shapes our minds.

Lack of empathy is one of the reasons public conversations have become so laden with vitriol and demeaning language. Instead of observing the desperate plight and pain of those outside our circle, the actual need of others can easily fade into abstraction. Since the inception of the world wide web the ability to write email, text, and interact with so many through the written word has increased. The joy of connection is mitigated by the magnitude of physical separation. Instead of action, we are reduced to words. Our words, as powerful as they are, limit us to understanding the world in a linear way. Linearity has helped make us into people who can think logically and critically, but to rest on the strength of words without experience is a set-up for destruction. To call Western civilization back from the brink we will need to address these forces of destruction with something other than guns, bombs, or rhetorical eloquence. Collectively, our mindset must change. The gift of silence is needed. Without silence the possibility of dialogue becomes more and more remote, yet this is an essential element needed for civility to return as a norm. Without it, in fact, all speech may be relegated to the instrumental and utilitarian. Thus, it is of essential importance to reinforce the benefits of speech and create a platform for the possibility of true communication in all its dialectical beauty and power.

Although dialogue is not all that is needed for a restoration of meaning it is a step toward regaining a living witness to the commonality we share in our humanness. Here Clifford Christians reminds us of a Habermasian concept, that communication is our "lifeworld." Communication "is the human mode of belonging together"(Christians 2020,p. 273). We live in communication with each other; that is our habitation. When communication is reduced to transaction *we* are reduced. When our habitation becomes the media environment in which we live, our souls are housed in the values of consumerism, individuality, and material gain. Growing acceptance of a utilitarian society has long been a factor in this reductionism.

Though the reach of dialogue can span much farther than one might imagine, the notion that dialogue is a panacea for the dysfunction in today's public media is untenable. Many other factors are at play. Format, frame, and the commercial goals of media conglomerates contribute to the steadily decreasing state of public discourse. When television programming executives actively work to reduce people to consumers and social media developers intentionally create addictive features, there is no discussion about personhood. Dialogue is dismissed. There is no room for it. Such objectification eliminates the person as subject, making each consumer a "thing" instead of a person. This has become crystal clear as the fractured mirror of public communication increasingly becomes the norm. We see ourselves in the broken glass, taking on a false sense of identity, one that has been shaped by the media landscape on which we traverse.

Taking time to rethink and rehearse the symbolic action that highlights our humanness will allow us to remember that which has been lost. In our world of highly differentiated cultures, it is challenging to always perceive the commonality or sense of "one-people." But just as a physical body cannot function when it is dismembered, we need to remember ourselves as part of one another. To "remember" is to gather oneself back to wholeness. This is somewhat akin to the wholeness—or gathering of itself collectively—of all of humanity. Staying awake to the collective Body, without which we become ill-equipped to remember, requires regular attunement to these proto norms and understanding of the profound power of our speech.

Contrary to much late modernist thinking, we make meaning together or die. The work or renewal and revitalization of our public sphere is a work that can only be accomplished together, for "language is not an agent of private meanings that individuals interpret esoterically" (Christians, 2020, p. 272). Rather, "language belongs to the community where its meanings are nurtured in the neighborhood, home, and school."[29] What is needed first is awareness of the desperate need for revitalization of all that is human. The awareness is just a beginning and must flow in undulating ripples into the public square. Although this book does not purport to be solutionary, the need must be called out again and again until we are able to each be a part of the answer. Collective effort spawned by individual awareness of the need to be better than we are—to return to a more civil society and carve a path for future flourishing—is a step in that direction.

Buber, Burke, Christians, Ong, and Ellul: Assigning these 20th-century thinkers the kind of importance I have allows a broader inquiry to be launched in the advancement of a philosophy of communication. What is especially relevant here is the way these communication philosophies intersect with the plethora of devices and numerous ways personal mobile media are presently being used. While in a certain sense, the high connectivity and interactive aspect of cell phone and hand-held digital devices might be viewed as enhancing relationship development rather than hindering it, the quality must be called into question. Certainly, each time the cell phone rings forth from one's pocket or belt loop it establishes a connection. While not face-to-face, the connection does provide the ability to participate in a verbal exchange and it does create a "sense" of being with another. The dangling question, however, is "what *kind* of connection is made, and does it involve living speech?" Is it possible or likely that people can experience fully this hopeful "moment of encounter" via text message? Does this method of message exchange make room for dialogue?

Conversely, when a person is engaged in dialogical listening and has intention to truly enter into a communication situation with another as other, an opportunity for what Buber calls "encounter" is made possible. With such face-to-face communication and high intentionality, the setting is now prepared for dialogue. Both speech and silence are present, parts of language that lay groundwork for what he calls a "revelation of otherness" to take place (p. 17). This sense of the other as subject is intimately intertwined with one's sense of self, the depths of which must be mined through silence, albeit a challenging thing to undertake. To take up the pick and shovel of an archaeological dig into one's own sense of self is a formidable task, but it is precisely where the interplay of meaningful communication begins and ends. This venture is often framed as a pilgrimage and embarked upon as a spiritual journey that requires fluency in silence and solitude.

The journey motif has been threaded throughout literature and is familiar terrain across all human experience, appearing in various instantiations, whether embodied or metaphoric. One example of this is the ongoing dedication to a journey through France and Spain called "the Camino." Pilgrims have walked the Camino de Santiago since the 8th century, each on a quest to disconnect from the noise of the daily grit of life to discover an elusive "something more."[30] The elusive "something" typically finds its goal in inner peace or purpose. Peace is an elusive gift; its lack is a key factor in conversations that tear people apart rather than bring healing and reconciliation. "When we are more at peace with ourselves, we will not be threatened by those who have different perspectives or beliefs."[31] To discover and then maintain such peace is intimately connected to one's inner dialogue. When that inner dialogue is obscured or muted it is especially challenging to speak with confidence, authority, or authenticity. Speech desperately needs its strong foundation of silence upon which to stand. Instead, its flimsy flooring can barely hold a conversation in which there is disagreement. Too much insecurity rules the day. This is the challenge of a silence that haunts rather than heals.

NOTES

1. Since 2012 a whole new generation of children are enjoying the animated spin-off from *Mr. Rogers' Neighborhood* called *Daniel Tiger's Neighborhood*.

2. In an excerpt from his 1999 induction into the Television Hall of Fame ceremony, Rogers revealed the reason for his persistence in bringing up subjects that were hard for children to talk about. He said, "We feel on the Neighborhood that whatever is mentionable is much more manageable. For children to be able to see us dealing with such things as the death of a pet, or the trauma of living through a divorce—these are all things that are allowed to be talked about and allowed to be felt. What some children can put up with, grow into, and then later flourish and help others with, is a wonderful mystery." Here, Fred Rogers is planting the seeds of dialogue in the soil of young minds, speaking directly to a generation of children who had largely been taught that they were to be "seen and not heard," or to "grow up" and stuff their feelings of insecurity. Fred Rogers helped his young audiences understand that it was okay to feel and to talk about it.

3. See James K. A. Smith. "The Intelligence of Love." p. 35.

4. The simplicity and basic human need for safety was built into every episode of *Mister Rogers' Neighborhood*: conversation; authentic, eyeball-to-eyeball, words ensconced in relationship—this is what Fred Rogers offered.

5. *Telos* also infers perfection, but not in the sense of that which is without flaw. The word points more directly to the "end" or "ripeness" of something. The fact that human perfection is impossible does not negate the reality that there is an innate desire to grow or develop into the perfection or end that will complete our lives.

6. The notion of "co-creation" of culture is rooted in an understanding that a human being cannot blink reality into being. Co-creation comes with the underlying and tacit knowledge that humans are born into the world with the ability to use symbols, but are not God or the force of the universe/nature to do this on our own.

7. Quentin Schultz. *Communicating with Grace and Virtue*. p. 87.

8. Consider the corpus of so many of those rhetoricians who are also known as philosophers, such as Jürgen Habermas, Kenneth Burke, Martin Heidegger, and Hans-Georg Gadamer, just to name a few.

9. See Neil Postman *Crazy Talk, Stupid Talk: How We Defeat Ourselves by the Way We Talk and What to Do about It*.

10. Quenttin Schultze. *Communicating for Life*. p. 19.

11. Josef Pieper. *Abuse of Language, Abuse of Power*. p. 15.

12. Max Picard's Hegelian and Heideggerian leanings are evident in his ontological approach to silence and speech, particularly in regard to Hegel's conception of being as spirit.

13. Max Picard. *The World of Silence*. p. 28.

14. Max Picard, the 20th century philosopher who wrote *The World of Silence*, reminds us that our flight from silence is really a flight from ourselves. https://herbertbaioco.files.wordpress.com/2017/02/the-world-of-silence-max-picard.pdf.

15. Much public and academic discourse concerning the fragmentation of postmodern society has been attributed to the spread of suburbia, the dual-income household, changing roles of men and women, the advance of globalism and ease of travel, etc. While each of these factors may play a role in the changing norms of society, the present fragmentation as an "outcome" is not the issue. That there is fragmentation is the issue. This frenzied, de-structuring/restructuring fragmentation and lack of anchoring

in traditional values may or may not have anything to do with the disappearance of silence in communication, but both phenomena are occurring simultaneously and certainly may have some correlative elements.

16. While divorce and crime rates in the U.S. are readily available, there are a number of variables skewing the statistics. In divorce statistics, the number of states reporting changed several years ago when four states removed their findings from the surveys of the U.S. Census Bureau polls. However, the United States also leads the developed world in divorce rate and in the increase of several other social ills. The writings of Francis Fukuyama point to possible reasons for the decline, one being what he calls "the Great Disruption." Fukuyama associates the divorce statistics, rise in crime, and the out-of-control pandemic of teen pregnancy with the decline of kinship in the 20th century. Part of the reason he cited for the dramatic change in social norms is the degeneration of cultural institutions due to the dramatic shift in population, changes in major economies in the West, and the onslaught of the Age of Information, which together converged in the West from the middle of the 20th century through the present. Fukuyama explained, "Although a majority of people in the United States and Europe expressed confidence in their governments and fellow citizens during the late 1950s only a small minority did so by the early 1990s. The nature of people's involvement with one another changed as well—although there is no evidence that people associated with one another less, their ties tended to be less permanent, looser, and with smaller groups of people" (Fukuyama, 1999, p. 1). Fukuyama, explaining his interpretation of the rapid and mass decline in social bonds and norms, may have touched upon an important factor in the disappearance of silence as it relates to mediated speech—the decline of kinship. In an extended excerpt from his *Atlantic Monthly* article on cultural, economic, and social ills, he wrote: "The decline of kinship as a social institution, which has been going on for more than 200 years, accelerated sharply in the second half of the 20th century. Marriages and births declined, and divorce soared; and one out of every three children in the United States and more than half of all children in Scandinavia were born out of wedlock. Finally, trust and confidence in institutions went into a forty-year decline [. . .] These changes were dramatic; they occurred over a wide range of similar countries; and they all appeared at roughly the same period in history. As such, they constituted a Great Disruption in the social values that had prevailed in the industrial-age society of the mid-20th century. It is very unusual for social indicators to move together so rapidly; even without knowing why they did so, we have cause to suspect that the reasons might be related" (p. 1).

17. I am borrowing the phrases "equipment for living" from Kenneth Burke, whose landmark essay, "Literature as Equipment for Living," is central to my understanding of the communication process.

18. Martin Buber. *I and Thou.* 91.

19. Although the first instantiation of it was found in his 1961 *Rhetoric of Religion*, Burke's full and final definition of a human is found in *Language as Symbolic Action* (1966). While I refer to this definition in the body of this work in its shortened form, Burke's fuller definition is as follows: "Being bodies that learn language thereby becoming wordlings, humans are the symbol-making, symbol-using,

symbol-misusing animal, inventor of the negative separated from our natural condition by instruments of our own making, goaded by the spirit of hierarchy acquiring foreknowledge of death and rotten with perfection" (p. 16).

20. It is the behavior which separates us from the beasts. Burke always used the phrase the "definition of man" (we forgive him for that). Women are a part of the human race but notoriously less attended to in cultural narratives during the 20th century.

21. Joseph Capizzi. "What Am I to Say?" June 24, 2020. COMMENT [June 25, 2020] https://breakingground.us/what-am-i-to-say/.

22. *Homo loquax*: Man, the speaker.

23. Discussion of the relationship between dialectic and rhetoric has a long history, and highly respected scholars differ greatly in interpretation. Some, like Aristotle, maintain that dialectic is a part of rhetoric; others, such as Plato, uphold dialectic as "higher" or more important than rhetoric, pointing to rhetoric as a means of persuasion through eloquence while dialectic involves argument and a more reasoned and respectable approach to truth. As a dialectician, Ellul's perspective seems to be the opposite of Burke's in that (as a Rhetorician) Burke positions rhetoric as replacing dialectic as the operative mode. However, in Burke's dramatistic theory of communication there are overlaps and intersections between Ellul's depictions of the tragedy and drama of life and the terministic screens through which people communicate. This train of thought may find application to the contemporary configuration and use of PMM in interpersonal communication, in general. The fullest expression of interpersonal communication makes use of both the rhetorical and dialectical modes. With the present use of these digital devices, it is evident that communication behavior requires an incorporation of both and may be especially so now as the tools of technology have become increasingly sophisticated and embedded in daily use.

24. This is from Jacques Ellul's chapter "Seeing and Hearing: Prolegomena" in the 1994 Anderson, Cissna, and Arnett volume, *The Reach of Dialogue.* p. 121.

25. Loren Wilkinson. "The Master and His Emissary: A Theological (and Theopoetic) Review." CRUX: Regent College, Canada. Winter 2015. Vol. 51, No. 4. pp. 2–11.

26. It is either "I-It" if one treats the other as an object or the "I-You" if one is fully present to the other and treats that one as fully subject. For Buber, the "I-You" is the most basic word pair (p. 53).

27. Other scholars of communication, philosophy, and rhetoric concur, writing about various aspects of such silence. Eric Watts (2001), for example, frames silence as "not muteness" (p. 191).

28. This statement was made by Richard Chaifetz, CEO of employee assistance firm ComPsych Corp in an interview with *Chicago Tribune* writer Barbara Rose.

29. Christians, 2020, p. 272.

30. This month-long, 500-mile walk has welcomed people for over 1,000 years to what is often called a "walking holiday" to disconnect from the noise and clamor of industrialized society and experience instead spiritual awakening or benefit from the relative silence and solitude. Originally, pilgrims set out to visit the burial site of St. James, and while some still set out with that intention, the "Camino" has drawn

pilgrims for a variety of reasons beyond adoration. Approximately 300,000 hikers of all ages and predispositions embark on the walk each year.

31. Jacobsen, Taylor, and Prater. *A Language of Healing for a Polarized Nation.* p. 87..

Chapter 5

Phantom Silence

When the Internet was young it was easy to fool most anyone. There was little reason to doubt that an email appearing on one's computer screen was not legitimate. Then came the flood of persuasive pleas from con-artists around the globe, each with untraceable email addresses hoping to pilfer funds from unassuming users. Many versions of email fraud emerged in the 1990s, but perhaps the most notorious came to be known as the "Nigerian Prince scam" where for more than a decade it operated in full throttle creating transnational havoc and much misery.[1] One version of this scam reads something like this:

> I am Mrs. Edward Impoya(ph), a member of the Movement for Democratic Change in Zimbabwe. I am so troubled. My spirit refuses to be at rest. The quick need for contacting you is because my husband has been killed unjustly, and I am sure if we don't act fast, head of the Emirates must come for our wealth and millions of American dollars will be seized. About $83 million U.S. my husband had in his private vault has been successfully deposited. . . . For this reason, I need your help. Kindly furnish us your contact information; that is, your personal telephone[2]

Many lonely people—and particularly, the elderly—were drawn into these scams by their compassion, each losing a bit their self-esteem along with their money. But fraudulent financial scams and snake oil schemes plagued humanity long before the Internet; from home burglars to bank robbers on horseback, masked men demanding cash from bank tellers to grifters and pick-pockets of every sort—the impulse toward dishonesty did not emerge in the late 20th century. What *has* emerged, however, is that remote communication via the Internet has made such trickery much easier. In fact, it was much earlier, when information became regularly separated from the person sharing it, that this trend began. During the 19th century the telegraph connected the continents, and it was there the great paradigm shift in communication began.[3] A much broader sense of world geography and history began to emerge as the telegraph deepened the public's perception of a silent stranger across the globe as someone they actually knew. Small bits of information about this fantastical unseen other captivated the soul of the West and we began in earnest to journey deeper into the forest of phantom silence.

FROM THE TELEGRAPH TO SOCIAL MEDIA

The telegraph connected the world, allowing access to people and problems far outside the scope of their immediate locale, changing the shape and perception of time, space, and reality itself. In 1985, educator and media ecologist Neil Postman (1931–2003) wrote about these changes and the psychological effects they fostered, notably, the major mental imbalance that occurs when a person hears about another's pain and is unable to move into action.[4] Public discourse, generally more civil and evolved, began to morph from reasoned argument and discussion to exclamatory reaction. "The telegraph introduced a kind of public conversation whose form had startling characteristics: Its language was the language of headlines—sensational, fragmented, impersonal. News took the form of slogans, to be noted with excitement, to be forgotten with dispatch. Its language was also entirely discontinuous."[5] Indeed, the social influence of the telegraph was monumental. In quite similar ways, the growing ubiquity of smart technologies has altered social life in ways that are at least as dramatic and life changing as the establishment of the telegraph.

Prior to the age of telegraphy, the ratio of information-to-action was sufficiently in balance so that most people had a sense of managing their output of energy with the amount of time available to address personal needs and responsibilities. In pre-digital America there seemed to be time enough to have a positive effect upon one's community and contingencies as they developed. If someone heard that a family down the street was out of work, she might make a meal and bring it down the street to them. If a neighbor needed a ride to the supermarket or pharmacy, it was not presumptuous for him to ask. Neither were simple requests such as "May I borrow a cup of sugar?" One could entreat one's neighbor without shame or fear. Stories of such neighborly interaction proliferated during the Great Depression of the 1930s in America and beyond. Discovering a bit of information about each other was useful and had action-value. But as the Age of Information took root, spawned by telegraphy, this sense of integration and purposeful action in the community began to wane. Today, such pro-social community sensibilities seem old-fashioned and increasingly uncommon. This is due, in part, because of the expanded reach of our personal lives. With the proliferation of the Internet and social media, many experience a social life that is saturated, overflowing with more casual contacts rather than a close circle of friends and neighbors.[6]

With the telegraph, the context for the news became the world instead of the local community. "Everything became everyone's business. For the first time, we were sent information which answered no question we had asked, and which, in any case, did not permit the right of reply."[7] Telegraphy, the "exact opposite of typography," dignified the trivial and irrelevant.[8] In many ways this was the beginning of incoherence in public conversation. For all the gifts of connection it brought, the telegraph introduced a new platform for communication, one that set the stage for fragmented attention and lack of focus. The overload of superfluous information began to have profound consequences in American life and throughout the world.

Expansive technological advancement and major innovation have taken place since the telegraph, but it was this invention that paved the way for the advertising age of radio and television in which wrangling with brief, disjointed bits of information became the norm. Now, as our media-saturated world moves more fully from television to Internet, social media, virtual and augmented reality, and beyond, the use of embedded smart technologies expands with greater pervasiveness and an even deeper thrust into the terrain of soundbite and meme is upon us. One of the outcomes of this shift in communication practices is the increased time spent using our digital devices for amusement. It is no longer unusual to interact with people we do not know across the globe or compete in digital gaming and "play" in virtual space against a non-human player. The myriad new ways we amuse ourselves have opened up an entirely new world of possibilities. In many ways it seems that everything has taken the shape of entertainment. From education, religion, and politics to family life, creative pursuits, and sports, these media have all taken on the patina of entertainment. Our digital media have not only increased our daily choices but have also co-opted the space and time for leisurely thought. "Head space," as it has long been known colloquially, is diminishing as clicking, sharing, and sending become the *de facto* way of being in the world. This trend will only increase as major tech corporations take us into the metaverse, an online immersive experience that is the next instantiation of the Internet. For a while we will be able to decide if we want most of our social interactions to take place in a setting of mixed reality, but as human functionality becomes more deeply enmeshed in the metaverse we will spend increasingly less time with others in physical settings, sharing the same air space.[9]

But more than the margins for daydreaming and free thinking have begun to disappear. Counterintuitive though it may be, as this new world of digital dominance has expanded, the room for civil public conversation has begun to shrink. Who would have imagined that immediate and direct interconnections with people throughout the world could diminish our collective ability to be civil? Though meta data suggesting this may not yet be available, the connection between social media and the need to stay connected to one's community has set the pace for such a confluence of these ideas. The joy with which we can now connect to others living in remote areas or at great distance adds something exciting to our lives but also puts us in contact with numerous others with whom we are not in community relations. Surely these media add something powerful to our lives but they also *change everything* (Postman, 1985). Social media open doors for reuniting with long-lost friends and staying in closer touch with relatives, but these media also foment a perfect environment for using language poorly, particularly in regard to the mobile phone. Instead of facility with words, we use shortcuts like memes, abbreviations, and emojis. These tools, while helpful in a pinch, too easily become the default manner of relating, and this is where communication breakdown and incivility begin. Now, to consider additional factors.

COMMUNITY AND CIVILITY

Though not the root of the problem, lack of civility is one of the first signs of disrespectful and barbaric treatment of others. What is the solution? Putting a halt to the damaging aspects of digital dominance is not likely but moving toward solution requires a number of clear-cut practices and the development of social protocols; the most significant, perhaps is a retraining and re-educating ourselves to seek human-centered answers rather than to uncritically accept every innovation as a cultural good. What is perhaps the most challenging factor here is that faith in technology continues to pervade the popular mindset, reigning over the collective despite near disasters and unproven results.[10] Continuing this false faith in technology and expecting that it will lead us to new, better, results is not logical.

Although his authorship has been questioned, Albert Einstein, has been credited to say that insanity is "doing the same thing again and again and expecting different results." Whether attribution belongs to Einstein or not, there is a reason the phrase has become axiomatic. A drastic—or at the least, radical—proposal involves laying hold of all that is available to us through the gift of communication. Such apprehension requires a strong understanding of the skills involved in meaning-making, but also an appreciation and welcoming of silence.

Reasons to welcome silence into the panoply of contemporary speech acts are many. Even more so than when Postman was theorizing, sensory imbalance has become more pronounced. Because using PMM to relate has become regular practice, what we say requires more interpretation and attention. Faster, more efficient means of communication such as email, social media, texting, airdrop, and a myriad of other channels allow for more tasks to be accomplished each day. Along with this ability to do more in less time comes the ensuing amped-up expectation to fit *even more* into the newly freed-up space. Additionally, many social spaces that traditionally make room for conversation have been altered to fit more cubicles in an office building, more cars in a parking garage, less room in most passenger airplanes, and more limitations on physical presence.[11] Consider the hiring process and the ebbing tide of face-to-face interviews. Uploaded resumes and automated machines choosing those applicants deemed worthy to find a place on the employer's desk—these processes are all geared toward efficiency. They are, in many cases efficient, but impersonal. This is the trade-off. The automated processes associated with digital media foster an environment that favors machines over people. They are inanimate but developed for the express purpose of material gain. In the case of the hiring process these efficient means of finding a good fit for one's company or organization eliminates the messy process of working through numerous resumes and interviews. It will also undoubtedly foster pre-meditated conformity among applicants that make little (or no) room for personality, character, or discovering a potential employee's creativity. Further, this very efficient automated process also contributes to normalizing machine-like communication, making it more challenging for people to treat each other as people.

In the not-so-distant past, situating oneself within the community was not something one had to strategize. Community was a place; something into which most of us were born. The sense of place—of being situated—was quite clear.[12] Being known was not metaphoric as much as it was something that occurred naturally, in proximity to one another. Communities had town halls and public squares; small, low populations were the norm. Today, *community* is a word that is in transition. We speak of "communities" that are far distant from one another and based on ideological agreement such as the "faith community," the "LGBTQ community," the "Black community," or the "hacker community," none of which articulate completely collective beliefs or action, but yet are connected by threads of ideological similarity rather than proximity or the common good. But the concept and practice of community has been changing for many years. When Robert Putnam's *Bowling Alone* (2000) was first published, the author addressed the unraveling of U.S. social capital and pointed to many contributing factors, such as the rise of dual income, nuclear families and the lessening of involvement in civic organizations. These changes in the social structure and community participation have long been developing. With each new technological development, the local landscape of human life has shifted. With the latest shift, the very definition of community has changed. Educator and community organizer Parker Palmer explains community as "a kaleidoscopic word that assumes new meanings at every turn—[it, *sic*] can evoke utopian images of a bygone era, a slower, simpler time when people lived side by side in villages and small towns. If community is to become an option for more than a fortunate few, we must shake off these romantic fantasies and create forms of life together that respect contemporary realities."[13] The form of life at its most basic instantiation is one of belonging. Human beings are social animals. We need others and we need a sense of belonging, but as the erosion of the local community continues it is not a far stretch to imagine a world of 8 billion lonely. Thankfully, this erosion is not complete. Many pockets of thriving communities still exist.

Many of the other factors contributing to this erosion are at work. Expansion into more of a global mindset instead of maintaining one that favors community investment and neighborhood involvement is one factor. Big box department stores, online commerce, and major search engines like Google and Safari have brought about cultural shifts in the perception and practice of community life. Each create convenience and novelty while contributing to the normalization of remote attachment to others, attachment that is often less vitalistic or engaging than everyday conversations in the marketplace and around town. The trickle-down effect is at work here in the gears of this mechanistic mode of being in the world. Lack of feeling a part of a closely-knit community contributes greatly to an attitude that easily breeds self-focus and hyper-individualism. As well, as the flow of information—relevant and irrelevant—continues, over-stimulation of the human sensorium increases thereby adding to the loss of stable and balanced interiority.[14] This overload of information encompasses not only that which we take in via digital channels, but through analog means. When small shops on Main Street are driven out of business because big box pricing and online delivery make it impossible for them to compete in the local marketplace, neighbors start seeing less of each other in public. Street relationships—those built by regular interactions and common regard for shared location—lessen; community ties begin to fray not because people decide to have less concern or empathy for their neighbors, but they remain strangers to one another. No one recognizes their neighbor. Whether significant information or irrelevant, the magnitude of the loss of these everyday interactions translates into stress, information glut, even sensory overload.[15]

This is not to say that the surge in mental illness, loneliness, and lack of close-knit community is a direct correlate of the rise of digital culture, but scholarly research suggests there is some connection. Analysis of several of the longitudinal studies examining the changes in empathy, for example, contribute to these insights.[16] In fact, many more recent studies reveal a parallel rise in unhappiness or loneliness that seems to correlate to the number of hours one spends on social media. It behooves us, then, to ask what might now be considered moot and a nearly unpardonable question. We must inquire about the ultimate worth of our digital devices. If these new media do, in fact, inadvertently create such hazards to humanity, is there anything to be done to address these adverse ramifications of extended use?[17] Answers may not be plentiful, but raising the questions is a start.

ELLUL AND *LA TECHNIQUE*

To further explore these questions we may begin with the following: Personal mobile media are efficient and helpful for immediate connection, but do they contribute to human flourishing? They add something to our lives, but what do they take away? Does regular use of these tools produce a desirable effect in our lives, our workplace, our land? Will habitual use of digital media lead to the flourishing of relationships, workplace, neighborhood, and wider culture? These are several of the questions that should be asked each time an innovative technology is introduced into popular use. The other, perhaps most significant question involves the underlying goal of digital devices. What is the desired end—the purpose—of being able to connect with others virtually anywhere and anytime? Although the history of innovation does not typically make room for questions of this sort, it behooves us to begin thinking seriously about ultimate ends. This is where the work of those who are experts in the philosophy of technology and the history of innovation can support such questions. One such thinker spent his life puzzling out these matters in the 20th century. French philosopher, social theorist, and interdisciplinary scholar Jacques Ellul spent his life studying the overarching societal patterns that emerge when technology stops being used as a tool and is substituted for human ingenuity and intelligence. A central idea in his thinking is *la technique*, his term for the non-human force of oppression into which individuals are caught and trapped by a systems-driven ethos of Efficiency.[18]

Ellul's concept of *la technique* involves the notion that our actions and ways of being in the world lose their meaning and helpfulness when they lose their *telos*, or ultimate purpose. Instead of values such as life, freedom, or love functioning as foundational principles, the rhythm of efficiency churns in mechanistic rhythm, weighing not the well-being of the humans involved in its processes, but rather the level of automated productivity to keep itself running. This, instead of broadening the possibilities for human thought and consciousness, works to cheapen and demean abstract thinking and human creativity. In this light, it is easy to see this dynamic at work as personal mobile media become the default means of communication, for the truncated, abbreviated interactions lead not toward civility and relational solvency, but to misunderstanding, division, and relational breakdown. As these dysfunctions become normalized they become automatic and the roiling rhythm of *la technique* begins to gain momentum until the ends are eclipsed and overtaken in the means.

La technique finds its force in the infiltrating folds of efficiency as a high cultural value. Its growing dominance in society moves us from the simplicity of using a method or *means* to meet a specific end, to losing the purpose (or ends) of a given goal in pursuit of the means. More definitively, John Wilkinson's 1964 edition of the book translates *la technique* as "the totality of methods rationally arrived at and having absolute efficiency (for a given stage of development) in every field of human activity."[19] Examples of this principle at work are found at every turn. The most recent at the time of this writing is Amazon's palm scanning program. The tech giant has begun a deeper reach into the lives of its customers through its identity recognition algorithms by collecting biometric data and storing that data in the Cloud. What is the purpose of this identity-invading means? Do the means justify the ends? Ends? Purpose? Have we stopped thinking about these questions and focused only on adopting the latest methods?

Another example is the fact that there are many places that no longer take personal checks. If persons do not own credit or debit cards, they may not be able to be served. Further, the cards are going away. It is more efficient to have an app on one's smart phone to pay for a coffee than to have to hunt for a card and hold up the line behind you. This, predicated on the assumption that everyone owns a smart phone and that they bring it everywhere they go, leaves a large number of the public out of the process. Possibilities for buying and selling shrink for a portion of the public until that portion capitulates and accepts the technology. That the technology reduces the freedom of travel to those wealthy enough to have phones and credit cards is part of the fallout, or the unforeseen consequences of the new technologies. Such fallout is dismissed as non-problematic because of the *greater good*, thus strengthening the utilitarian thread that increasingly binds up the organic (and often messy) processes associated with our humanness.

As a driving principle the rhythm of efficiency is clearly in operation within the systems of every sector of society—education, government, politics, and corporations, to name a few. Seen in the reliance—even veneration—of increasingly complex organizational methods, Efficiency has often become an end, and seems to have taken root in the outworking of each of these sectors, boxing in every human endeavor to fit within its parameters. "Like a fish's perfect adaptation to its water environment, we are enveloped in data, absorbed into a mono-dimensional world of stereotypes and slogans, and integrated into a homogeneous whole by the machinery of conformity."[20] Almost 60 years later such technological machinery is in full force, and the act of conformity nearly complete.

SILENCE

Silence is a misnomer in an age of such grand efficiency. It is counterintuitive to the domination of means. The disconnection between silence and the technological society is increasingly apparent, and although Ellul (1964) did not theorize formally about the role of silence in communication, the correlation exists in his work with an emphasis on the ways language and symbol systems are used to persuade, provoke, and keep discussion and debate to a minimum. This, we find in his thoughts regarding the use of propaganda, which is another way *la technique* makes itself known. Here Ellul suggests that one of the ways the state influences public opinion in favor of war and civilian involvement is through nonstop communication, that is, communication that takes place without room for a breath or reflection. He notes that this sway could "only be properly produced by the enormous pressure of advertising and total propaganda on the human psyche. It was necessary to use the so-called obsessional technique, to subject the citizen to propaganda without letup, never allowing him to be alone with himself."[21] Referring to the propaganda of the 19th and 20th centuries, Ellul becomes granular in describing the way this worked: "In the street people are confronted with posters, loudspeakers, ceremonies, and meetings; at work, with handbills and [catchphrases like, *sic*] industrial mobilization; in his amusements, with motion-picture and theatrical propaganda; at home, with newspaper and radio propaganda. All these means converge on the same points. All these exert the same kind of action on the individual and are of such overpowering magnitude that he ceases to be consciously aware" (1964, p. 366).[22] The engulfment makes it nearly impossible to push back from the press of words. A mental image of words in flight comes to mind, surrounding us like seagulls descending on a lone fish that's washed up at the shore. It is a foregone conclusion that the fish has no chance.

Caution about message-overload must not be limited to electronic and digital culture alone. Ellul, writing in the middle of the 20th century, concerned himself with the plethora of words and their proliferation through propaganda and popular culture, while today the expansion of such has become oppressive, saturating virtually every layer of contemporary social life. Whether words, images, electronic games, texts, emails, or social media—exponential increase of information and ensuing saturation is bleeding through every fiber of society. Here, silence becomes increasingly important, for as a sturdy background and foundation of speech it also creates a necessary pause in the mass of information washing over the average person.

Silence also creates a favorable environment for meaningful conversation. As Max Picard reminds us, "Speech came out of silence, out of the fullness of silence" (Picard, 8). It rises from the bed of silence, making room for the word to stretch into life. In its proper proportion, silence soothes conversation and makes it pliable. Whether the bit of pause is offered to allow speech to emerge or it is simply restorative for the individual speaking, there is much to be gained. The added time necessary to interpret messages shared through virtual spaces may also be construed as quiet space or silence, and it can be, but is no substitute for, regular intervals of silence to center oneself. Just as sleep rejuvenates our bodies and brains throughout the night, silence—during waking hours—has the potential to calm us. Along with this much-needed respite from "too many words," apprehension of regular intervals of silence may be the elixir needed to combat the effects of message-overload in public discourse and personal relationship. One antidote for this is intentional gathering in a place where one's presence is not mediated by a screen but occurs face-to-face.

Since the start of social media in particular, the decreasing ability to carry on complex conversations is noted with greater frequency (Turkle, 2015). In the last twenty years this is particularly true as digital natives—the children of the 1990s—move into mature adulthood. The first step toward reclaiming the art of conversation is to regain the solitude that we have let ebb away from daily life. In her 2015 book, *Reclaiming Conversation*, MIT researcher Sherry Turkle states plainly the need for silence and solitude: Without it "we can't construct a stable sense of self. Yet children who grow up digital have always had something external to respond to. When they go online, their minds are not wandering, but rather are captured and divided."[23] The increased concern of scholars and other observers of the new dynamics in communication point to additional impediments to conversation, citing the increased pace of social exchange as well as the annoyance of noise in the public square. While some of these noises are less obvious because people have become habituated to them, other examples of blaring, distracting sound are still obvious. This is apparent, for example, when an oversized truck with windows rolled down and speakers pulsing pulls up next to your car at a traffic signal. The sound vibrations ring through the air and it is impossible not to be distracted.

NOISE AND ITS ASSOCIATES

Popular newspaper and magazine articles have begun to focus on these problems with increasing regularity. One *USA Today* weekend newspaper columnist described what he framed as the growing scourge of noise pollution and discussed the myriad ways people are being dehumanized or feeling physically sick simply because of too much noise. He suggested that much of the new technological gadgetry appearing on the market is designed to shape sound, eliminate extraneous noise from the average person's personal space, and create access to and interactivity for people using the new media. The journalist wondered rhetorically,

> How unnerving will it be to hear voices inside our heads? I don't want Ronald McDonald nudging me to "supersize it" or a vending machine babbling, "taste me, taste me." And hearing someone whisper in my ear from across the mall could be downright scary. Now, more than ever, we really may need a cone of silence.[24] (p. E5)

Futuristic speculation of this sort has long been a part of literature and film, but as smart phone data-gathering technologies and location capabilities increase the growing sense of having "no place to run" to be alone is becoming a reality. This "phantom silence" has long been the stuff of science fiction such as in Huxley's *Brave New World*. He writes:

> "But people never are alone now," said Mustapha Mond. "We make them hate solitude; and we arrange their lives so that it's almost impossible for them ever to have it." The Savage nodded gloomily. At Malpais he had suffered because they had shut him out from the communal activities of the pueblo; in civilized London he was suffering because he could never escape from those communal activities, never be quietly alone. (1931, 235)

When Huxley first warned readers about the unnerving lack of solitude and silence used as a means of control and dehumanization, his fiction could not have been more prescient. His insights, while using the vehicle of fiction, are uncannily appropriate for our day.

The growing need for silence in a culture that is increasingly characterized by distracting or oppressive noise is an example of Ellul's self-propelling force of *la technique* and the way its progress affects human well-being. The French philosopher's contentions concerning this nervousness with which modern men and women must cope are clear in Huxley's implicit observations. Because of a constant drive toward efficiency and the push toward unbounded busyness, Ellul wonders about the plight of modern men and women and asks, "What does he find [when he gets home from work, *sic*]? He finds a phantom. If he ever thinks, his reflections terrify him."[25] Ellul's apparent pessimism is a part of his activistic approach to the threats associated with technology. It is what he terms "active pessimism," a posture that does not tone down or attempt to lighten the weight of the problems associated with technology-as-panacea.

Along with Ellul and Postman, the notion of too much information has been a consistent theme in the work of many other scholars and thinkers, but perhaps most notably in the mind of Marshall McLuhan, whose view of media as a totalizing force, enlivening or deadening the whole sensory apparatus of the human brain, was the subject of his greater body of work. In his classic *Understanding Media*, McLuhan explained that the human brain cannot stand detached and unmoved in its interaction with media, a dynamic that has increased exponentially as we have soared into ubiquitous and pervasive use of digital devices. McLuhan writes, "In the electric age, when our central nervous system is technologically extended to involve us in the whole of mankind and to incorporate the whole of mankind in us, we necessarily participate, in depth, in the consequences of our every action. It is no longer possible to adopt the aloof and dissociated role of the literate Westerner."[26] Like Postman who posited that an inability to act upon this information increases the sense of personal helplessness and adds to a psychological state of stress, McLuhan's premise that media are extensions of our faculties affecting the human sensorium is an idea that has continued for over 50 years. Communication scholar Paul Soukup links this idea with Walter Ong's work in secondary orality. He explains, "Products of secondary orality demand more, not less, interpretation since they involve a deception—the hiding of the text on which they depend. Digital materials, as being yet more abstract, require more interpretation."[27] One more recent example of this is emerging research about the use of screen technologies such as Zoom and FaceTime. During meetings that take place on these platforms, the image of the other is present and social interaction made possible, but the lack of touch, smell, and proximity creates a mental fatigue and resident anxiety that is not present when working and relating in proximity to one another. Without greater intention to distill and interpret our words we risk falling more deeply into the chasm of cultural chaos and decline of mental health.

The need for face-to-face communication is generally a given, and not only in the context of intimacy or close personal friendship, but from a business perspective, as well. There, particularly among executives, meeting face-to-face is certainly tacit knowledge. Millions of dollars are spent on business travel when technological solutions such as Zoom, FaceTime, and a growing number of other aps are available. Ulrich Kellerer, author and former CEO of the German corporation Faro Fashion, in an interview with Forbes explains why. He writes, "While sending emails is efficient and fast, face-to-face communication drives productivity. In a recent survey, 667 percent of senior executives and managers said their organization's productivity would increase if superiors communicated face-to-face more often."[28] People need people, intimate relationships, and the nonverbal communication cues to help maintain predicable outcomes in communication as well as navigate the realm of emotion in personal interactions. Can we survive without face-to-face communication? The overarching results of the global pandemic are yet to be seen, but the rapid adoption of technological solutions such as Zoom conferencing, education online, and tele-medical office visits suggests a change in this tacit knowledge. Human beings are ultra-adaptive, and it is quite likely that we will adapt to these new conditions; yet without a solid sense of belonging in human relationship, something is missing, and loneliness ensues.

Indirectly, these maladies associated with the heightened pace of life also contribute to the current demeaned state of public discourse. This happens for at least two reasons. The first involves basic human nature and the second is purely media ecological. While civility is necessary for civil discourse, it is diminished when we don't see each other's faces. In his analysis of the lack of civility, Yale professor of law, Stephen L. Carter points to a time prior to the television era, the 18th and 19th centuries when "television had not yet destroyed the attention span."[29] Carter's ideas pinning morality to civility are not new to philosophical conversations but help reveal the connection between modern media's ubiquitous display of the image and the imagined world where our instincts rule us rather than we them.[30] The moral implications here may not be obvious immediately but are present and will be addressed in a later chapter.

Understanding that technologies come with an inherent bias goes back as far as Plato where within his dialogue, *Phaedrus*, the Greek philosopher notably distrusted the newest technology of his day—writing. Plato voiced his concerns that one's ability to recall what was said will be greatly affected using pen and papyrus.[31] Internationally recognized ethicist Clifford G. Christians suggests that all technologies are value-laden. The mistake is to see technology as neutral.[32] Ellul made similar observations, pointing out the socio-psychological effect of the rise of the image and its part in truncating meaning and skewing human perception.[33] This he did long before the breadth of today's media landscape emerged as a collective new way of functioning; he described the process as social propaganda. Some of it has a positive effect on public health, such as the campaign to stop smoking inside buildings and restaurants. Other social propaganda is less explicit, foisting new norms into public acceptance without anyone consciously choosing them.

A recent example of the degradation of choice may be found in the following: Traveling from West Palm Beach, Florida to Miami on the Brightline transit system provides a delightful and refreshing experience in train travel. The new station gleams. Its waiting areas are beautifully decorated and comfortable. Its wine bar, candy counters, and ticket machines are available, but one cannot purchase anything with cash. A credit card is the only acceptable way to make a transaction. While most people carry credit cards, those who don't cannot purchase a train ticket, buy a bag of peanuts, or enjoy a glass of wine at the station without a credit card. Choice is being eliminated. If the trend continues, a cashless society is soon to follow without public approval. This issue is not specifically problematic because a cashless system may seem more favorable to some. Nor is it about stretching beyond one's comfort zone to discover new ways of doing things in the world. Rather, the issue involves personal agency and collective choice. Ellul's argument surrounds the encroachment of a technocratic society. To address it involves taking the time to notice the diminishing returns of a social system that quietly erodes freedom. It is as if a poisonous but invisible odor is wafting its way through the atmosphere—a silent phantom or ghost in the machine appears and surreptitiously works within the image-based, propagandistic media to undermine life.[34] The dominance of the visual over the spoken word contributes to this erosion. Ellul frames this dominance as triumphal victory, emphasizing the importance of speech in an image-laden world. "In our common experience seeing and hearing are related and the proper equilibrium between the two produces the equilibrium of the person, so it is dangerous to favor one, in triumphant fashion to the detriment of the other. Yet this is exactly what is happening today, as we witness the unconditional victory of the visual and images" (1985, p. 2).

Another example of acquiescence and forced compliance is in the growing use of texting instead of communicating through speech. Sending short and abbreviated messages instead of calling has become the norm. The same is so with the practice of announcing personal information through social media. It has become the norm. If one does not use social media it is seen as an anomaly. There must be conformity. This happens because our social environs are saturated in a particular idea. Fifty years later such technological machinery is in full force, and the act of conformity nearly complete. To address this, let us briefly explore the rise in use of the cell phone.

As of 2019, 5 billion[35] of the world's population are regular mobile phone users. Everything from media and medicine to retail, banking, and relationships is quickly becoming mechanized and automated. While the human brain has a tremendous capacity to filter unnecessary information, the shift in major social functions continues to bring new challenges for the individual and society. Today, with the many strong and strategic methods of persuasion collapsing public dialogue into memes, tweets, and other snippets of information, the study of silence may offer something of an antidote to a world so abuzz with words—words that seem to hold increasingly less credibility as our media yet provide more and more means by which to speak. Aside from the immediacy, there is the distraction factor. *Boston Globe* journalist, Maggie Jackson addressed this subject at length in her study of social media and young people and concluded, "Amid the glittering promise of our new technologies . . . we are nurturing a culture of social diffusion, intellectual fragmentation, [and, *sic*] sensory detachment." Since the publication of her book, may other studies bear these points out. Jackson's work is but one of the studies that point to a need for more solidarity and open dialogue. The need is great to have conversations that have long been unheard. Fear of rejection, disapproval, retaliation, bullying, or being ostracized from one's in-group are just a part of the things that hold us back. Whether these unheard conversations center around gender inequity, political propaganda, global injustice, or the need for racial reconciliation, these healthy, world-changing conversations will continue to go unheard unless we bring our full selves to the conversational table and make a commitment to civility. Silence can help lead the way. Cultivating a habit of daily intervals of silence will be just as important to our mental health, and perhaps even more so in the future.

The mediated, phantom silence available to us on social media platforms appears to provide the quietude necessary to live in interior equilibrium. We may even turn the speakers off and spend hours keying into conversations in what appears to be a quiet space. But phantom silence is qualitatively different than that of the contemplative's inner silence or the silence necessary to be an attentive listener. The relative silence of sitting on the banks of a quiet lake is a lovely respite in a noisy world of means and clatter. The richness it brings to a busy, active mind cannot be bought or sold, but is ours to grasp if we do it with intention. Interpersonal relationships suffer for the lack of silence and need respite, as well. To this we now turn.

NOTES

1. Though one might imagine everyone has been cautioned about the "Nigerian Email Scam" it is still raking in major money. As recently as 2019 Australians reported over $6 million dollars lost in this fraud and others like it. In America, citizens reported a loss of $703,000 to these frauds during the same year. CNBC "Make It" website by Megan Leonhard, April 19, 2019. Report [March 24, 2021] https://www.cnbc.com/2019/04/18/nigerian-prince-scams-still-rake-in-over-700000-dollars-a-year.html.

2. This snippet is an example of the many varieties of the email scam. It is an example from "Talk of the Nation," a National Public Radio station broadcast from a Miami, Florida station on May 22, 2013.

3. "Technology doesn't just add something to the environment, it changes everything." Neil Postman.

4. Neil Postman *Amusing Ourselves to Death.*

5. Neil Postman. *Amusing*. p. 70.

6. Kenneth Gergen's *The Saturated Self* is an excellent resource to investigate this trend further.

7. Neil Postman. *Amusing Ourselves to Death*, p. 69.

8. Postman. *Amusing*, p. 69.

9. Set in 2071, my own fictional depiction of this metaverse was published in 2016 in the trilogy *Within the Walls.* Mark Zuckerberg has been discussing this move to

metaverse publicly since 2018 and in 2021 launched Meta—the new umbrella corporation to house all of the company's social media platforms. The move to mixed reality social life is occurring much earlier in the century than I envisioned.

10. Carter. *Civility.* p. 186.

11. The exception here is the major Silicon Valley corporations such as Google and Facebook that create space within the work environment for exercise and entertainment such as pool tables, ping pong, work-out rooms, and gaming areas. These in-office perks promise to keep employees happier, more relaxed, and more productive. By staying in the office for good food and a break, FB and Google employees are reported to stay on campus longer with less time away from their desks. Famous for this techy "in-office culture," these companies have been making moves to create different kinds of perks for a post-pandemic workforce.

12. Joshua Meyrowitz's book *No Sense of Place* is an excellent resource for further exploration into this idea.

13. Parker Palmer, *Hidden Wholeness.* p. 73.

14. Venus Bivar. The Chicago School of Media Theory. The Committee on the History of Culture University of Chicago [June 6, 2019] https://lucian.uchicago.edu/blogs/mediatheory/keywords/senses/.

15. Ted Koppel. CBS News Interview with Nicholas Carr. "Overload: How Technology Is Bringing Us Too Much Information?" [May 29, 2019] https://www.cbsnews.com/news/overload-how-technology-is-bringing-us-too-much-information/ 2018.

16. University of Michigan longitudinal study of empathy. [April 25, 2021] https://news.umich.edu/empathy-college-students-don-t-have-as-much-as-they-used-to/.

17. Whereas information overload may cause stress, sensory overload stems mostly from competing sensory input in the brain. Too much light, noise, strong odors, or emotional stimuli can push a person into sensory overload. While there is no substantive evidence, information overload has also been linked to part of the cumulative effects of sensory overload. For more information, see MedicalNewsToday.com [April 25, 2021]. https://www.medicalnewstoday.com/articles/sensory-overload.

18. For Ellul, technology is not the problem, but becomes a problem when we make an idol of it and "bow" to its power. His concept of *la technique* speaks to this. Conceptually, *la technique* is difficult to grasp, for although it is inanimate, its force is one to be reckoned with and once it has been set in motion is difficult (if not impossible) to defeat. The idea gains clarity as we see the desire and drive for greater efficiency at every level of human life being preferred. Again and again, efficiency is chosen despite ends that lessen universal human values such as honesty, love, kindness, and equality. This is evident in every sector of society: online education, the virtual church, and eCommerce are but a few of the trends that have gained social acceptance in the last two decades, each conceived of through technological innovation and driven by the increasing demand for efficiency.

19. Jacques Ellul. *The Technological Society.* From the translator's introduction by John Wilkinson. p. ix.

20. Jacques Ellul. *The Technological Society.* p. 163.

21. Ellul. *The Technological Society.* p. 366.

22. Ellul's thoughts on *la technique*'s manipulation of human freedom are far from the first example of this line of thinking in the history of ideas. Two hundred years before Ellul, Jean-Jacques Rousseau (1712–1778) wrote extensively (and famously) about the dehumanizing effects of civilization. He won first place for an essay in this regard, which is known as his *First Discourse*. Later, in perhaps his best-known work, *The Social Contract*, Rousseau begins with the following: "Man is born free; and everywhere he is in chains. One thinks himself the master of others, and still remains a greater slave than they. How did this change come about? I do not know. What can make it legitimate? That question I think I can answer. If I took into account only force, and the effects derived from it, I should say—'As long as a people is compelled to obey, and obeys, it does well; as soon as it can shake off the yoke, and shakes it off, it does still better; for, regaining its liberty by the same right as took it away, either it is justified in resuming it, or there was no justification for those who took it away.' But the social order is a sacred right that is the basis of all other rights. Nevertheless, this right does not come from nature, and must therefore be founded on conventions" (First Book, public domain, 1762).

23. Sherry Turkle. *Reclaiming Conversation*. p. 6.

24. Reference to a "cone" of silence (rather than "code") is a colloquial reference to a 1960s television series called *Get Smart* in which the secret agents would walk into a soundproof "cone" and speak openly so as not to be heard. The author of the piece is from an October 2003 newspaper article in the Morristown, NJ, *Daily Record*. [February 24, 2021] https://www.newspapers.com/newspage/255854399/.

25. Jacques Ellul. *The Technological Society*. p. 376.

26. Marshall McLuhan. *Understanding Media: The Extensions of Man*. Cambridge: MIT Press, 1994.

27. Paul Soukup. "Looking Is Not Enough."

28. Carol Kinsey Goman, "Has Technology Killed Face-to-Face Communication?" *Forbes*. [June 11, 2019] https://www.forbes.com/sites/carolkinseygoman/2018/11/14/has-technology-killed-face-to-face-communication/#1ab9d968a8cc.

29. Stephen L. Carter. *Civility: Manners, Morals, and the Etiquette of Democracy*. p. xiii.

30. Stephen Carter, *Civility*. p. 187.

31. In speaking about writing, Plato wrote: "If men learn this, it will implant forgetfulness in their souls. They will cease to exercise memory because they rely on that which is written, calling things to remembrance no longer from within themselves, but by means of external marks." **Plato (c. 429–347 B.C.E).** *Phaedrus* **(c. 360 B.C.E.). Trans. Reginald Hackforth. pp. 274c–275b.**

32. See Clifford Christians. "Technologies Are Not Neutral, but Value-Laden," in *Media Ethics and Global Justice in the Digital Age*. p. 21.

33. See Jacques Ellul. *The Humiliation of the Word*. p. 2.

34. *Ghost in the machine* was originally used in philosophy to attend to René Descartes's mind/body dualism. Today, it has come to infer a force working within a device, computer, or person that is unexpected and insidious. Is a program, computer, or technology running contrary to expectations or goals? If so, there is a "ghost in the machine."

35. Numbers reflect 2019 data Pew Research. [February 15, 2020] https://www.pewresearch.org/global/2019/02/05/smartphone-ownership-is-growing-rapidly-around-the-world-but-not-always-equally/.

Chapter 6

Relational Silence

From the 1960s through the 1980s there bloomed in America a burgeoning belief in the need for communication. Suddenly, it seemed, the world woke up to the fact that communication is more than talk. In fact, awareness of the need for communication skills in business, education, family, and romance expanded to a "communication is everything" mentality, the panacea for all relational ills. As the subject was elevated to a place of relational utopia, communication then became invisible again. Today, in light of the wellspring of writings about the efficacy of communication and the massive connections occurring online, the idea of bringing silence back as a relational good might appear foolhardy. But despite the plethora of books and the buzz surrounding them, the practice of effective communication has yet to show its full strength. This is the primary benefit of relational silence.

In chapter 2 silence was addressed as an inward phenomenon, *vis-à-vis*, a part of spiritual formation. Chapter 4 dealt with the ontological grounding of silence. Chapter 5, a silence lurks in the background of our lives but is not revitalizing or generative. Here, as we explore its relational dimensions, we find that the power of silence in the intrapersonal realm of language usage has a definitive place in all communication behavior, not just in contemplative repose. Intrapersonal communication overlaps, recreates, and informs that which is being spoken. The strong, functional, structuring apparatus of the intrapersonal is necessary for relational health, for without it conversational coherence seriously lacks. Taking some time for quiet, restorative silence can pave the way for relational longevity and ultimate happiness simply because when one brings a more peaceful self to a friend or partner there is a greater chance it will be reciprocated. Additionally, a more centered, secure, and peaceful self is less likely to project onto others what is in turmoil within, or to introject.[1] In this way, silence as a fixed feature of relational vitality and an active factor in interpersonal exchange plays a dynamic and essential role in the communicative process (Bolton, 1990; Jaworski, 1994; Picard, 1952; Scott, 1979, 2000; Tannen and Saville-Troike, 1985; Wolvin, 1993). Thus, the overlapping connection between the intrapersonal and interpersonal gains clarity. The realm of intrapersonal communication not only includes identity development but analysis, interpretation, evaluation, and reflection; it is interlaced with the entire thought process. The thought process cannot be neatly sequestered into its own canister, but there is much room for intentionally creating periods of quiet in which to reflect.

INTRA- AND INTERPERSONAL OVERLAP

The "silent time" one spends in reflection is not empty space, but essential for human beings living in a civilized world. Whereas present trends and behaviors might refute this as necessity, "time spent thinking, reflecting, is not wasteful," explains John Stewart (1990). Just as silence is necessary to ground oneself intra-personally, it is equally helpful in creating space for thoughtful discussion, conflict management, and overall relational maintenance. In fact, silence is critical; whether alone or engaged in an interpersonal exchange, the need for a measure of quiet is essential. Could lack of silence and solitude be exactly what is missing from the theater of public discourse? Is it possible that speech untethered to this grounding silence is the very reason public address creaks and cries out for nourishment? This type of silence may be the very lifeblood that courses through relational discourse without which the relationship, like the human body, becomes stiff and brittle. Without room (i.e., time and space) for reflection the communication process is compromised in so many ways. It is perhaps what Max Picard (1952) perceives when he writes of reflective silence as foundational and the "friendly sister of the word" (p. 33).

As in other areas of human social interaction, silence in relationship can be disconfirming as well as confirming. A silent pause is often used to calm and de-stress during moments of high tension, but it can also be used as a weapon to push away or punish another. In friendships and romantic partnerships, silence can also be a hiding place, one that is used to protect oneself from being known. An example of the vast chasm between the positive, nourishing experience of generative silence and its fearful, mercenary cousin is explicated in the difference between the silence of solitary confinement in a jail cell and the sought-after silence discovered in a monastic cell or hermitage. Whereas monastic silence can be rich, fostering a state of inner harmony and centered peace of mind, the silence of solitary confinement is grueling, punishing the one for whom social interaction has been removed.

Much of what has been explored thus far involves the positive uses of intrapersonal silence. Going forward, these benefits have application as we relate to others. This chapter brings silence more deeply into the interpersonal realm and addresses the impact of too little silence along with the negative impact of distractions to relationships. But rather than beginning with the distractions, we focus first on positive aspects of silence as it is used to build and maintain relationships.

As that aspect of the communication process that helps create the reality of speech, silence is not unnecessary; it is not passive (Scott, 1979). Rather than merely the absence of noise, it is a phenomenon in and of itself, quite necessary for continuity, cognition, and comprehension of what is being articulated (Jaworski, 1994; Picard, 1948). Some scholars involved in silence research emphasize the acoustical tension of speech and silence and suggest the essential role of silence in finding meaning within a verbal exchange (Ong, 1982; Merton, 1947; Strate et al., 2003). Adam Jaworski, author of *The Power of Silence*, outlines an interpretive, socio-pragmatic perspective that locates silence as a powerful communicative function in all types of communication behavior. He argues for a contextual, "non-essentialist stance and refuses to define silence as an absolute or discrete category (e.g., as existing in complete opposition to speech)" (p. 2). The dialectical *necessity* of speech and silence may not be easily grasped. However, Jaworski contends that although silence may be construed as the most ambiguous form of communication, it is not the antithesis of speech; rather, silence and speech overlap in their functions and are complementary (p. 62). The two intertwine with an almost visceral push-and-pull to overcome awkwardness, relieve social pressure, and work toward meaning-making.

COMMUNICATION AS MEANING-MAKING

What is the core of relational communication? The core is making meaning—together. As Quentin Schultze affirms, "At the heart of all this humanly created culture is a system of meaning—what people think and believe."[2] Without the desire (and perhaps the ability) to make meaning, one can be reasonably sure that miscommunication and conflict will arise in a relational context, but much of the disconnect between relational partners stems from many other sources. One of the most significant aspects of silence scholarship, at least in terms of this work, involves the matter of communication coherence. The logic and consistency of the message being sent and received is based on shared symbol systems and a desire to come together. It is hardly possible without a strong, intentional motivation to attend to what is being said, but there are numerous elements to also consider. As discussed in chapter 3, listening becomes imperative to the process of communication, but nonverbal cues, as well, make a major difference in one's ability to make meaning. Without the gestures, physical movement, eye contact, and tone of voice, the process of communication suffers greatly. The possibility for meaningful communication diminishes.

Meaningful communication is a phrase wrought with ambiguity for what one individual perceives as meaningful, another may perceive as nonsense. It is not quite the same idea as meaning-making. Meaning-making involves coherence. I see communication most fundamentally as meaning-making that is accomplished in sundry and manifold ways. Primarily, it involves:

- Communication behavior that is viscerally *coherent*. It accurately "makes sense" of the disparate bits of information exchanged in interpersonal interactions. Whether or not the language is properly used in terms of politeness, diction, grammar, or vocabulary, meaningful communication occurs when people conversing understand one another. When understanding occurs, meaning takes place. This happens verbally and nonverbally. It includes the setting, the channel, the human receiver, the human sender, and feedback.
- Communication behavior that fosters *relational* development or maintenance. Rather than the notion that meaning is found in words, interpersonal communication takes place in the coming together (however awkwardly or imperfectly) of at least two people and does so by locating and sharing the space between them.
- Communication behavior that goes beyond transactional interchange of information. It occurs between at least two people and creates a greater *awareness* of "the other."

Awareness and attentiveness to "the other" are equally fundamental in engaging in meaningful communication (Arnett, 1986; Buber, 1970; Friedman, 1974). Coherence, relationality, and awareness: these characteristics represent part of the necessary rationality that is inherent to the communication process. Much practicality may be found in the limitation of these terms. Without these elements there is too much room for meaninglessness. Everyday life is wrought with numerous opportunities to make meaning. When we do not accept and heed boundaries and limits to what can be said, and where, the result is a communication process that is trivialized and broken, undermining the possibility of relational security and satisfaction. It is here, as well, that silence can function as a salve to create the break or breath needed to maintain the goal of meaning-making.

Most everyone in relationship has found themselves saying the flippant quip, "I just need a little peace and quiet." It is a common rant, one that most people understand intuitively even if it is not verbalized. While not the product of a necessarily over-busy person, it is typical of the person living in a hyper-technicized culture, especially one that has moved from a loosely controlled system of dependence upon its technologies to one that has a totalizing effect, dubbed by Neil Postman as a "technopoly."[3] In such a society it matters not so much whether one lives on a farm or a metropolis, because it is the interior quiet that is missing. The busy mind, jumping from thought to thought like a monkey swinging through a rain forest, does not miraculously change when one moves to the country or a less populated area. This is because the kind of quiet necessary for a centered life comes from within, not outside of one's self. Although it may be much more pleasant to have a conversation with as little extraneous noise as possible, once an inward silence is gained, much of the noise that litters the paths of strong conversational resonance typically no longer presents a problem. The well-being associated with a centered, focused mind is part of the reason for the sharp incline in mindfulness courses and its seepage into our institutions. Bringing a peaceful, uncluttered mind into each of our interpersonal relationships is our launching point to discuss another way reflective silence is connected to conversational coherence and intersects with interpersonal communication and intimacy in the relationship.

Just as speech has empowering properties, silence has soothing properties. Numerous examples of this exist. One is the way psychotherapists use silence. Listening in non-judgmental silence is a major aspect of talk therapy. Silence blankets the room and allows the patient freedom to bring forth words unhindered. Another example comes from the medical profession. In the lives of seriously ill babies, "intensive care nurseries have found that special headphones that block noise reduce the stress caused by the sounds of respirators, ventilators and other hospital machinery" (Wood, 2004, p. 147). The relative quiet provides an environment that is conducive to health and growth.

Equivalent results are often seen relationally. When one person has paused to reflect on the words just spoken, the momentary silence can create the necessary relational space for meaning to take place. Silence allows "breathing time" in conversation. That is, a conversation punctuated by silence allows the mind to provide the "gentle nudge" that prompts the conservation to expand, deepen, or linger, specifically because *there is time* for reflection (Bolton, in Stewart, 2006, p. 188). This type of punctuation is quite natural. Different cultures have cues and social protocols indigenous to their own patterns, but a natural conversational flow arises both verbally and nonverbally. Yet, in spite of the organic apparatus available to each one of us, *vis-à-vis* smell, sound, sight, etc., if one has never seen conversational style modeled in the early speech community, the punctuating pause of conversational flow will take some time to emerge, just as speech takes time to develop in a toddler.

THE SPEECH COMMUNITY

Without a strong speech community modeling the punctuating pause it will take intentionality and discipline in learning this skill. When a moment is taken to allow what was spoken to register, it has the potential to create space that otherwise would not have existed—a space for heartier conversation and a deepening of the dialogue. Conversely, without it, the tendency to jump ahead with one's own words before truly comprehending what the other has to say snuffs out dialogue, eliminating the possibility of coming to a place of mutual respect and meaning. This is seen every day on interactions that take place on social media platforms. Whether Twitter, Facebook, or the latest platform for remote public conversation, the lack of holding one's tongue reduces conversation to ash. Instead of meaning-making, what passes for dialogue is reduced to crazed, uncomely, and disrespectful name-calling, subtle put-downs, and blatant attacks.

Returning to face-to-face settings, silence finds an equal place of significance. Along with the possibility of deeper, more sustainable dialogue, respecting the importance of this reflective space can work positively as a route toward intimacy in friendships, in marriage, in the family, at large. So often a word is blurted out of pain or insecurity but does not reflect the truth of one's feelings or commitment to the relationship. The breath of silence can help us stay true to what we know in the deepest places of our knowing. The ancient axiom reads "from the fullness of the heart the mouth speaks."[4] But how often is the human heart shrouded in pain and confusion? What lies resident in the heart is so often covered up by self-preservation and fear that many of us don't even know our own hearts. Reasons for relational conflict are often rooted in the misplaced words that are random projections of one's own insecurities. Another reason is the risk factor—the risk of being known and unreceived. Though silence doesn't guarantee it, the pause makes room for our truest feelings and commitments to be seen. Silence makes space for sensitivity to the rhythm of the other and allows the listener to experience less risk when communicating personal information. Self-disclosure is more apt to take place when reflective space is evident.

This dynamic is key to establishing strong conversational flow. Without the time or conversational "space" allotted to determine whether or not it is safe to self-disclose, it is likely that relationships of depth will take much longer to develop, or not develop at all. This idea conflates with Bolton, who infers a strong link between emotional equanimity and conversational flow, explaining that "silence on the part of the listener gives the speaker time to think about what he is going to say and thus enables him to go deeper into himself. It gives a person space to experience the feelings churning within" (p. 188).

This "churning," which is a natural part of the ebb and flow of interpersonal relationship, must be managed or processed, and it is part of the dialectical tension that takes place during an interpersonal encounter. It is an important part of the communication process (Rhodes, 1993, p. 224). Self-reflection, listening deeply to one's own inner voice, listening attentively, and observing the other are all necessary elements of close relationship (Redmond, 1995), but more "relational goods" are needed to build and maintain intimacy.[5] True intimacy involves the unmediated knowing and interdependent association of one person with another. Knowing the other *as other* necessitates knowing more than what one says or writes about oneself. Whether one's perception of self is shared in cyberspace or in a conversation on a cell phone, the limits of such knowledge are more pronounced when not sharing the same physical space. There are a number of reasons for this. First is the inherent power in the spoken word. Why self-disclosing through one's own voice is so much more powerful than using the written word has much to do with the breath upon which the spoken word is carried but is also partially because the dialectic of silence is operating at all times in the reflective silence of the intrapersonal. Secondly, truly knowing another person involves sharing a life. The embodiment of the word *vis-à-vis* speaking while in the physical presence of the other—is more important to meaning-making than what those advocating virtual and mediated communication propose. Intimacy is much more than sharing mental processing; it involves sharing life together.

To move more fully toward this level of intimacy it is necessary to employ silence as a regular component, appreciating and respecting the other's need to process and interpret meaning. Thus, the intentional use of silence far exceeds punctuating silence, active listening, or conversational turn-taking. It is a type of attentive listening that has been referred to as relational listening, that is, listening with a goal to foster relationship rather than to simply gain information (Rhodes, 1993). The practice of relational listening is such that one is already listening attentively, but also intently, that is, with the intention of furthering or developing or maintaining relationship. Listening intently is one part of the communication process, however. When communication breakdown occurs, it is not always because one or both parties are inattentive, uninterested, lacking desire for greater relational closeness, or distracted by the sounds of the acoustic environment. Sometimes the problem lies in the misreading of boundary markers, those cues that let the other know if he or she has entrée to more personal information or permission to close the space gap in physical proximity and/or touch. Assessing these boundaries is another place silence can help advance relationship. Attentive silence allows for cognitive processing. It is in the few moments or milliseconds of interaction that help to establish boundaries in conversation. These are not immediately evident when conversation occurs via the cell phone, and often entirely lost.

RELATIONAL LISTENING

The gifts of digital culture make it all too easy to ignore or miss boundary markers because of all the lacking nonverbal elements and other variables coming together. For example, using a mediating device such as the cell phone to discuss important matters may create more tension or conflict than the expedience and convenience that the mobile phone facilitates. This may seem somewhat counterintuitive, particularly where relational intimacy is concerned, but there are times in relationships when immediate discussion may foster more reactionary and inflammatory exchanges rather than rational, productive ones. One blurts a quick concern because another person is approaching and wants to maintain privacy, but the tone sounds too direct, even hard and is mistaken for offense. This is especially so when a discussion involves issues of intimacy and/or conflict within the relationship, thus interlocutors may discover the combination of their emotionally charged state and the use of the cell phone as medium of communication is not a good mix to advance effective communication behavior. Also, the speed with which contemporary conversations take place via PMM has increased exponentially and continues to accelerate. It takes a bit longer to discern meaning when not speaking face-to-face. This, too, plays a part in the overall hindrances to listening. Another aspect of relational listening involves interest. To listen relationally requires that the individual be interested in relationship-level conversations, which is not necessarily required in every aspect of communication. We often must listen well to discern the goal of a work project that holds little, if any, relational interest. But listening with empathy to a friend whose story is of little genuine interest is an act of kindness, even love. This is relational listening.

Many of the traditional approaches to communication such as that of Carl Rogers (1980) ascribe a good deal of relational health to listening rather than speaking. One Rogerian concept that points to this is "congruence," which he suggests is an aspect of healthy relationships that is discovered through experiencing the moment and being able to "reflect on the dimensions of experience that deserve communicating" (Stewart, 2006, p. 657). Relational listening incorporates regular intervals of this reflection and congruence.

A healthy relationship requires a level of concentration and focus that is not always possible in the type of information and media environment surrounding most 21st-century, Western interlocutors. No matter the setting or channel, it does involve "hearing and being heard" (p. 658). This process involves the actual physical hearing as well as the ability to interpret the symbols used (whether text or voice), something Carl Rogers referred to as *hearing deeply*. He explained that hearing deeply means the thoughts, the feeling tones, the personal meaning, even the meaning that is below the conscious intent of the speaker. Sometimes too, in a message which superficially is not very important, I hear a deep human cry that lies buried and unknown far below the surface of the person. (p. 659)

Other theorists, such as Erving Goffman (1956) are of heuristic value, suggesting the importance of understanding the social situation (or setting) in order to be able to communicate effectively. The need to establish a role for oneself creates an environment that leads to effective interpersonal communication. In an analysis of Goffman's work on communication, institution, and social interaction, Joshua Meyrowitz (1990), explained,

> we need to know whether the situation is formal or informal, happy or sad. We need to know the various roles of the other people, whom we should speak to and whom to avoid, and whether or not we are welcome. Conversely, people in the situation need to know something about us. What is our reason for being there? What role will we play in this situation? (1990, p. 67).

Meyrowitz advances Goffman's notions of the "situation" but differs from his "place-bound" system of thought by suggesting that since face-to-face encounters are no longer the only way people interact it is important to look "at the larger, more inclusive notion of 'patterns of access to information" (pp. 88–89). Certainly, the pervasive and growing presence of personal mobile media makes Meyrowitz's argument increasingly plausible. As interpersonal situations expand across platforms, analyzing the individual environmental variables in mediated encounters will prove helpful in understanding how PMM may best be used to maintain civility and sanity in human relations. As in the focus of this project, the increasing denouement of silence in the blurring of public and private spaces creates various new situations in which it is more difficult for interlocutors to hear each other, understand what is being said, or even begin to develop a stable assessment of the "role" and the "scene."[6] However, there are many other variables to consider as well.

The boundaries eliminated or altered by PMM convey other messages to interlocutors and may be part of an overall societal shift, for as Meyrowitz (1994) explains, the "spatial and temporal limits help to define the nature of social interaction" (p. 150). This applies greatly to relational silence. The desire and need to listen relationally traditionally involves being in proximity to the other, but the rules and social protocols for this kind of listening are in flux due to so many of our interactions occurring on social media. Today, one can be present with another via FaceTime or a Zoom connection, seeing each other's faces, hearing each other's words, the communication mediated by the screen. This sense of one's presence, what one might call "partial presence," has been theorized in different ways throughout the years, however the phrase that most typically differentiates these types of being with from being in another's physical presence is known as "co-presence" (Goffman, 1963). With co-presence, there is the sense of the other through voice, text, or image, but the full presence or full attention of the other is absent. Many words or too few are offered to cover for the lack of presence. What to do about this is yet unknown, for pulling back the technologies that enable co-presence is not an option. But "whether the effects of such media on our society are good, bad, or neutral, the reprocessing of our physical and social environment is revolutionary" (Meyrowitz, p. 145).

As in every other technological revolution, it is not only the mode of communication or devices used that change. People change. Culture changes. Humans adapt and prevail. The current revolution, however, is occurring so quickly that it appears human beings are not quite catching or adapting as quickly as necessary to maintain decency, order, and relational sustainability. Meaning-making is diminished in many ways. In a culture saturated with social media, we appear to be more in touch with the performative aspect of words rather than the formative aspects. Among so many other losses, much coherence is lost.

According to Rhodes (1993), in order to maintain coherence in communication it is necessary that both the sender and receiver will be listening and receiving. One is sending the message; one is speaking and receiving feedback. Further, Rhodes suggests that to truly embark on relational listening one must concern oneself with various appropriate responses. He names five types of responses that are appropriate and work toward effective relational listening. To start, it is necessary for the one who is listening to make a remark that is either "understanding," "probing," "supportive," "interpretive," or "evaluative" (p. 224). Without these elements relational listening is diminished. The missing beat of silence is a partial antidote. Such silence does not provide an entire solution for many other factors exist, but the moment or two taken to process what is being said is essential. This is relational silence, and it is in order here, for each of these relational dynamics is quite impossible without a fitting amount of pause (or quiet) in the exchange. Time to reflect—even a moment—is necessary in order to choose what is appropriate. Craig, Tracy, Flood, and McLaughlin (1984) concur, claiming this type of listening is necessary to maintain conversation coherence. Without it, the relational process will be hindered (Rhodes, p. 240).

For Don Idhe (1976), listening relationally involves silence. To listen with a desire to further relationship is a process that is different from abstract listening, in that it necessitates a certain measure of silence, for, he explains, "silence is the hidden genesis of the word" (p. 202). Idhe suggests that "the presence of the word already there for listening is also what I find if I inquire into myself" (p. 202). The association he makes between the intrapersonal and the interpersonal aspect of communication is evident. To clarify this, he uses the term "communicative silence," which is akin to my own use of the phrase "relational silence." The type of listening associated with such silence, and that which must occur in order to invite speech, suggests that listening is primary. Such listening precedes meaningful conversation. Idhe posits that this type of listening is a primary part of learning and communicating and begins in the womb.

> Long before [the child, *sic*] has learned to speak he has heard and entered the conversation which is humankind. He has been immersed in the voices and movements which preceded his speaking even more deeply in the invisible language of touch and even that of sound within the womb. Listening comes before speaking, and wherever it is sought the most primitive word of sounding language has already occurred. (Idhe, p. 202)

Learning to both speak and listen are essential ingredients in the social and psychological development of a child. The fact that "the conversation" begins in the womb is an intriguing concept, for even there, it is relational, yet without words. Built into our nervous systems is all the apparatus necessary to speak, but no specific language. Once the child is born and moves from the warm bath of intrauterine development to interaction with his/her external environment, the next essential element in the acquisition of language is integration into the speech community. A child's *speech community* is a "technical term [that, *sic*] refers to a social group whose speech is relatively uniform and whose homogeneity is a direct result of the group's members having common experiences and common interpretations of the experience" (Shachtman, p. 17).[7] Speech acquisition comes from within the community as a child listens to the sounds going on around him. He listens until the sounds he is hearing begin to emerge from his own lips. The community is not just a promising idea or a help. It is absolutely essential. Both speaking and listening have long been considered by communication scholars as "the most intimate and personal way that we commune with one another."[8] What is fascinating about this among other things, is the absolutely necessity of community to bring forth language. As Schultze suggests, "Relationships formed in orality are the most enduring forms of interpersonal interaction and are the cross-generational glue of culture in any place."[9] In those speech communities in which fewer people are involved in day-to-day life, or there is less communal time speaking, a child's ability to speak is hindered and he or she will undoubtedly come to speech later than those immersed in active, lively, speech every day.

Moving from individual speech acquisition to the communicational health of the group (and then wider culture), the same principles of listening apply; interpersonal relationality increases as those within the community regularly practice listening to each other. Here we may observe the way families get along together when they develop habits of relational listening. This is where relational silence is a strength, for coherence and overall communication effectiveness is about much more than just getting the meaning correct. Ron Arnett (1986) expands on this theme with movement from dialogic encounter to community. His explanation of dialogue as that which helps to dispel the sense of existential mistrust so prevalent in these postmodern times is another aspect of the connection between silence and effective communication and the furtherance of community.

The best, most personable, and harmonious relationships are those in which there is trust, safety, and a sense of peace. Instead of being in a hurry to blurt out information, people wait for one another to finish their sentence, avoid interruption, and respect the other's thought process. This tacit bit of "best practices" in family life is, according to Thomas Shachtman, fading in America. Part of the problem, he explains, has to do with the substitution of language for images. "We are shown a thousand pictures rather than offered a single insightful word. The direction and emphasis of these changes are in all cases the same: away from precise, reasoned, thoughtfully argued, verbally adroit, idea-laden communication" (pp. 1–2).

Shachtman argues we are in a "crisis of eloquence" brought about as dominance of and dependence upon visual stimuli takes precedence over the spoken and written word. He suggests that while over-reliance on images disrupts the logic and rationality of linear thinking, denigrating the value of the spoken word, there yet exists a residue of the word, which is connected closely with the values brought about by the dominance of literacy in the 18th and 19th centuries. When analyzed on a larger scale Shachtman's ideas are consistent with what Walter Ong refers to as *secondary orality*, that speaking culture dependent on earlier forms of communication, specifically literacy. As he explains in his classic *Orality and Literacy*, the newer modes of communication such as (in his time) television, radio, and telephone, are dependent "for their existence and functioning on writing and print" (p. 11). While the spoken word is by no means disappearing, the alternative dependence on text-based media for conversation has the potential to erode the embedded strength and gifts of literacy as has become apparent in Twitter wars, de-friending from Facebook, and the inability for many people to conduct a respectful conversation in which they disagree. Amid the sometimes-pithy posts that provide a chuckle or bit of charm exist countless messages launched into the public forum via Internet platforms, disparaging anyone with a view different than one's own. Like a virus spreading rapidly throughout the human body, each one chips away at the ability to participate in public conversation with any sense of safety. As a result, a culture of disease emerges with Death to all-important public discourse knocking at our door.

If the ominous tone here sounds dramatic, *it is*. The relationship between interpersonal interaction and public address is tightly knit. In the 1990s access to the world through the world wide web was new and exciting. The 2000s brought expansion and fun introducing us to social platforms. By the time social media became a *tour de force* in the 2010s public address was rapidly falling from dignified, meaningful discourse to the often silly and mean-spirited throwing of barbs. Today, the fun factor is all but gone and the digital environment is rapidly devolving into a new algorithmic reality. Today's Internet has been a key component in creating a public sphere that is corrupting free speech and meaningful conversation. The pressure to post is part of the very human need to be seen and be known, but the mechanistic, tightly controlled underpinnings have done little or nothing to advance meaningful discussion in the public arena. Those areas where artful and honest conversations have been taking place are to be applauded, however the damage being done in the name of commerce and corporate gain is pitiful.

Part of the solution to this conundrum brings our discussion back around again to silence. If we are to reclaim the space (public and private) for civil, healthy, meaningful discourse we must become comfortable again with a measure of quiet. Shachtman explains part of the reason for this is that "aural and visual noise drown out other stimuli, and when they do, quiet decreases apace."[10] Incrementally, the need for quiet becomes greater as PMM become more pervasive. This shift toward visual noise exposes the need for more than the quiet that "is associated with words like calmness, inactivity, and peace"; It is also necessary to maintain equilibrium in both personal and public relationships.[11] Without it, we can expect continued frenzy and fitful rants via social media.

Public places, as well, are replete with tidal waves of sound ushering swells of information into relatively boundary-less spaces that were once deemed virtually sacred. As we move in expedient, harried reaction to the quickened pace of society, we are incrementally giving up the very skills that make us an articulate society. It is time to take a breath. Whether friendship, marriage, or familial relationships, no one can sustain endless words, even if those words are harmonious. There must be some silence kneaded into each relationship so that the communication behavior maintains a flexible elasticity. Without it we are likely to give up on the hope of rich dialogue. Without it, the mediated techniques of media will pull against the strong connective tissue inherent in human relationship and weaken the ebb and flow through practiced non-presence. Instead of habits that include awareness of others, an isolating autonomy begins to emerge that draws us into the delusional notion that we can "make it on our own." Instead of preparing ourselves for lifestyles of shared responsibility and care, we are tempted toward isolation and independence. The reasons for this retreat from others are many, one being the ease of independence. Collaboration is a challenge. The more people involved in an endeavor the more opportunity to be slowed down or stopped by another's question or input. Thus, we lean toward it. We lean toward the myth of independence—the *self-made man* or the *wonder woman.*

Interdisciplinary scholars such as Michael Bugeja (2017), Philip Thompson (2000), Rob Anderson (1994), Joshua Meyrowitz (1994), Robert Bellah (1985), and Thomas Merton (1979), along with Postman (1993), Ellul (1990, 1985, 1964), and Buber (1969) are among the many whose work make evident the myriad snags in relationship that occur when human beings reify the inner longings and needs through words alone. The push-and-pull of silence helps to work against the current tendency to objectify the relationship. In this way silence, along with action coming forth from the words, helps deconstruct the socially constructed notion of a relationship being a *thing.* To treat a human relationship as a product to be had or a "thing" to be consumed is grossly problematic to the effective functioning of relationships. Programming such as ABC's *The Bachelor* or *The Bachelorette* reinforces this objectification. Although the shows have mass appeal and major audiences throughout the globe, they are just one piece of a puzzle that contributes to a false sense of relationship.

Whether platonic or intimate, instead, healthy relationships are processes, part of the overall communication process and emerging from a shared space of curiosity, attraction, and/or commonality. As use of our screens to mediate these relational practices become normal social practices it may be argued that they objectify human relationships more than serve them. A growing body of research substantiating this points to these problems suggesting the distractive and addictive properties associated with PMM contribute to the objectification (Lanier, 2009; Turkle, 2015; Twenge, 2016; Rushkoff, 2020). The work of earlier communication and interdisciplinary scholars Martin Buber (1965), Joseph Walther (1995), and Julia Wood (2004) advance this idea, as well.

Along with harmonious relations, as discussed previously, silence is used to structure speech and is an anchor for conversation (Scott, 1979, pp. 1–18). Placed intentionally in the way of pauses and accents, silence also helps to define meaning (Scott, 2000, p. 108). Without an appropriate amount of silence (both interior silence and in the external environment), interpersonal interactions using PMM may—over time—become increasingly more impersonal. This can be further illustrated by noting what John Stewart (2006) described as the five key elements of interpersonal communication.

These areas of functionality are intricately woven into the communication process, most specifically, the interpersonal realm. The term "interpersonal labels the kind of communication that happens when the people involved talk and listen in ways that maximize the presence of the personal" (p. 38). For Stewart, the meaningfulness of interpersonal communication is dependent upon five key areas of relationality. These are: responsiveness, addressability, response-ability, immeasurability, and uniqueness (p. 38). Each of these factors contributes to communication that may be considered interpersonal.[12] Each element, however, incorporates additional meaning. One, for example, is the response-ability factor. Unlike the similar word "responsibility," to be response-able means that one has the "ability to respond" and does so (p. 24). If the ability to respond is hindered, either by external noise, internal overload, or some other variable, one must wonder if the ability to be "response-able" is present (p. 24).[13]

The myriad contexts and settings available through PMM make this factor particularly salient. Is it really possible to listen and carry on a conversation "response-ably" with another who is involved in coaching their child's soccer game? Or the increasingly common practice of using one's automobile as an office and missing the turn signal at a traffic light because answering emails and checking Instagram is possible while driving. These social phenomena point to a practice sometimes referred to as "continuous partial attention," a type of communication practice that never focuses on one person or issue but is constantly multitasking.[14] Texting while on a date and checking in with one's Instagram account at the same time is an example of this hyper-attentiveness to never miss anything. The acronym FOMO (fear of missing out) has become associated with this behavior, a way of being in the world that does not adequately shift the cognition process between activities. Canadian media ecologist Ellen Rose explains what happens when we capitulate to continuous partial attention. "Our minds and eyes, as we use the computer to write papers, prepare presentations, read documents, or participate in online courses, are always scanning the periphery for incoming e-mail, instant messages, and other communications and contacts. Like video game players, we are constantly on the alert, our eyes darting, our fingers twitching, anxious not to let one message, one fragment of information, one potential contact with a virtual friend slip by."[15] Such nervous energy does several things to one's ability to communicate. Along with an increased squirt of cortisol, the brain's ability to focus on one item is hampered. It is unsurprising that the ability to concentrate is lessened. Over time, the heightened but fractured awareness of incoming information creates diminishing returns on relational solvency. As friends, families, and partners acculturate to the partial attention they are receiving, relational sustainability lessens.

Messages may be transferred, and transactions completed, but do "wireless encounters" with the information of others count as true encounters in the Buberian sense? That is, are they unique, expressive, and creative forms of using language in which the two meet in a new, "third space" that exists between them? Other questions of effectiveness emerge as well, concerning such elements as the visual and tactile properties of human communication. Are these elements necessary for communication effectiveness? The immense advance of video technologies has led to greater communicative effectiveness for those who use them (think: Zoom meetings, FaceTime, and VideoChat). If silence works to order or structure speech and is used as an anchor in conversation, what are the means by which one may apprehend the time that is necessary to maximize the interpersonal exchange, particularly if the conversation is taking place on the run? How do interlocutors measure the interest and enthusiasm of the other without the fullness of speech? Is the mediating channel more dominant in a conversation than the conversation itself? These questions present themselves and are worthy of deep consideration and research. The many variables associated with them are intricately intertwined with the need for communication coherence and quality, and each has an influence and outworking on an interlocutor's ability to notice, receive, and fully embrace "the other."

DIALOGIC LISTENING

Certainly not all listening is relational. Some listening is more pragmatic or perfunctory, but relational listening requires an empathic impulse. Such listening involves greater focus than simply being attentive and aware of nonverbal cues. Philosopher and theologian Martin Buber (1990) contends that listening is a primary element involved in fostering relationship and necessary to engaging in true dialogue. Sensitivity to the other is very much a part of relational listening, yet Buber described a type of listening that emphasizes "the other" on a deeper level, a listening style that has come to be known as "dialogic" (Anderson et al., 1994; Arnett, 1986; Friedman, 1974; Buber, 1970).

Dialogic listening requires attentiveness, as well, but much more. To listen dialogically requires forethought, intention to meet the other in true presence (Buber, 1970; Ong, 1985; Strate et al., 2003). Presence requires much more than simple attention from the interlocutors and, in turn, provides more than a simple, informational verbal exchange. Unlike attentive and/or relational listening (which each describe a various type of listening), "dialogic listening involves a crucial change from a focus on *me* or *the other* to a focus on *ours*, on what is between speaker(s) and listener(s)" (Stewart, 2006, p. 230). While empathic listening attempts to understand the feelings behind another's words or nonverbal behavior so as to encourage or maintain relationship, dialogic listening attempts to encourage a response to something that has already been said (p. 230). One listens dialogically to find a common ground, a way to move forward in the conversation. And, in the same way that the noise permeating our contemporary media environment undoubtedly effects the ability to listen deeply, other factors contribute to the success of dialogic listening. One is the mobility factor.

The mobility factor is a major part of the dynamics involved. Essentially, those using personal mobile media are always in two different geographic places when interpersonal communication occurs, a factor that allows a degree of connection but removes the dynamics of one's full presence. The mobility factor enables us to connect with others at vast distances, but also increases the number of hindrances to listening making it increasingly difficult to listen dialogically. In fact, all the technology-induced distractions or "noise" that have been described in previous sections interfere with any effort to advance dialogue. Remedies for such would seem to extend beyond using silence in the interpersonal exchange process; however, the need for silence remains and perhaps even increases. Without the ability to focus or concentrate on that which the other expresses of himself or herself both verbally and nonverbally, it is increasingly difficult to enter into the practice of dialogic listening or have much consideration of "the other" as other. Interpersonal communication that continues without this focus may serve as a strong inhibitor to the mutuality and connectedness that dialogic listening inspires. This is precisely why the intentional use of silence in pauses, turn-taking, gestures, and listening "with the heart" may be part of an antidote for the instrumentality fostered by personal mobile media.

One of the downfalls of dialogic listening is that it takes more time than other types of listening. Allowing the measure of silence necessary to think deeply on a matter is not expedient, at least in the short term. Thus, dialogic listening becomes even more difficult as increased levels of noise fill the conversational setting. Yet, the untold benefits of slowing down the conversation to make room for more thoughtful response is just the beginning of change that is desperately needed in advancing relational richness and a healthy public square. The concept of "mutuality" is intricately woven into this type of listening. It is a type of listening that "values and builds mutuality, requires active involvement, is genuine, and grows out of a belief in and commitment to its practice. Dialogic listening is that which is needed if one is to engage in dialogue, that practice which inheres desire and understanding to communicate with a goal of finding meaning together. Dialogue does not necessitate agreement, nor does it preclude it, but the goal in dialogue is to further the conversation and continue an ongoing discussion of a subject important to both parties. Ideally, dialogue will result in one party moved to action, but dialogue doesn't begin with the goal of persuasion.

In this chapter, we looked carefully at the various functions of silence in establishing quality and meaning in interpersonal communication. We also examined the ways in which the silent components of nonverbal communication aid the interpersonal process and looked carefully at some of the challenges presented by the current media environment. Of the many challenges mentioned, this chapter brings to bear the dynamics of the new media landscape and argues that the increasing press of sounds, images, and information may serve as more of a distraction to the listening that is vital for the advancement of interpersonal relationship. I argued that while personal mobile media may give us exceptional tools for exchanging impersonal messages, these media are not the best choices for use in establishing dialogue and the other necessary components of interpersonal relationship. Additionally, I contend that the complexity of interpersonal communication in establishing meaning, quality, and the goals of relationship with another or a public create a need for concentration and focus, two elements that are directly related to dialogue but rarely found among those interlocutors excessively using personal mobile media. Finally, I suggest that listening is at the forefront of the process of interpersonal communication. This is true whether people speak face-to-face or in mediated situations. However, the skills and surroundings necessary to be an apt listener necessitate the full attention of both parties and are easily compromised when using personal mobile media.

As significant as listening is to this relational approach to interpersonal communication, being relational involves more than the silence sequestered in attentive listening, more than reflective, healthy self-talk, more than making room for the other to speak. Such communicative effectiveness involves a mentality that might best be described as non-instrumental and requires a certain participation and attitude that is not always possible in a world where words are exchanged hurriedly and at the heightened pace of today's communication systems.[16] The type of transactional exchange that today passes for communication has its roots in many factors but emerges more recently from a post-industrial push for efficiency and is complicated by an exchange of the ends for the means or methods used to communicate. The result of this switch in purpose funnels into moral territory where the presence of an ethical foundation in interpersonal communication is weak and full of cracks. Implications to civility and personhood are many. And so, to ethical silence we now turn.

NOTES

1. The practice of taking on the pains, problems, and issues of a relational other into oneself and appropriating them as one's own lack is introjection. To introject is vastly different from projecting one's own issues onto another.
2. Quentin Schultze, *Communicating for Life*. p. 20.
3. In a technopoly people still possess the impulse to create or innovate, but this impulse is lessened by the surreptitious removal or slow erosion of a stabilizing meta-narrative such as that which religion or politics provide. In the wake of the collapsed or shrunken meta-narrative the tools that once served human beings begin to establish sovereignty over the thought world and perceptions of a population, shaping and re-forming what is valued and what is not.
4. New American Bible (revised edition) Luke 6: 45b.
5. Many interpersonal communication theories/theorists might apply in some way here, but discussing each of them goes beyond the scope of this study. It is important to acknowledge, however, some of the most salient ones in the following list: From Cicero's Science of Conversation, which he differentiated from formal discourse in his essay "On Moral Duties"; the helical-spiral model of Frank E. X. Dance, 1967; the Self Disclosure theory of Sidney Jourard (1969); Charles Berger and the theory of Uncertainty Reduction; Mark Knapp's Staircase Model (1978); the Social Penetration Model of Gerald Miller; Baxter and Montgomery's Relational Dialectics, 1998; Rogers, 1995; and Steven Duck's theory of Relationshipping (2006). There are numerous, helpful models and theories of interpersonal communication.
6. Erving Goffman's dramaturgical theory depicts interpersonal communication as performance. The ground upon which interlocutors perform is a "stage" that separates communication behavior into regions. In the front region or backstage, "performers" play roles that are dependent upon the audience and the place (setting.).
7. For expansion on this phenomenon and an enlightening understanding of the process of speech acquisition, see Thomas Shachtman's readerly and highly accessible book, *The Inarticulate Society*.
8. Quentin Schultze. *Communicating for Life*. p.70.
9. Ibid.
10. Thomas Shachtman *The Inarticulate Society*. p 144.
11. Thomas Shachtman. p. 144.
12. John Stewart, *Bridges not Walls*. p. 38.
13. John Stewart's (2006) explanation of response-ability brings greater clarity. "You are response-able when you have the willingness and ability to contribute in some way to how things are unfolding, rather than ignoring what's going on or dropping out of the event" (p. 24). As smart phone technology advanced in the early 2010s the mobility factor became even more important. As the ability to multitask became easier, the need for responsibility became more evident. This is particularly salient in regard to PMM and most specifically to the use of cell phones where the exchange is often abruptly interrupted or halted completely due to what is termed a "dropped call."

14. Former Microsoft and Apple executive Linda Stone came up with this term in the late 1990s. [April 24, 2021] https://lindastone.net/2009/11/30/beyond-simple-multi-tasking-continuous-partial-attention/.

15. See Ellen Rose. "Continuous Partial Attention." p. 43.

16. From Quintilian's "a good man speaking well," to Kenneth Burke's use of words to "induce action," there are numerous definitions of the word "rhetoric." And, while some scholars take issue with using the word to refer to anything that is not implicitly persuasive, others separate instrumental rhetoric (or, most simply, public speaking) as audience-centered, or that which is primarily focused on convincement. My use of the word "instrumental" refers to an explicit desire or design on one's audience to inspire action or a change of mind. I am using it loosely in juxtaposition to the idea of "relationship talk" where the intention to persuade is not primary. Persuasion can (and does) occur within interpersonal relations, but the differentiation focuses on the desire for conversion/persuasion and the desire for knowing the other as an end in itself.

Chapter 7

Ethical Silence

There was a time in the not-so-distant past when a forthright, honest conversation could reasonably be assumed to be private. One-on-one discussions over nettling matters in the workplace, painful family problems, and ongoing relationship conflicts were held in unspoken trust that what was shared was not for public consumption. When confidence was breached, it was a serious matter, one that could end a friendship or start a war. Today, the lines between what is public information and what is private are completely fluid. No longer just blurred, they have all but disappeared from the map of conversational legitimacy and the space to have an old-fashioned private conversation is disappearing. It seems nearly everyone on the street or in a discussion forum has a ready camera and recorder in the palm of his or her own hands. Now that our media travel with us, we can share our private matters in public, and indeed we do! Ethical issues surrounding PMM are numerous, and silence plays a major role in most of them. From privacy and cyber-crime to online bullying and catfishing, there are ever-new means of stealing, hurting, cheating, and harming our neighbor. The expansion of new media has allowed the general public access to places, people, and opportunity like never before in the history of civilization. Along with this expansion the opportunity to slip into moral regress is exacerbated. Thus, the hegemonic pervasiveness of new media presents not merely a technological problem that needs fixing, but an epistemological condition from which emancipation is needed.

The super-saturated, often anonymous, situation with which we conduct online conversation has fostered a crisis, indeed, but the crisis we face is not the hardware, software, or particular infrastructure of any of the major companies involved. Rather, the crisis is what media ethicist Clifford Christians explains, is "a technological understanding of being"[1] (Christians, p. 44). The moral quandaries interposed throughout online settings are evident but do not always ring with clarity. Countless opportunities to become tangled up in obfuscation and breeches of trust exist at every turn. A crisis, indeed; it is one that denigrates the commonplaces of our humanity such as honesty, compassion, and concern for a common good. James K. A. Smith sees it pointedly as a disease, explaining that "the pathology [besetting, *sic*] us at this cultural moment is a failure of imagination, specifically the failure to imagine the other as neighbor."[2]

With each new technological innovation and software update the learning curve increases. But the problems involved therein are more complex than simply straightening out the most egregious behaviors or mandating particular social protocols. There is challenging work that can be done and steps that can be taken to create communication protocols that protect our social trust. These may be partially addressed by adjusting the technologies themselves, but the ethical quandaries associated with the digital age require more than a technological solution. What is needed are solutions that put our humanness in the forefront. The prevailing principle of utility as it operates in the technological system instills a technological ethic that eclipses a teleological one, and it manifests itself in behavior that is not pro-social, but highly individualistic and utilitarian.

The ethics so often associated with technological innovation do not keep humanness in the forefront of discovery and development, and in fact, in many ways serve to incrementally diminish it. Examples abound. Instead of building social media networks to advance human flourishing, it is the pursuit of efficiency and individual achievement, technical grandiosity, and corporate control that spawn much of it.[3] Christians (1980) suggests this technical artifice is not merely "one more arena for philosophers and socialists to investigate, but a new foundation for understanding the self, human institutions, and ultimate reality."[4] This new foundation provides fertile ground for the expansion of digital culture, and it does so at great speed and without attention to what is being eliminated.

In accord with Christians, Darrell Fasching describes this technological ethic as a threat, corroding the fresh flow of freedom. Instead of prioritizing human agency, the ethic of efficiency begins to usurp and undermine it (Fasching, 1997). This ethic of efficiency is the crux of what is underpinning a new, multi-tasking way of being-in-the-world, and as it becomes the norm, the ability to focus on one thing at a time not only becomes passé but is eventually no longer available or no longer allowed. This idea may be challenging to apprehend because freedom is not violently taken away by force, but in order to comply with the demands of the technological system choices become limited. Eventually, choice is not available at all. The clearest example of late may be observed in the now notorious political engagement during the 2020 presidential election in the United States. Instead of actual discussion, what passed for public conversation plummeted into what may only be described as a free-for-all, the bulk of which took place without context, fact-checking, or listening to one another on social media. Truth was scarce. Willingness to patiently listen was almost completely absent.

In the last few years social media have become portals of pontification and do not favor or foster civil discussion, democracy, or an overarching "good" to society. Mudslinging and manipulative language are not new, but in just a few decades, public discourse has morphed from well-reasoned speeches, carefully constructed essays edited for mistakes and typos, and hearty conversation to silly memes, soundbites, wild rants, and promotional stories that have little to no regard for meaning, let alone truth. The heft and harangue of social media favors unrelenting contentiousness in the same way that television and other visual media favor drama. One example is the worldwide melee that began in the U.S. in the wake of several egregious instances of police brutality during the spring of 2020. Even as I write these words, cities throughout the globe are literally ablaze in protest with destruction and bitter hatred for those whose views on politics, race, religion, and the news differ from their own. Law and order are sacrificed and of little concern to vocal, violent groups, hurling words that feel like rocks, aiming to crush the other in the public square as one might have done in the arena at the ancient Roman Games. This emerging culture of contention does not reflect, I believe, what is legitimate protest against social inequity. Nor does it represent the hearts and minds of most people, but it is fomented in a competitive media environment that seeks attention, personal data, subscriptions, and ultimately dominance. Roots of this contention are found in greed, the desire to put financial gain above the common good. Without attention or attempt to address this cacophonous free-for-all, words become weapons and weeds grow up through the soil of a healthy society. Although their culpability is clear, laying all the blame for this erosion of civil discourse must not land at the feet of the corporations and companies. The public choose to use these media, and as other options for discussion become obsolete, the situation worsens.[5]

Attempts to voice opinion in this culture of contention do not generally address any problems; they serve only to create more pain, creating spectacle and exacerbating the problem. Thomas Shachtman concurs and explains part of the reason for this shift lies in the advance of the image over the spoken word. He explains, "We are shown a thousand pictures rather than offered a single insightful word. The direction and emphasis of these changes are in all cases the same: away from precise, reasoned, thoughtfully argued, verbally adroit, idea-laden communication" (pp. 1–2). Indeed, words without action are no substitute for justice, but the need to address injustice must be done without resorting to aggression, insurrection, or violence. Instead, much of what passes for public conversation involves a mélange of images that disseminate information through video and photography. The rise of the image advances on the heels of the technological age and has major impact on how we process reality. Henri J. Nouwen makes the point that how one sees oneself is connected to the images we view externally. This has a rippling effect on our social interactions and ability to experience true dialogue. He explains, "When it is true that the image you carry in your mind can affect your physical, mental, and emotional life, then it becomes a crucial question as to which we expose ourselves or allow ourselves to be exposed."[6] And, as our knowledge is mediated through decontextualized videos, we perceive something to be *true* when it is but a snapshot of reality. This limited, bounded information is not enough to claim one knows the truth of a situation with certainty, yet verbal wars and disconfirming actions take place every day instead of deliberation and dialogue.

The factors involved in the demise of dialogue are many. Another aspect of what slows the advance of healthy public dialogue stems from uncertainty of the future, and what Ronald C. Arnett frames as lack of confidence in the ability to make a difference.[7] This "background of trust" is something that is necessary for healthy public discourse but has been sorely compromised in the digital age. Arnett suggests that this background of trust is largely situated in the assumptions we make in conversation, particularly those being the most basic, that is: we will listen to one another, and we will take turns to speak. Another is the assumption of honesty. Truth must be a part of this trust. The hope of dialogue is made possible when those coming together are open to gaining perspective on the truth the other brings, for "truth lives in dialogue, in the discussion, in conversation."[8]

Problems are guaranteed to arise when this trust is not present. "When the background of our communicative ecology is not based in a realistic sense of trust, two major interpersonal consequences are invited; a hermeneutic of suspicion and narcissism."[9] Memes, tweets, fake news, and the rest of the messages that are disseminated without care for context or facticity are good reasons to be suspicious, but without a ground level of trust between those conversing there is little to hold back the base reactionary result. Ethical silence speaks to this issue and can often lead the way to address such problems. Is there always a need to respond with a retort, correction, or adjustment? No, there is not. Silence can be a proper and legitimate antidote for the trust issue; it is one way to change the tide of a conversation that has drifted into brackish waters. Deciding to respond without retort or with an extended pause will not provide the satisfaction of making one's point, but it may provide a way in which to build a more solid ground for conversation. What must be noted is that the choice to respond in silence can easily be interpreted incorrectly. This is especially so if one is functioning within a culture of silence where problems are habitually buried, ignored, or denied. Silence surely does not fit every situation and must not be used as a panacea for conflict. In an unhealthy situation it will have the opposite effect, producing a toxic culture of habituated abuse.

Clifford G. Christians is a noted ethicist, media scholar, and part of the U.N. project on universal human rights who has worked internationally to offer communication solutions to globally diverse people groups in stalemate and conflict. Christians has done much to advance the practice of ethical communication. His work spans the globe and is centered in a philosophy of communication that is non-instrumental but underpinned by a deep respect for human life. Other scholars concerned about the absence of ethical speech readily contribute to the ongoing conversation to advance dialogue as the necessary astringent and salve for a world divided by ideology and cultural diversity, among them, Arnett (1994), Makau and Marty, (2013), Cissna and Anderson (2003), and Buber (2003). Going forward, we will feature some of their erudite ideas.

DIALOGUE AND MEANING

The purpose of dialogue is to further relationship, to find common ground to discuss a particular subject. Dialogue infers high worth placed on the value of the word. The word is capable of summoning justice and mercy or sowing condemnation and deceit. In a Buberian sense, it is this aspect of the word that enables two individuals to experience the actuality and uniqueness of each other, wherein truth, freedom, and relationship become possibilities. As these human goods emerge, they do so as a result of the experience of dialogue, a type of conversation that flows forth from a mutual desire to know and be known. But dialogue is rarely a natural occurrence and must be learned whether formally or through experience. Listening to one another with a genuine desire to understand and make meaning together begins ideally with the speech community, and it would seem that the greater grasp of language, the more likely it is that two will find company with one another, resting in the equanimity and harmony of dialogue. Here Ellul notes the importance of language and frames it accordingly:

> Language is an affirmation of my person, since I am the one speaking, and it is born at the same time as the faint belief, aspiration, or conviction of liberty. The two are born together, and so language is a sign bearing witness to my freedom and calling the other person to freedom as well. (1985, p. 24)

The reach of dialogue spans far beyond the linguistic mechanics of conversation and is intimately associated with ethics that respects personhood. Dialogic ethics is a lived ethics that inherently respects the other, *as other.*

This means—among other things—that dialogue doesn't simply happen when two people come together to converse. Inherent in the meaning of dialogue is the idea of mutuality and the otherness of the other. Dialogic morality does not objectify the other but insists on the value and sacredness of human speech. It meets the other as other, in true presence. Ethics is the place dialogue and silence meet.

To best address this interchange, one must apprehend a definition of communication that is inclusive of the whole of humanness, and one that speaks to its ontological roots. But such a definition is rather vast, seemingly unreachable. Yet, attempt it we must if we are intent on speaking and writing in meaningful ways. Honoring the process of communication and taking time to use it with respect and civility in a world bedazzled by materialism and celebrity will take time. But, as a society much less weight is placed on learning the art of communication than is given to other subjects. Instead of education, weighty arguments, and essays written about the need to adapt to these changes in the media environment, public commentary typically amounts to bits, bytes, truncated pieces of poetry, song loops, articles, and memes. This is vastly different from the elements of dialogue.

First, it must be noted that not all conversations are dialogic. Dialogue is a very specific type of conversation, one that is typically more formal than a discussion or lighthearted exchange. It is equally distinguishable from debate. Dialogue involves use of language between two or more to seek meaning, independent of agreement. Using a dialogic approach may yet involve a stark difference of position between interlocutors, but it is not debate. Makou and Marty (2013) explain one of the elements that distinguish the two is that debate is competitive. It "is oppositional: two sides oppose each other and attempt to prove each other wrong," while dialogue "is collaborative; two or more sides work together toward shared understanding" (2013, p. 69). Dialogue infers high worth placed on the value of the word as well as the person speaking. Its purpose is to maintain ongoing discussion and find common ground in addressing a particular subject The word is capable of summoning justice and mercy or sowing condemnation and deceit.

In a Buberian sense, this aspect of the word enables two individuals to experience the actuality and uniqueness of each other wherein truth, freedom, and relationship become possibilities. As these human goods emerge, they do so as a result of the shared experience of dialogue, that which flows forth from a mutual desire to know and be known. Without these goods, it is unlikely that community life will flourish. With them, community ties are strengthened and the possibility of living in peace is advanced. Today, perhaps more than ever, people are afraid of disagreement, but disagreement is not the crux of the problem. Rather, the inability (or unwillingness) to cultivate a culture of respect lies at the root. Nurturing a dialogic culture requires ethical sensibility that is not afraid to deal with disagreement. Arnett suggests that it is in "balancing relationship sensitivity and a willingness to encounter conflict in resolving a problem."[10]

Dialogue can occur in a number of ways, but it is most favored and possible when meeting face-to-face in an unhurried setting. Part of the reason for this is the notion of facial primacy, that aspect of communication that gives more weight to the face than other parts of the body. It is more difficult to ignore or disregard another when one looks into his or her eyes. Because the eyes provide a primal reflex, the information gained from eye contact can indicate credibility and genuineness or the opposite. In a study published in *Computers in Human Behavior*, the authors note that among the chief contributions to online flaming, eye contact was the most prominent disinhibitory variable.[11] This factor underscores the importance of facial primacy and speaks to the desirability of presence in a dialogic situation. Although technological substitutes for meeting face-to-face, such as Zoom, FaceTime, and newer voice-centric apps, bring the image of another to a conversation, interacting with a grid full of faces mediated through a screen is not ideal and diminishes the possibility for effective communication.

Another contributing factor in dialogic success involves the sound of the word being spoken. The bias of the spoken word toward presence is not to be minimized, its power has long been standard for dialogic credibility. The sound of a person's voice is essential in communicating mood, meaning, context, and genuineness. It is integral to the development of relationship and community. As Ong so aptly writes, "Man communicates with his whole body, and yet the word is his primary medium. Communication, like knowledge itself, flowers in speech."[12] Such flowering includes the nuance and excitement of hearing one's voice and subsequent voice of another. Emerging from the breath of one's being and rising from the lips of one's mouth, voice carries with it a dynamic that inheres intimacy.

> Voice is for the person the paradigm of all sound, and to it all sound tends to be assimilated. We hear the voice of the sea, the voice of thunder, the voice of the wind, and an engine's cough. This means that the dynamism inherent in all sound tends to be assimilated to the dynamism of the human being, an unpredictable and potentially dangerous dynamism because a human being is a free, unpredictable agent. (Ong, 1969, p. 638)

The freedom to speak is activated by the voice, and although it is an immeasurably powerful element, voice is not the sole key to successful dialogue. Willingness to listen and the exchange of ideas occurs in writing as well as in speech. Some examples are evident in discussions carried over a period of time within journals, academic papers, and official documents. Weighty conversations about world health, climate change, scientific research, or the ongoing conversation surrounding racial reconciliation, each are examples of this type of dialogue.

THEORETICAL ROOTS

Understanding the elements of dialogue is primary to the advancement of ethical communication. When speaking about the common good, dialogue must be employed. Dialogue is the vehicle through which a healthy polis is governed, bringing stability and the maintenance of freedom. To participate in dialogue is, in a sense, to choreograph the common good. An ethics of dialogue is not based on outward or external rules and principles, but is situated deeply within, upholding the sacredness of life as an underlying principle (Christians, 2019). With respect for the other *as other* being of chief importance, and the dialogic principle upheld, dialogue is yet not the foundation of ethical communication praxis. Rather, an ethics of personhood and the dignity therein is the foundation for dialogue. Such grounding established by deontological sensibilities and communitarian action are weighted acknowledging a responsibility to the other—a duty to maintain the value of personhood and human presence. This thinking is firmly found in the principles of universal human proto-norms established in the work of Clifford G. Christians. Christians provides solid ground for dialogue in the digital age through his media ethics scholarship and has been at the forefront of the project since its inception. His theory of media ethics is based on a moral philosophy that finds its center in the sacredness of life itself and an understanding that technologies are not neutral, but value-laden (Christians, 2019, p. 21).

Rather than political or economic underpinnings, Christians explains that, "Theories of global media ethics ought to be ontological instead. One theoretical model compatible with human centered technology is the sacredness of human life as a worldwide proto-norm. This is a different kind of universal, one that honors the diversity of human culture while advocating cross-cultural norms" (Christians, 2019, p. 29). Communication that is grounded in the sacredness of life has the potential to reach into the hearts and minds of people of all cultures to provide sturdy basis on which to stand with another even when disagreement on particulars is strong. Life is sacred, all life. The dignity of human life, the importance of truth, and the essentiality of non-violence provide ways to discuss the common problems of all humans and work together toward solutions (Christians, 2019). Christians speaks of these as proto-norms with historic precedence and explains their universality arguing that "concrete human existence is inscribed in the vitalistic order as a whole."[13] This perspective pushes back hard against the transactional ethics of utility and offers a way to enter into dialogue that is open, honest, and accessible.

Much more has been written regarding the types of dialogue and theoretic constructs therein.[14] Interdisciplinary scholars such as Michael Bugeja (2017), Philip Thompson (2000), Rob Anderson (1994), Joshua Meyrowitz (1994), Robert Bellah (1985), and Thomas Merton (1979), along with Postman (1993), Ellul (1990, 1885, 1964), and Buber (1969) are several among the many who emphasize the importance of keeping humanness in human communication. As such humanness is understood and practiced, dialogue is apt to increase, and a groundswell of respectful, relational conversation is more possible. In this way, dialogue is an extremely helpful part of the solution to avoid aggression, violence, and war. However, dialogue is not a formula and holds no guarantee to work 100 percent of the time, nor does it heal all wounds.

The theoretical roots of dialogue run deep but moving from chaotic "crazy talk" to communication that is dialogic is as much a matter of character as it is understanding the principles of effective communication. Warring against the high moral ground of universal proto-norms and civil discourse are the myriad dynamics created by our digital tools of communication. Just as the "noise" of too much information hinders the listening process, the dynamics at work in the use of personal mobile media create entirely new areas of conflict and communication breakdown in interpersonal exchange. One in particular involves the objectification of human relationships. As addressed in the earlier discussion of Buberian thought, viewing a relationship as "a thing" is to engage in a wholly instrumental way of perceiving the other. This mistake occurs in countless ways. Whether they are familial, romantic, or professional, platonic or intimate, healthy relationships emerge from a shared space. They do not become reality through the touch of a magic wand but are part of the overall communication process. Depending on the nature of the relationship, they flourish and take shape as two share a common space of curiosity, attraction, and/or mutual interests.

Along with leading with an indubitable foundation of respect, willingness to wait one's turn to speak as well as continuing to make listening a priority are two areas that require awareness and discipline. As Wayne Jacobsen explains, "Speaking the language of healing isn't a matter of semantics alone; it's also a matter of developing your character."[14] Myriad snags in communication occur when human beings reify the inner longings and needs through words. This is not only evidenced in the flagrant abuse of language, but in its improper use. Desire for honest relationships of authentic character is jeopardized and thwarted when careful attention to words is ignored. As Josef Pieper reminds us, "The natural habitat of truth is found in interpersonal communication. Truth lives in dialogue, in discussion, in conversation—it resides, therefore in language, in the world."[15] The unfortunate human tendency to treat relationship as a product to be had or a "thing" to be consumed is grossly problematic.

Another way to understand this aspect of dialogue is to approach everyday conversations more seriously. Something important is missed when the seemingly trivial, everyday interactions with neighbors, grocery clerks, and bank tellers gives way to text-based, digital exchange. Losing those often cumbersome and mundane activities to the anonymity and ease of doing it all from a home computer or mobile device removes an essential element of social cohesion. *Small talk*, although far from the ethics of dialogue, is not beyond its reach. It is one of the ways we learn to see the other in front of us as a subject and are thus less inclined to perceive them as just a name on a screen—an object. This is not a completely novel problem. In the history of technological innovation these same elements have slowly eroded, and we have largely learned to adapt to life without the pleasantries of small talk. Everyday conversations in physical proximity to others help us stand in what Parker Palmer calls "standing in the tragic gap."[16] Without this type of social interaction, that gap, created by differences of opinion and belief, grows to a chasm of endless separation and divisiveness. It is then much more difficult to pursue dialogue. It is indeed tragic when hope is lost for harmonious relations with those people and ideas that differ from our own. But hope can be restored—along with meaning—when we hold to a belief that human life is sacred. As lovely as it is, this notion of restoration is fraught with complications and tension. To revive (or maintain) hope is to acknowledge its complexity and bear with it in each other, rather than be dismissive or give in to defeat because there is so much lack of clarity. Again, Palmer assures us with encouragement to go beyond placing faith in only what we see before us. He writes, "Hope is holding a creative tension between what is and what could (and should) be, and each day doing something to narrow the distance."[17]

Many other variables are at work in the discussion of dialogic ethics. The intersection of relationship in the use of personal mobile media is a significant one. Walther (1995) discusses the selective self-presentation of social media users. Another is the dishonesty of presenting a completely false sense of self or intention such as exhibited in the practice of "catfishing" (Kottemann, 2015).[18] As of yet, a consistent body of knowledge that unilaterally depicts the use of PMM as detrimental to relationship has not emerged, but many examples of the stilted, decontextualized nature of interpersonal exchanges in the use of personal mobile media are a growing norm. One is in the sparseness and immediacy of text messaging on a cell phone or the use of Instant Messenger on e-mail programs. A normative practice among many users is to highlight, copy, and paste the messages into a virtual storage container on the desktop. E-mails and personal information are saved and increasingly forwarded all over the world.

The interpersonal ramifications of this practice are many; some are obvious, others, less so. Consider one example: the matter of forgiveness. If a person has received a hurtful message from a dear friend, that message can be revisited verbatim, again and again, making it much more difficult to forget. On the other hand, an encouraging, positive message can be reviewed, too. The same dynamic is present with less recent media, such as the telephone. Telephone messages are saved on message retrievers and can be played and replayed. Recorded messages on telephone answering machines, digitally recorded clips of video or audio messages, and numerous other permanent records of "what was said" are often filed and kept in the same way that diaries and photo albums helped to memorialize important moments in the past century.[19] Now, however, these messages are available in a moment with the stroke of a key or a pull-down menu and much more easily stored and retrieved. In the present media environment, there is little room for "necessary forgetting" that is so very much a part of Western relationship maintenance.[20] Forgetfulness is one of the important elements with which Picard (1952) concurs in respect to relationship:

> There is oblivion in language, it seems, so that language should not be too violent. The supremacy that language has over silence is thereby mitigated. The sinking of words into oblivion is as it were a sign that things belong to us only temporarily and can be called back to whence they came. When a word sinks into oblivion it is forgotten, and this forgetting prepares the way for forgiveness. That is a sign that love is woven into the very structure of language: words sink into the forgetfulness of man so that in forgetting he may also forgive. (p. 28)

Another example may be found in the business sector. Consider the number of e-mails saved in a folder on a computer hard drive in nonsocial settings. Colleges, universities, corporations, and businesses now regularly hire entire teams of consultants as data managers, many providing in-house support to make sure the computer connections are properly configured so as not to "clog the network." What is written or "texted" in a casual manner is typically saved by the computer system and can be retrieved for investigation. Many employees are not even aware that their supervisors (or others, such as administrative aides) have access to read their e-mail. In a sense, current communication technologies have made it difficult for not only individuals but organizations to forget words that have been expressed.

Numerous other variables influence the possibility for dialogue, many are not especially communicational but pertain to accessibility, poverty and wealth, social status, and education. Many, however, are explicitly informed by communication. Privacy, trust, conversational tone, context, and setting are each elements that influence the prospect and promise of dialogue. Each may operate as both an indicator of motive and a factor in the ethics of dialogue. Other blockages to building trust and the advancement of dialogue involve algorithmic preference for a pre-determined set of specifications. The preconceptions and unconscious biases coded into Internet search engines and social media platforms create an unequal field for constructing a solid sense of self or pursuing relationship, whether it be with a future friend, partner, or employer.[21]

One area of metacommunication that is often missed is the principle of utility at work in the reversal of means and ends.[22] In the fervor to accommodate new technological platforms and their social uses, the importance of physical embodiment (really being there) and the spoken language as a way to appropriate meaning is often perceived as insubstantial, even insignificant. Unfortunately, this cavalier lack of attention to the seriousness of presence creates a misappropriation of the tools used to communicate. Instead of becoming a useful means of communication working toward healthy, effective, and relational goals, the proliferation of these media fosters unilateral use for any occasion and confuses the means with the ends. As described earlier, in this absence of awareness conversations are much more susceptible to becoming little more than *crazy or stupid talk.*

Substitution of the means for the ends must not be understated for "our interpretive dimension forms an organic whole with our deepest humanness, and its validity or oppression inevitably conditions our wellbeing."[23] The significance of this substitution becomes especially apparent as the principle of utility more completely underpins our social interactions and eventually overtakes them. The ends are eclipsed by submersion in the means. Typically, the progression of this takeover happens so subtly over time that it is barely perceived as anything but an annoyance of adaptation. And adapt, we do. In the case of PMM, the reversal is happening much more quickly and steadily, leaving little time for the body politic—or individuals—to think critically about the ramifications. Relationally, the unchecked use of technological devices to mediate communication seems only to exacerbate an unwieldy condition of the objectification of the individual, removing interlocutors from each other in proximity as well as emotional and psychological distance (Arnett, 1994; Friedman, 1974; Sontag, 2003).[24] Ultimately, then, without due respect for face-to-face interaction and a working knowledge of what is lost in communicating remotely, human communication begins the downward spiral from objectification toward barbarism, and the chance for healthy, flourishing relationship diminishes.

The question may rightly be raised, "Aren't we smarter than this?" or "Don't we know better?" Cries of techno-determinism often echo the halls in which these questions are raised, with declamations of certainty such as "We are more intelligent than insentient devices!" To which, we may reply, "yes, we are"—however, we are not merely symbol-*using* creatures, as Kenneth Burke posits, we are *human* beings, those who are also inclined to abuse and misuse of our symbol systems. Burke's definition of human as the "symbol-using, symbol-abusing animal" reminds us that we use language symbolically "to act"; it is very often through misuse of our language that we "act" poorly. The negotiating of meaning through language is essential to maintain culture and a civilized society, and historically, we fail as much as we succeed. If then, through excessive and pervasive use of the mediating tools of our digital devices, people initiate and maintain relationships with increasingly less face-to-face engagement, it may be argued that there exists nothing less than a potential crisis of civilization. A statement this strong is likely to be viewed as an overstatement, naïve to the power of technology to correct itself. Perhaps, it is. However, human communication behavior moves from the novel to the norm rather slowly and awareness of the changes in consciousness, perception, and social interaction are often unaccounted for until the changes are complete. Our role in changing speech and relational patterns may be inadvertent, yet it is inevitable, for how little do we stop to think critically about the reality we are shaping for ourselves? I am afraid it is not often enough, yet the unintended consequences of our changing speech patterns and use of digital media do much to radically change our world.

One example of this is the accelerated attitude toward utility as an operational value. Rather than quality in our relationships, we seem increasingly willing to opt for proliferation and scattering of relationships, choosing what is most useful and efficient over what might best serve our neighbor. In spite of the prosumer sloganeering that has encouraged the use of PMM and even led (perhaps) to an increase in personal interactions among individuals, these devices help to create an environment that diminishes civil communication and exalts utility. By providing access to people as goals, objects, and tasks, we become *things to do* instead of beings who are set apart or differentiated from the world of inanimate reality. As this sense of objectification advances, individuals come to expect to be treated as something less than subjects. Notions of "the other" become buried in the black box of daily business. Conversation is reduced to message exchange. Texting, truncating words, collapsing sentences into three letters and emotions into smiley faces become a technological imperative, reducing the purposes of connecting to others via PMM to a fascination with and exploitation of the means. In this way, the principle of utility seems to set the pace for communication, exchanging the purposeful "end" for the means. As with any mediating device, psychological distance is unavoidable, but this distance—or lack of intimacy—is exacerbated when the unspoken rules of the semantic environment are ignored.

Human personality accounts for much of the communication breakdown that occurs online, but the ineffective, transactional means of exchange must be taken into account as well. We must remember the bias inherent in media, for "technologies are not neutral, but value-laden" (Christians, 2019, p. 21).

CONVERSATION AND TRUST

Along with opening up a broader range of interpersonal dynamics, the expansion of PMM begs the question: *What is conversation for?* Use of these devices may be responsible for promoting as much social regress as advancement, particularly in regard to the development of rich, satisfying human relationships (Bugeja, 2017; Postman, 1993; Yaross-Lee, 2003). Whether it is blogging, text messaging, or e-mailing, the end result of such a paltry way to communicate on serious issues leaves much to be desired. Friendship, family, and business each require trust; this must be built. Even when relationship is strong, there is room for misinterpretation. In the same way that television as a medium requires drama to make it "good television," e-mail "conversation" requires those engaging in it to be "good" writers. Because it is a text-based medium, the importance of writing well cannot be overlooked or minimized. Yet, so often it is just this "missing link" that is overlooked, causing people to "flame" each other, misrepresent what a third party has said, and more easily project one's own feelings and positions onto the other. Worse, it is nearly impossible to really "know" someone via e-mail or social media. It is easy to know information about another person, but to know the other, *as other,* is hardly possible. Buber's sense of the rich, mystical otherness of another is fostered by dialogic listening and being fully present with the other as subject. The challenge is heightened as platforms for engagement are reduced to digital options. To speak with a company representative, we must log on with a password; to engage with a doctor for follow-up information we must download the app; to pay for a train ticket we must do it online. To resist is to subject ourselves to ridicule or major inconvenience. Yet, we must comply if we are to engage at all. This is the principle of utility at work. The longing and need for connection and relationship keeps us engaged in communication practices that we know are not sufficient. Longing for something more than information, many give up trying and succumb to the truncated social life that is available online. Until we understand the importance of mystery as part of the human experience, we are apt to miss the ongoing and beautiful dialectic of silence and speech, a process to which we must ever be vigilant.

One must ask the questions that now arise. How, then, might the advance of dialogic morality factor into a silence that is ethical and supportive of the goals and expectations in a civilized society? Having discussed the legacy of the Desert Fathers and Mothers and their dependence upon solitude, Quaker Silence and their practice of "waiting for clearance," the emergence of the new monastics and mindfulness practices, attentive and relational listening, one must now consider how these practical examples of silence-in-action might help to inform speech acts that work toward renewed civility. A detached silence—apathetic to the concerns for a common good—will not do. That passivity plunges one into self-focused hyper-individuality, not helpful to anyone. But dignified silence, that which bids one to remain without words at the ludicrous bombast of what has been said, is sometimes an option. The 1986 Nobel Peace prize recipient Elie Wiesel (1928–2016) refused to speak with Holocaust deniers. Moving into argument with those who have closed their ears in staunch ideological obstinacy does not make sense. There, dignified silence may be the most propitious choice. Parker Palmer addresses the question of "how" by pointing us inward with his musing on the notion of the practical wisdom necessary to walk in ways that lead to peace, non-violence, and human dignity. He writes: "[E]veryone has inner wisdom, and one of the best ways to evoke it is in dialogue when we knock down the walls that keep us apart and meet in that in-between space" (2018, p. 39). Although here Palmer refers primarily to making sense of the confusion that arises in discussions of age and gender, his thoughts about dialogue may be applied to every gap in people's experience. Race, culture, class, politics, religion—all these ways of perceiving the world can find the space between. And when they do, dialogue becomes possible and from there, an opportunity to see a greater good emerge. Helping each other find and practice that inner wisdom will be key to advance these goals.

THE ETHICS OF SILENCE

The responsibility to speak up against hate is tacit knowledge, though bravery and discernment are needed to bring such knowledge to action. It is a virtue to use one's voice for the weak, for the victimized, and for the unheard. However, there is also a time for silence. As a response to someone who is determined to use hate speech, silence guards the integrity of the truth by refusing to give breath to hate or nonsense. To do so, one must take silence seriously and use it to open a space for dialogue. Without it, progress is just a word, change, an illusion. When dialogue is impossible because one or more parties will not participate on the basis of any or all of the universal proto-norms it may be more productive to be silent and let the gravity of a subject sink deeply into one's soul. What is the answer? There is none and there are many. Merton, whose monastic silence was an activist response against embedded oppression and injustice, pointed readers inward. Here he emphasizes attitude and mentality as integral to this inward journey. "Instead of hating the people you think are war-makers, hate the appetites and disorder in your own soul, which are the causes of war. If you love peace, then hate injustice, hate tyranny, hate greed—but hate these things in yourself, not in another" (1949).

Finding answers to the problems surrounding habitual use of our PMM will not be attained in a technical solution. This will require a new mentality. Instead of pressing forward with more words, formulas, or persuasive tactics, it is time to retrieve and restore the place of silence in our speech toolkit. Silence is something we sometimes mistakenly believe we can do without, at least for a while. By the end of a busy, hectic year, the average individual realizes that he is in great need of some solitude. This may more likely be interpreted as a need for vacation—time off—or taking a break from "the rat race." Like so many other aspects of culture, the manner in which "free time" is presently perceived is changing radically. In fact, there is less and less free time because increasing numbers of people "take a break" *with* their digital devices in tow, never far away from the office call or others who want to connect with them through the PMM of our time. These days, a "break" from work seems less a break than a change in setting. An example of this shows up in the most recent findings of the Pew Internet Research group. In their analysis of the data, the MediaPost research group reported that "Americans are using their cell phones to shift the way they spend their time. Forty-one percent of cell phone owners say they fill in free time when they are traveling or waiting for someone by making phone calls" (p. 1). Scrolling, as well, has become a pastime that consumes many hours. Screen time is up. Many mobile devices send a daily or weekly message to let us know how much time we spent on the device. The deluge of words and information to be processed, organized, and assimilated often sweeps over us like a tsunami, rolling over the landscape of our daily lives.

In this chapter we have discussed and reviewed ways in which silence functions as a part of a practical philosophy of communication. This approach creates new avenues of investigation, revealing new considerations to be made when deciding what types of media are most effective and appropriate for individuals, relationships, communities, and nations. Going forward, it will be essential to grapple with the ways in which the media-rich environment not only adds something positive to our ability to communicate but diminishes key elements of interpersonal effectiveness. Along with a shift in mindset, attending to specific ways in which we might rework our involvement and integration with these media is part of the way forward. Clearly, more scholarship in this direction is necessary. I would be remiss to take this discussion further without addressing the use of silence that is unethical, and so turn now to a more careful look at the places silence is weak, uncalled for, and unhelpful.

NOTES

1. Clifford G. Christians. *Journal of Media and Religion* 1, 1 (2002): pp. 37–47; p. 44..
2. James K. A. Smith. "The Intelligence of Love." p. 35.
3. One example involves the algorithms and coding purposely developed to manipulate social media users to increase time spent scrolling. There is a growing body of literature studying the additive properties of such media and culpability admitted by many tech-insiders. For an interesting exposition of this see the 2020 documentary *The Social Dilemma.*
4. See Clifford G. Christians, 2005. p. 121.
5. Again, I refer the reader to the Public Television release of a documentary in 2020 called *The Social Dilemma* that provided an insider view of the addictive properties purposely built into such social networks as Facebook, Twitter, and Instagram. Big-Tech opened the eyes of many Americans who believed falsely that social media is free and exists for the public's pleasure. The 90-minute film is available on Netflix and free on YouTube. [February 20, 2021] https://www.netflix.com/title/81254224.
6. Chris Glaser. *Henri's Mantle.* p. 67.
7. See Ronald Arnett. "Existential Homelessness." pp. 234–235.
8. See Josef Pieper. *Abuse of Language.* 36.
9. Ronald Arnett. "Existential Homelessness." p. 237.
10. Ronald C. Arnett. *Communication and Community.* p. 7.
11. Noam Lapidot-Lefler and Azy Barak. "Effects of Anonymity, Invisibility, and Lack of Eye-Contact on Toxic Online Disinhibition." *Computers in Human Behavior* 28, 2 (2012): pp. 434–443, ISSN 0747–5632, https://doi.org/10.1016/j.chb.2011.10.014.
12. Walter Ong. *The Presence of the Word.* p. 1.
13. See Clifford G. Christians. *Media Ethics and Global Justice in the Digital Age.* p. 100.
14. See Wayne Jacobsen, Arnita Willis Taylor, and Robert L. Prater. *Speaking the Language of Healing.* p. 87. After each chapter in their book the authors share active ways to practice the language of healing. Whether we crawl, walk, or run, there is a rhythm to the work of dialogue, and it always involves the art of listening.
15. Josef Pieper. *Abuse of Language and Power.* p. 36.
16. See Parker Palmer and Carrie Newcomer. *The Growing Edge Podcast.* January 6, 2021.
17. Parker Palmer Podcast. *The Growing Edge.* Conversation with Carrie Newcomer, January 6, 2021.
18. See K. L. Kottemann. "The Rhetoric of Deliberate Deception: What Catfishing Can Teach Us." University of Louisiana at Lafayette, 2015.

19. The apparent and opposite outcomes of these practices seem too obvious to mention, such as immediate access, greater spontaneity in response (using the cell phone), and a way to be "playful" or informal without the anxieties of face-to-face uncertainty. However, I do not think the benefits and challenges of this media use are equal in influence on communication effectiveness.

20. There are certain relationship "commonplaces," that is, dynamics of relationship in the West that are understood without explanation. Without the ability to begin each day anew, minus the baggage of past failures, relational conflict, friendships, marriages, and professional relationships have less chance of enduring. The often unspoken "give and take" between relational partners stems from an ability to allow the memory of such failures to subside. As any counselor or relationship professional knows, the daily (or regular) rehearsing of carelessly spoken or harsh words is the death knell of that relationship's life. For elaboration and broadening into public discourse, see Jacques Ellul. *A Critique of the New Commonplaces,* 1968; or the new legacy edition with a foreword by David Gill, 2012.

21. See interview with Joy Buolamwini. "How Do Biased Algorithms Damage Marginalized Communities?" National Public Radio (NPR), October 2020.

22. For further reading on this reversal of means and ends, see Jacques Ellul's *The Presence of the Kingdom*, and Clifford G. Christians, *Media Ethics and Global Justice in the Digital Age.*

23. See Clifford Christians. "The Sacredness of Life." *Media Development* 45, 2 (1998): pp. 3–7.

24. Buber's (1970) explication of the It-World fits with the relational implications of *la technique.* His picturesque language depicts the process of objectification that Ellul is arguing occurs as a result of unchecked technological advancement. He explains here: " [B]ut in sick ages it happens that the It-World, no longer irrigated and fertilized by the living currents of the You-World, severed and stagnant, becomes a gigantic swamp phantom and overpowers man. As he accommodates himself to a world of objects that no longer achieve any presence for him, he succumbs to it. Then common causality grows into an oppressive and crushing doom" (pp. 102–103).

25. The notion of producer-consumer has been given some traction in the vocabulary surrounding online interactions, particularly in the world of VR, Mobile Commerce (such as eBay, Amazon.com, etc.), and digital gaming.

Chapter 8

Unhealthy Silence

As central as is the place of speech to human development and culture, when language is used to bully or coerce it can easily morph to patterns of domination and control. This happens when boldness shifts to arrogance or persuasion moves to manipulation. This is also an example of unhealthy silence. Loudly and clearly, it must be stated: Where there is oppression and abuse, one must not be silent.

Because the breath of silence can be such a salve to agitation or conflict in relationships, it is easy for some personality types to default to silence no matter the situation. This, too, is unhealthy silence and can cause much harm. There may be good reasons one is more comfortable and secure choosing not to speak, but as a default mechanism it remains unhealthy silence. For example, when relational conflict is buried and critical issues are masked, solutions to the myriad of life's nagging problems are inadvertently lost in a sea of non-generative silence. This is the silence which covers up, denies, ignores, masks the facts, eliminates context, and attempts to unilaterally shape a narrative. No one else is allowed to speak when unhealthy silence reigns. Whether implicitly understood or explicitly stated, the one (or group) in the weaker position is told to be silent . . . *or else*! Frequently this scenario is a result of a dominating personality, one whose desire for power and control outweighs the respect, affection, or care for the other. The one remaining silent may know it is better to reveal the truth but chooses not to because of a desire to save face, shield someone, or protect themselves. It may feel safer to be silent, but it is not a solution when harm is being done. This unhealthy silence is evident throughout the world and is fraught with complexities, many involving oppositional politics, different perspectives on education, religion, generational wounds, and trauma of all sorts. It may be found anywhere but flourishes in places where honor culture is high and is particularly egregious when it is promoted as moral high ground.[1]

The long song of forced silence does not make for a healthy family, marriage, or society, nor does it promote equality or well-being. A person who routinely uses this tactic to manipulate others into quiet submission disregards the dignity of our mutual humanness. This is the sort of toxic silence that reigns when domestic violence is allowed to go on unhindered, or human slavery is upheld as lawful or necessary. It is the punishing silence that a woman feels in a workplace where non-male opinions and concerns are seen as superfluous or ignored completely. Guilt, turned in on the weaker, shame for raising a voice; traumatic repercussions of all kinds reign when this unhealthy silence is breached by the words a brave soul offers to counter workplace, familial, or systemic injustice. This harmful silence is rampant.

Calls to "be civil" often mask such abuse. This is one of the reasons civility has suffered a bad name, so much so that civics classes have all but disappeared in public schools, and calls for civility are often met with derision or mockery. And while the need for polite, well-mannered speech is desperately needed to return as a social norm, kind words that mask underlying hatred do no good. Civility is indeed an important part of the solution to healing the ragged edges of our frayed public discourse, but not as a sole factor, and most certainly not as a means to cover up the ugly evidence of oppression, exploitation, injustice, and the many other social ills people of all cultures experience. Civility is not the only way forward; it cannot walk alone, but it *is* one of the missing ingredients that make possible the healing of collective wounds and generational trauma. *How?* Openness to each other is key. Hearing each other's stories is part of the path forward. Prioritizing time for each other—time to truly listen—coaxes us to take another step forward and can pave the way for open, honest, questions which is a much-needed precursor to healing broken communication. As we diligently embark on this road we will find Civility a constant companion, one that allows us to listen long enough to the viewpoint of another to revive the kind of conversational durability necessary for managing conflict and walking in peace with our neighbors.

SILENCE AS BALM, SOLACE, OR STRATEGY

As a communication tool silence may, at times, be the most appropriate response to those whose wounds are so egregious that their tone and overall message is offensive or discourteous. Silence can function as a temporary salve or as a gentle breeze in the midst of a stormy encounter. But there are storms that relentlessly beat against the house—those that require someone standing up to raise the alarm, shutter the windows, and act with bold directive to avert disaster. One such major storm landed on the shores of the Americas and barreled through the U.S. long before its establishment as an independent nation. That storm involved the enslavement of thousands of Africans ripped from their families and continent of origin, thrown into forced submission. Although slavery was eradicated in the United States, its long tail continues to sweep through areas of the country in subtle and sundry ways. The bane of slavery continues to bear down on humanity in numerous ways and places throughout the earth.[2]

Well into the 20th century and more recently in the wake of protests against police brutality, the rippling effect of the atrocity of slavery continues to rage. For generations, the work of racial justice and harmony has made conciliatory and effective inroads, but more healing is needed. Many who have watched and celebrated the progress of race relations sit befuddled and frozen, unable or unwilling to discuss the ongoing inequities. But discuss it, we must. Without telling our stories and listening to those of others, we stand with faces looking in opposite directions, falling into a silence that is deadly. One particular personal moment in time provides context for this and affords some insight into the subject. It took place when I was much younger. This is the story in short:

Wrought with angst and confusion, the 1970s brought robust measures of desegregation throughout the U.S. in hopes of enacting the equality promised to African Americans during the Civil Rights Movement. Some states were quicker to adopt measures of integration; others lagged sorely behind. No matter the approach, each people group experienced its own challenges and though much progress was made, much more change was needed. In my own heavily desegregated community, the pangs of oppression hit me hard when an African American girl my age began shouting obscenities and ugly racial slurs at me in the junior high cafeteria. I was stunned and stood there dumbfounded, looking at her in disbelief because: 1) It was a very large school and I had never seen her before, and 2) the expletives and accusations she hurled at me had no basis in reality. I did not know her. Before I had a chance to tell her that it must be a case of mistaken identity, she landed a powerful punch to the left side of my face. My lunch tray went flying. My ear throbbed in pulsing pain and my pale face turned fiery red. I was mortified. In a flash, the lunchroom monitors pulled her and her cousin off me before any further violence took place, but the stinging shame and confusion of that moment stayed with me for some time. I walked the halls of my school that year afraid of another attack and unsure why I was hated just because of the color of my skin, something I couldn't change. The punch hit me squarely in the face but lodged deeply in the seat of my emotions. I was more scared than angry, but to be sure, angry enough. Because I was blessed with a mother who kept her cool—an educator who understood the results of generational oppression and displaced anger—my pain was short lived. Mom taught me not to retaliate. She reminded me who I was and taught me that my response to violence said more about me than what was said about me. She taught me about human dignity.

Not everyone has such a mother. Nothing I did deserved this woman, but as the recipient of an upbringing that denounced racism with every breath, I learned by example. So much of the racial unrest of that era stemmed from decades of an African American community trying to make sense of an irrational and unethical history of oppression and slavery, asking, "Who *are* we?" and "What is our social identity?" Much, not all, of the misconception, conflict, tension—even hate—often stems from never having answered these questions. And much is simply rooted in the inability of a white majority to fully embrace equality.

Howard Thurman (1900–1981), theologian, professor, and mentor to Martin Luther King, Jr., framed the marginalized Black community as "the dispossessed" or the "disinherited," as those who lived in a white world with fear that penetrated every aspect of their daily lives. The fear, he suggests, was different than typical fear. He explains it as a "resident fear" . . . one that feels "like a climate closing in; it is like the fog in San Francisco or in London. It is nowhere in particular yet everywhere"[3] (1949, p. 26). After years of living in this type of fear and adapting to it in order to survive, it is challenging to step out into a clear space and trust that one's voice has a place. The rights and privileges of citizenship are available to all, but when one's voice continues to go unheard, it is easy to fall into a desolate despair. This is unhealthy silence. As a result, some resort to violence, but many more allow their unheard cries to plunge them into silence as their *modus operandi*. Silence becomes anathema; an unsatisfying solace that masks the pain; it is a silence that gives up trying. Such silence punishes oneself as well as those who need to gain perspective and are stuck in an unseeing web of denial. This *punishing silence* exhibits itself in a number of ways, one way is by simply giving up. When people no longer have hope that their voice will be heard, they often choose silence. The ongoing remnants of racial disharmony in the United States are just one example of this behavior.

The poor and homeless are also among those whose backs are against the wall. So often treated with contempt, their basic needs unmet; they have lost their voice and the silence is riddled with despair. Women have experienced this throughout the world for generations. Even in the West when a woman is welcomed into a position of leadership it takes time to dispel the resident fears of rejection, subjugation, or outright oppression she receives in the workplace. There are members of every people group who are overlooked, used, or abused. Choosing to remain silent about these needs because we cannot provide total solution or because "we have come so far" does not work to mitigate against the damage done, nor does it move our world toward greater harmony. But addressing these wrongs is not as simple as becoming aware and concerned. Symbolic action is necessary. This is the power and place of speech. American evangelist Beth Moore's 2018 "Letter to My Brothers" and ensuing departure from the Southern Baptist Convention in 2021, broke the silence surrounding exclusion of women preachers in the largest Protestant denomination in the U.S. It remains to be seen if her courageous action will pave the way for more equal treatment of women in Christian churches, but the fact that Moore spoke out against the rude and undignified treatment of her male counterparts is a step in that direction. Hers is a noble example of breaking through the institutional silence that has long kept many women from walking in the fullness of their gifts and skills.[4]

The role of language in giving voice to our concerns is immense. Language is not the only factor, but it has a major role in shaping reality. The words we use are powerful symbols that are suffused with action. For the world to change, the abuse and misuse of language must be addressed. One of the reasons well-intentioned people fall prey to abusing the language is because it is easier to react to offense and misunderstanding rather than respond. As mentioned in the last chapter, reaction typically stems from the emotional center of our brains with a busy amygdala kicking into action, igniting the sympathetic nervous system to fight or flight. This type of reaction is often referred to as our *gut*, or *knee-jerk*. When we're faced with something unfair, unwarranted, or counter to our core beliefs it is all too easy to react this way. Response, however, is reasoned. It calls upon the judgment center of the brain—the prefrontal cortex. Surely the amygdala and front lobes are essential for top brain functionality, but over-dependence upon the emotional center of the brain does not provide what is needed to avoid abusive speech or make meaningful dialogue. There is breath between the fiery feelings of offense, disagreement, or fear and that breath is silence. Taking a moment to breathe, to think, to ponder, to ask a question—this is how silence can serve.

Reaction instead of response is not the only reason for entrenched conflict and division among us. There are myriad abuses of language, each leading to a different social ill. Use of language that corrupts one's sense of decency and order easily devolves into ways of being that demean others by objectifying them and losing sight of our common human condition. Josef Pieper explains that "word and language form the medium that sustains the common existence of the human spirit as such" and that it is the "interpersonal character of human speech" that anchors us in reality (Pieper, p. 15). Without it, we drift. We are anchorless. Without it we can forget the most basic decencies.

PERSUASION

Hierarchy, power, and control are embedded in language. One cannot pass over these deeply entrenched elements of context that affect our ability to maintain healthy relationships of mutuality and respect. Persuasion is one such element. The subject has long remained at the forefront of the study of speech and is part of the human way of being in the world, but the need to persuade has become all-encompassing. In fact, we have become part of what Deborah Tannen has called an argument culture, the "pervasive warlike atmosphere that makes us approach public dialogue, and just about anything we need to accomplish, as if it were a fight."[5] The metaphor of war using words and phrases such as don't "shoot the messenger," "going in for the kill," and "fight to the end" are just a few of the ways politicians and corporations talk about messaging. This is quite evident in our public rhetoric, but obvious, as well as in personal conversations.[6]

Because the ability to speak and use language meaningfully is a key and distinguishing characteristic of what it means to be part of the human family, it is necessary to underscore its importance. This one aspect of our humanness is so powerful that to invite silence often feels as though we are inviting a type of death, for it is the diminutive and implicit presence of silence that reminds us that in spite of amazing and magnificent strength, we are fragile and weak, limited by the conditions of our humanness. Thus, silence is something we sometimes believe we can do without, at least for a while. Who but philosophers and poets spend time even thinking about such things? And the disappearance of silence, why would this be a problem? For one day, or perhaps for a week, the disappearance of silence may go unnoticed, but by the end of a hectic season or busy year, one soon realizes that some solitude is needed. Typically, this thought emerges as the need for a vacation—taking time off—getting a break from "the rat race." In these post-industrial, 24/7 computer-mediated days, however, the manner in which "free time" is presently being spent is changing radically. Actual leisure may be less available because increasing numbers of us take a break *with* our digital devices in tow, never far away from the buzz or ringtone that keeps our minds back at work. Our devices become our lords. We cannot do without them. This is a good example of the Ellulian *technique* discussed earlier. It provides unambiguous evidence of the way silence and solitude tie into our individual sense of being, gives us the ability to conduct meaningful relationships, and offers an overarching touchpoint in the maintaining of civil public discourse.

TOXIC SILENCE

Another way of understanding the silence that works against human flourishing is the notion of *toxic silence*. While explicit and overt slavery is most definitely a poisonous evil, the term used here applies more generally to the destructive and harmful ways one experiences everyday indignities in the midst of a free society. Toxic silence is more about the games people play, the strategizing to exert power and control in what is idealized as being an open society, one that allows representation and expects participation.[7] This *participatory culture* refers not only to a free and representative government but reflects the sort of *ethos* that exists in the healthiest marriages, friendships, teams, and small groups. Team meetings at the coffee shop, department meetings in academe, church services and other religious gatherings—even families—are involved in active participatory cultures, or they are not, and instead, moving in one version or another of the power-control dynamic. Developing a participatory culture takes more time and is less efficient than using a hierarchical method of relating, but the time and patience involved mitigates against toxic silence.

The *ethos* of participation sets the tone for decision-making and interaction and seeks to actively include the voices of every member. In the workplace one team member might be the established leader or have ultimate charge for a project's success but using lead status to assert control will not work toward creating an atmosphere of participation. Instead, cultivating a participatory culture welcomes input, discussion, and ideas. This type of leadership more readily establishes a sense of shared responsibility and works toward retention. In addition, it makes for a more pleasant work environment. Participation is one of the ways a culture of mutuality is cultivated; it is one in which all voices are welcomed. When this ideal is corrupted by an overly competitive spirit or the push for status and control, it is destructive to any relationship, people group, government, or society. Without participation, voices are unheard. When this becomes habitual, the potential for collaborative strength dries up, making the team or group weak and ineffective. Unchecked, the toxic silence begins to poison partnerships, destroy marriages, pit neighbor against neighbor, and cover up unfair treatment, injustice, oppression, and crime.

Some of the most insidious types of toxic silence occur when sexual harassment and domestic violence are covered up. This is evident in abusive marriages where one of the two threatens the other with leaving if he or she speaks. It happens in the workplace when racial or gender inequities continue unchecked. The threat of losing one's livelihood is always an undercurrent. In the face of ritualized oppression such as domestic abuse, pedophilia, sexual exploitation, and other atrocities against humans, toxic silence is a scourge. Typically, those who remain silent do so because they feel threatened, fearing that they will be harmed, humiliated, or even killed if they speak up. Incredibly, such egregious silence often goes unnoticed by those untouched by it. Others, who may be aware or even observe such injustices, often do not speak up because they are blinded by a false narrative. Examples are numerous such as, "The rape was her fault for wearing such a short skirt," "the poverty is something they choose because we all have opportunity," or "he could have kept his job if he just kept quiet."

There are times when unhealthy silence becomes deadly and the magnitude of what is taking place is undeniable. Students learning the history of World War II read stories of the Holocaust and see photographs and film depicting the political soldiers of the Nazi regime standing in silent complicity as hundreds of innocent Jews marched daily to a grisly death. Studying these atrocities opens their eyes to the toxic nature of this type of silence. One does not have to look far to observe the silence that steals human dignity. Whether it is closing our eyes to the abrupt dismissal of a woman's voice in the workplace, keeping silent when a colleague is falsely accused, or maintaining the "status quo" just to keep a roof over one's head in an abusive marriage, toxic silence destroys confidence and well-being. It mitigates against happiness and mental health. This silence is toxic to the one who knows it is time to speak but remains silent out of fear or shame.

When there is no room to discuss the tensions that keep us at a distance, silence can quickly turn from polite quietude or necessary reflection to punishing toxicity. It is like a fire that destroys every healthy tree in its way, blazing a path of destruction. If allowed to continue, it is this type of silence that foments despair. It is this kind of silence that can erupt into violence. Whether turned inward against oneself or aimed at others, violence prompted by unwillingness to address a problem can have life-threatening results. This is why openness, and creating safe, comfortable places for conversation is so important. Conversations on social media and Internet platforms get heated and harsh so quickly because those involved are generally reacting to statements, not people. The anonymity and lack of face-to-face presence make it extremely difficult to read silence correctly. When face-to-face, a tell-tale sign of this dynamic is when conversation evaporates; the door is closed, arms are crossed, the other refuses to speak. In digital settings the silence lacks clarity. One may be at work, in the shower, out on a date, or at the bottom of a manhole investigating the city's underground plumbing. Where is that debate partner? Why hasn't she come back with a counterargument? Because there is no immediate response, these are questions one wonders when staring at a screen. These are some of the questions that cause mixed messages and communication breakdown.

When people give up trying to be heard the silence that ensues is deadly to relationships, to groups, in the workplace, and in a nation. It is unhealthy when people stop trying to give voice to their pain. It is unhealthy silence, and it must be broken. Silence is also a formidable foe to an interpersonal relationship when the invisible struggles and relational concerns are muted. It may not be considered toxic but is unhealthy and oppressive, easily capable of poisoning even the strongest ties. In marriage and family, a very unhealthy practice is the sort of relational dysfunction that uses silence as an escape or a weapon. Either metaphorically or physically they separate themselves through silence. This is but one among the many destructive ways silence is abused. It is the manipulative, punishing silence of being ignored. Relational damage due to this type of silence happens among people groups as well; Democrats and Republicans, progressives and liberals, those advocating the European Union and Brexiters, Palestinians and Jews, to name a few. It is a misuse and abuse of the rich resource of silence. Instead, the strong dialectical push-pull of speech and silence is necessary. Reflective, articulate silence has the power to break the natural tendencies which create these patterns of punishment. No one is exempt if the patterns of dysfunction are permitted to continue unchecked. College roommates, siblings sharing a room, married partners sharing household responsibilities all represent relationships that suffer greatly when silence is misused or abused. Such dysfunction hurts children as well, particularly when they are regularly exposed to abusive behavior in the home and suffer in silence. Or, on the playground, children are bullied and often kept silent by threats of public humiliation or social isolation. These are some of the worst examples of unhealthy silence, for a child is less equipped to handle such suffering, especially when it occurs in what should be the safe zones of home and school.

The renewed discussion of racial injustice that is occurring all over the world is another example of the need to embrace the dialectic of speech and silence. The fact that people and organizations are creating space to discuss the social inequities experienced by many under-represented groups is a positive step toward lifting the lid of unhealthy silence. Progress remains a challenge, however, largely due to the inability to listen to one another. This is particularly so in a media environment in which there are no safe spaces to speak, where bullying and rejection can occur simply by posting a quote on Twitter or "liking" a song, children's classic book, or film on Facebook. People become afraid to speak, fearing loss of reputation, rejection, or watching an out-of-context soundbite go viral. In the present environment it is easier to submerge oneself beneath a sea of silence than plunge out into the deep of conversation that is riddled with opposing ideas, tension, attacks, and hate speech. As safe as that type of silence seems, it is an illusion. Eventually it will destroy.

Such unhealthy silence is destructive to relationship, reputation, and self-respect. It is akin to what the Hebrew Preacher of the Old Testament must have been feeling when these words were penned several thousand years ago:

> When I kept silent, my bones grew old
> Through my groaning all day long.
> For day and night Your hand was heavy upon me;
> My vitality was turned into the drought of summer[8]

It is easy to associate this type of silence with the most egregious unethical behaviors such as the sex trafficking industry or exploitation of children, but the misery of keeping silent is kneaded into some of the most innocuous situations as well, such as *on the job*. Workplace silence is anathema. It is another flagrant example of the insidious power of unhealthy silence. The unspoken pressure to ignore familial needs in favor of working 24/7 is a way we condition ourselves to press forward while ignoring the very reason we work (*La technique* rearing its serpentine coils!). This has been especially prohibitive for women in the workplace, but more recently has spilled over to intimidate men who may be single parents or simply co-parenting with as much responsibility as their wives. Or the voiceless misery that one must hold while a colleague or superior undermines their work. This is another kind of unhealthy silence, chipping away at one's confidence, stealing whatever joy one might have at doing a job well. There is little room for speaking up about such untoward behavior for it often worsens the situation. The result is acute dissatisfaction in the workplace which easily ends up in loss of position, outrage, depression, and despair.

Unhealthy silence is not new. Systemic and institutional dominance are each part of the reason it continues. This silence is a major part of the problem and occurs readily when a dominant voice or majority quash the voices of the oppressed. This practice reveals its ugly head in the history of all institutions. Whether education, government, armed forces, the church, or any other institution, abuse of power by the dominant group has long created misery for the person of lower social status. When not addressed, unhealthy silence becomes a hotbed for violence. Positive public address, that is, rhetoric used in its highest and most noble form, has long been used to reveal such lapses in judgment and abuses of power. When words, well-spoken and delivered for the good of the community, are used to rally the good and correct the wrong, wars have been averted. Neighborhoods, villages, cities, states, and nations have benefited from the good word spoken well.

RHETORIC AND THE PUBLIC SPHERE

When the "good word" is absent and reasoned argument is no longer appreciated or used to marshal cooperation, social unrest begins to gain prominence and chaos is an almost certain outcome. Now, after 25 years of growing digital ubiquity and dominance a chaotic public discourse is making itself known. The raucous and restless way words are used today is an example. This is largely due to the current online communication environment which inhibits reasoned discourse and weighty argument for all of the reasons noted thus far. Though lawful freedom of speech may exist, our PMM create an environment that is not pro-social. The words, untethered to community, inhibit meaningful public discourse. The combination of emotionally charged unreflective messaging and rapid-fire media foist the prospect of dialogue into a whirling dervish of unanchored rants that create fortresses of would-be conversations—those that never make it off the street onto the table of mutual discovery and dialogue. As the noise grows, bullying and rejection rise and an unholy silence is the result, one that takes place where people no longer feel safe or welcome to speak. Voices quashed in the cacophony. Here, silence is not golden. It slinks and stultifies, landing a blow to once harmonious relationships, democracy, and sanity itself.

So much of the reason for this social dysfunction stems from the speed with which we communicate. In an online social media network, one has a few moments to state a case for change in health care insurance, immigration, racial reconciliation, politics, or any number of important issues facing the world. In a blink, that one will be mocked and disregarded, often shamed with a quick and nasty expletive or deftly placed put-down. What ensues is one of two distinct phenomena, both being corrosive to the human soul. What began as a simple remark or casual conversation quickly flares to a contest and a war of words begins to rage. One side will win, the other lose. Or, the discredited one—along with massive numbers of those who see things the same way—slinks away in a silence that sets the tone for every other dissenter to remove his or her voice from the mix. This outrageous and anti-productive communication behavior has become commonplace. We can bemoan it, and well we should, but perhaps instead of defaulting to outrage, we might employ a real solution toward positive change. It is not that feelings of outrage are unusual or unacceptable, rather that verbal outrage is largely ineffective. Does outrage change behavior? Does outrage persuade people to listen? Instead of positive change, outrage is often met with more outrage, stalling progress or fomenting violence.

Some claim anger and outrage are the only options left, that burning buildings and violence are acceptable means of protest. Former NPR social science correspondent Shankar Vedantam suggests that this sort of "outrage leads to engagement, but not change."[9] When change is necessary, we must find a way to express our outrage without resorting to violence. Here again, space for dialogue makes itself known. We must invite dialogue to the table and make room for voices of the oppressed and disenfranchised to be heard. Reflective silence provides an opportunity for us to breathe and pause before we speak. If the answer were as easy as just taking that moment to pause, our world would be a more just place. But it is *not* easy and *has not been* easy. We do not like silence because it is humbling. It makes us feel weak. This is where a spiritual silence may come into practice with greater intentionality and flow into the other spaces of everyday life, thus creating greater equanimity.

To work toward changing the many social ills existing in our world we must move from outrage to listening, from reaction to response, and from despair to hope. There is hope to be discovered in dialogue, hope in an alternative way of talking about difference. This is not discovered in a unilateral choice to speak or to remain silent, rather it is discovered in discernment. Part of this hope involves the apprehension of difference as a gift rather than something to be tolerated. In welcoming silence as a regular daily practice, we might find a way to receive the otherness of the other and through it learn about ourselves. Envisioning a world where difference and diversity don't destroy but help us engage in the beautiful mystery of life is a project that requires hope-filled communicators to stand against unhealthy silence and raise a voice to speak truth.

THE DIALOGIC IMPULSE

The impulse to stand and proclaim truth in the face of a lie is natural part of the deep human search for truth, goodness, beauty, and love. When unhealthy silence reigns and voices go unheard, a just society tumbles into disorder. Unaddressed, disorder encroaches and without a turn toward dialogue, eventually hope fades. To grasp the residual effects of this loss we once again draw wisdom from Howard Thurman who understood the hopelessness that entrenched itself into the hearts and minds of so many African Americans during the Jim Crow years in the United States. There, even after emancipation and laws passed to ensure equality, their voices continued to be trampled and ignored. Their friends and families continued to be lynched and attacked. For years, the humiliating presence of public shaming rituals magnified the mortification they endured. Forced segregation in the use of public toilets, restaurants, and athletic clubs worked like a virus to expand and foment a type of human misery that continues to have a lasting effect today. Unable to voice complaint without further degradation, these former slaves and children of slaves had to cope with a deeply disconfirming social condition, suffering in silence and hopelessness. Such silence not only hangs on the hearts of those who are shamed into silence but erodes confidence and self-esteem. Many in the majority culture are just beginning to realize the lasting presence of this gaping wound and how it has embedded itself in Black consciousness for generations. When hope is lost, despair is not far behind, and the promise of a culture of healthy public discourse evaporates.

Unfortunately, this scenario is a common one throughout history. When one people group dominates another to the point of disallowing alternative opinions, communication breaks down and chaos ensues. Such was the case with the 2020 United States presidential election where the ideological divide became so narrow that conversations between many otherwise like-minded, liberty-loving individuals came to a screeching halt. Shame, guilt, and bullying were inflicted on those with differing perspectives on the role of government, the mission of the nation, and the way to pave a path to future success. The attacks and barbs hurled on social media became so fraught with dissension that many on both sides of the ideological aisle just stopped talking and dropped out. Friends came to an impasse with lifelong friends. Even among families the walls of division arose, some members refusing to share a holiday table. Once sociable neighbors closed their doors and some even changed their street address to remove themselves from judgment. This is the situation we find ourselves in the world, and in the U.S., home of free speech and land of opportunity for so many, the situation is just as toxic. This leads our conversation about civility and silence to the root.

Communication best practices are the outgrowth of something even deeper than the ability to make meaningful conversation or learning how to use silence beneficially. Without exception everyone in the world needs to love and be loved. When broached in academic circles, we write about the topic from a distanced, theoretical viewpoint. Ideally, however, it is the love of all creatures great and small that would propel humanity successfully into the next age, one that supports the flourishing of all humans, helping us to live together in harmonious accord. To discuss love as an idea without the tenacity to live it authentically is an oversimplification and not helpful. Thus, we will address the subject here. Love is an action word, not a concept. Love is not the impossible dream; there are steps that will help take us there.

Taking "the first step toward love is common sharing of a sense of mutual worth and value. This cannot be discovered in a vacuum or in a series of artificial or hypothetical relationships. It has to be in a real situation, natural, and free."[10] Howard Thurman spoke these words in the heat of the Civil Rights Movement in America. Much has been accomplished to resolve unsettled issues of racial inequality in the last 60 years, and most of it has come as a result of conversations built around the values of truth, mutual worth, human dignity, nonviolence, and the sacredness of life. These conversations moved from words to action. Therein is the progress. Dialogue has been both an underlying premise and an emergent good for it provides actual space to notice the commonalities between us and the impulse to seek these cultural goods. To take such love out of the stratosphere and let it land in the realm of real relationships is a major undertaking. It begins with a willingness to know the other, accept the stranger, and understand the one with whom we disagree. The deep, luminous richness in silence can serve such ends.

This type of rich, generative silence has long been a part of the devotional path for those in traditional religious communities and those seeking a path of enlightenment in traditions as wide-sweeping as Zen Buddhists and Christians to Jewish Kabbalists and indigenous people groups. This is because silence provides a way of knowing that contrasts with our modernist, rational mind and helps us in wordless presence to access those parts of ourselves normally associated with the heart. As one moves more deeply into silence practices, greater integration between mind and heart generally follow. Undoubtedly, inner integration is exhibited in encounters that are dialogic, and essentially, in more effective, enduring interpersonal relationships.

DIALOGUE

Just as the place and need for silence is not a new idea, neither is dialogue. But the state of public discourse is such that a reclamation of dialogue is necessary. As Martin Luther King Jr. often reminded us, "Those who love peace must learn to organize as effectively as those who love war." Arnett, Holba, and Mancino suggest that each "historical moment announces questions that give meaning to philosophies of communication that emerge and re-emerge across time and context."[11] The questions here are many, but *this* moment of time warrants dialogue in action. Unfortunately, dialogue is not possible unless more than one party agrees to reason together. That being said, it does not mean that effort toward it should be lax. Mutuality, truth, the common good, and emphasis on *the other* are at the center of dialogic speech, each presenting movement toward repair of the degradation of the word in this century. A revitalization of dialogue and renewed interest in doing so will do much to foster a genuine respect and quality of communication, and therefore is a noble goal in public address and interaction. Additionally, an appreciation for diverse or alternate views may be more likely because focus is on negotiated meaning or meaning that emerges "between" the two parties speaking. On a very practical level, then, dialogue has the potential to pave the way for greater relational potentiality and ultimately less conflict.

When applied to public situations, dialogic rhetoric advances such potential to help polarized parties and groups to exist without coming to battle or a standstill. Concurring with Buber, Jeanne Cuzbaroff (2000) sees dialogic rhetoric as essential in the understanding and apprehension of this project and explains:

> Instead of a pragmatic or epistemological orientation, dialogical rhetoric takes an existential-ontological orientation to the situation of human beings in relation to each other and to all beings. Dialogical rhetoric especially in its recognition of the spoken word which emerges in the address and response between persons captures the profound person-forming, community building, and world creation functions which mark our communicative and rhetorical relations. (p. 182)

According to Riikonen, the word "dialogue" bears two different senses. One is its cognitive sense. That is when dialogue is seen as an "exchange of rational arguments among (more or less) equal persons" (p. 601). The other is seen from "the perspective of connectedness and inspiration" (p. 601). Additionally, he posits that

> dialogue stands in opposition to everything that is destructive for curiosity. The main enemies seem to be objectification processes related to various forms of "knowing already." Knowing already dissolves the need to look beyond averages or categories. It is the prime source of nonparticipation. (p. 601)

The communication process being discussed here is non-instrumental. It is a type of communication behavior that is conversational, confluent, engaging, and endued with relational potential. Framed as "dialogic rhetoric," this type of speech may be recapitulated into a type of dialogue that includes silence as having a distinctive role, *vis-à-vis*, silence as having its own voice. Jeanne Cuzbaroff discusses this dynamic, expounding upon the differences between instrumental and dialogic rhetoric. There is nuance involved between two modes: "Where instrumental rhetoric differentiates between irrational and rational persuasion, dialogical rhetoric distinguishes between rhetoric of 'not doing' and rhetoric of direct confronting."[12] Dialogic rhetoric proceeds with a sense of allowing that which already "is" to emerge. It involves less persuasion and/or argumentation which is a key feature of the traditional approach to rhetoric and more of a realization that difference is not the enemy; that there is a meeting ground somewhere in the space between us. It has the power to take us from hostility to hospitality. Emerging from the interaction between audience and speaker or, in the case of interpersonal communication, it occurs *between* the two conversing.

In comparing and contrasting dialogic rhetoric with a more instrumental type of approach, several differences are clear. One involves the conceptualization of Truth. Truth arises, according to Cuzbaroff, "in dialogical encounter as we hear and respond to what the other says to us, [however, sic] it is a truth which does not provide us certainty, partly because it is not generalizable beyond the immediate situation."[13] Thus, the pressure to exact meaning or to provide a specific, singular understanding of a message is not foremost in dialogic rhetoric. Rather, whether in public address or conversation, motivation is key. There may be a desire to communicate compellingly, but, Cuzbaroff explains, the speaker "is not motivated by particular needs or goals and does not have a present particular message."[14] Instead, it is the discovery of what exists between or in the midst of the interlocutors that become the "central achievement of dialogical meeting; [it, sic] is the continual discovery together of the truth for each in their common hour. Always, this truth is unique for each participant."[15] One would hope that a similar dynamic would play out faithfully in the use of PMM, however, given the auditory obstacles and lack of nonverbal communication cues, it does not seem likely that without determined intentionality this level of encounter could be a generally realizable goal. When viewed from this perspective, it is clear that attaining (and maintaining) conversational coherence necessitates engaging in the spoken word along with as many nonverbal communication cues as possible.

Another aspect involves a less evident hindrance to coherence. Because digital technology has advanced exponentially in the past 10 years, video, audio, and newer text-based features help to ameliorate the lacking cues, thus creating a more enjoyable interpersonal experience. This can easily cloak the underlying hindrances, giving one or both conversational partners the impression that the communication process is strong. To the average user, it may not be immediately evident that personal mobile media are counterproductive. As well, it is important to note that during conversation, the need to listen attentively to the other and to one's own interpretative processing simultaneously is ongoing and occurs at many levels all the time. The interwovenness of the intrapersonal with the interpersonal is not always apparent, especially in a casual conversation.

This brings us back to reconsider the place of listening in this entire process. Awareness is essential and all too easily banked at the dock of tacit knowledge. We do not realize how unaware we are of our own subconscious wrangling or those struggles encumbering others. Parker Palmer explains this well: "If silence gives us knowledge of the world, solitude gives us the knowledge of ourselves."[16] Without it we are lost and blind. Becoming aware of *what we don't know* along with awareness of the grief and loss of others whom we do not know well is important motivation with which to approach this dialectic of speech and silence. There are as well the larger contexts of these personal dynamics such as learning to communicate with an abiding awareness of the inequities, wounds, and harm exacted upon those who have been oppressed or unheard. Keen awareness and attention to these dynamics will help all who endeavor to understand and make use of the beautifully dialectical nature of speech and silence. Such awareness might be seen as the first note in an orchestral performance—the downbeat—that will open the door to the symphonic delight of melody, harmony, and live musicians playing with skill and passion. Through it our eyes open to the full beauty of diverse instruments joining in one major chorus of excellence and grace. To extend the metaphor, a second note involves being intentional about creating space for dialogue, and that requires a hard look at the power dynamics in each of our lives.

Changing the power dynamics that drape over our lives and those of families who have lived in oppressive silences for generations is a feat that warrants ongoing attention and activism. The unethical means and machinations that foster the toxic, oppressive, and punishing silences of injustice will not change overnight, but there are ways to address and chip away at entrenched abuses. After awareness and intention to change, a switch in attitude must be made from the understandable desire to "do something big!" to doing *something*, daily. Positive, lasting change necessitates more than a blazing social movement or bombastic protest. It takes grit and discipline to work a rhythm of dialogue into our lives. As our circle of trust expands, a second note in the grand orchestral dialectic might mean going out of one's way to listen to the stories of those unlike oneself, remaining curious and open to each other, actively pursuing opportunities for conversation and relationship. Each of these may appear much less significant than a splashy nationwide campaign but are definitive, major ways individuals can pursue positive change. The heavy de-personalizing effects of the digital age lose some of their girth when we sit face-to-face and listen to the story of our neighbor. Waiting to hear these stories will undoubtedly require patience, which leads us to a final note, one that rings out with clarity as we remember that no matter how much one has advanced in the art of listening, dialogue often needs to be coaxed.

Encouragement in the daily pursuit of justice, kindness, and decency weigh more than decrying the problems in Twitter wars and Facebook rants. If there is no one available to encourage, we must encourage ourselves and begin providing the open and fragrant breezes of an attitude of the heart and mind that remembers we are a part of one another. A single beat of silence before speaking, a light pause to consider the other's view, an extra breath to weigh one's words: each of these small communicational steps help to plow the ground for a dialogic environment. The presence of the word is curious; it responds to an exchange endued with the vitalistic energy of another's genuineness. The word emerges from something far more significant than the need to convey a message or represent reality. It just needs to be nurtured and given room to grow.

Silence is not a one-size-fits-all solution to the ills of our age. No, a panacea it is not. It is, however, a hearty idea, marinated in desire for harmonious, life-giving relations and the common good. It is one that has the potential to restore meaning to our lives. Reconciliation between people of opposing ideologies is not an idyllic dream. Healing is possible, but we must take care to cultivate an environment that fosters it. As the ancient proverb makes clear, "reckless words pierce like a sword, but the tongue of the wise brings healing."17 My hope is that this book will do its small part to help readers avoid unhealthy silence and embrace the silence that is generative and full of potential for good. This is the silence that encourages speech in another, welcomes words that move us toward healing, and honors all that it means to be human.

To this day I am thankful for a mother who sat me down and taught me that aggression does not demand aggression. She made it clear that returning hatred for hatred was wrong. After the aggression I experienced in high school, my parents did not respond with outrage or a lawsuit, nor did they demean and disparage the girl who hit me, but they did act. The following year we moved to a new district, one that would allow me to concentrate on schoolwork instead of living in fear of another attack. I did not want to move. All my friends were in the school system I left but keeping me safe was my parents' priority and I did not have a say in the matter. Moving was an option for a hard-working middle-class family living in the late 20th century in America. While it was inconvenient and presented sacrifice, it was possible. Not everyone had the benefit of that option, especially those tangled in the sticky web of systemic poverty. For many, the option to find a better school was simply not a possibility. Understanding this is important.

Listening to the stories of those with competing narratives will take patience and a belief in humanity. It will mean staying curious about the unknown other, moving past a first impression, and taking a second look. In Latin, the word for "to observe or to look" is *spectare.* It is the root of the word *spectator*. It may be helpful to remember this etymology when struggling to listen respectfully to one with whom we disagree, for to respect (or, *re*-spect) infers to look again. In practical terms this might mean asking a clarifying question rather than reacting with immediate judgment. It may be a challenge to withhold judgment when words fraught with opposition or loaded, slanted meaning are sent our way. But taking a moment to breathe, nod, and let the other finish his thought may be one very small step, but it is a step heading in the direction of dialogue.

Listening well to the stories of loss and lament is also part of the road to healing, and whether it involves listening to those whose stories surround racial inequity or to the very personal stories of friends and neighbors, silence gives them room to speak. When it is time for words, may we let them flow, but may they flow from a rich interior sanctum of silence that listens to the inner voice of love and leans in with genuine care to the one who is speaking. There is no one-size-fits-all solution to the numerous problems threaded throughout a shrinking public discourse. There is, however, an unrelenting hope in which we would do well to embrace. The hope of life-giving, respectful speech, spoken from the deep well of silence can help pave the way for the conciliatory meeting ground called *Dialogue* where a compassionate, harmonious world of human flourishing is possible. Without this hope we risk losing the great strength of a free society. Actually, we risk even more—our collective sanity. Living in a crazed world of cacophonous uproar, unstable and uncertain at every turn, is untenable. No one wants that. Greater apprehension of dialogue is an idea and a practice that must push its way through the birth canal of the Digital Era. No matter how treacherous and painful the labor, for a civilized world to sustain itself, Dialogue must breathe; it must be birthed anew each generation.

The changing shape and practice of dialogue is exhibited throughout the history of rhetoric and must continue to re-shape itself to meet the needs of a changing world. While silence is not always the answer, it *is* part of the solution toward more meaningful, life-giving, ethical communication. And there are times, even as we are experiencing tension and unrest in our closest interpersonal relationships, we may find silence a satisfying helper. Momentary (or temporary) silence can work as a buffer to calm jagged emotions. When passions are high and trust is low, taking some time to listen in quiet attentiveness can create a receptive climate for future conversation. I close then, with a familiar word from the Old Testament lexicon, one to keep close, perhaps even commit to memory: "To everything there is a season and a time for every matter under heaven [. . .] A time to keep silent and a time to speak."[18] Discerning the difference is the key.

NOTES

1. Cultures that place the highest value on reputation and honor are more apt to default to unhealthy silence but it is by no means only those known as "honor culture" that use and abuse silence to maintain domination over the weak, marginalized, and powerless. Silence can also reaffirm the power of institutional or systemic abuse as reported in the study titled "Success without Honor: Cultures of Silence and the Penn State Scandal," by Cheryl Cooky.

2. Over half of the countries in the world today have no law penalizing slavery. The country with the highest number of slaves today is India where forced labor, marriage, and commercial sexual exploitation are common. The treatment of women as

property or used for "legal prostitution" in Misyar marriages in the Middle East, the exploitation of women and children sold in the sex-slave industry, and the trafficking of children in the brickyards of Northern Africa are just a few of the ways slavery continues today.

   3. Howard Thurman. *Jesus and the Disinherited.* p. 26

   4. Moore spoke but not without cost. She has been the object of derision and slander ever since the letter was written. https://www.npr.org/2021/03/11/976124629/prominent-evangelical-beth-moore-announces-split-from-southern-baptists.

   5. Deborah Tannen. *The Argument Culture.* p. 3.

   6. An example of this is the 2020 election campaign in the U.S. One rhetorical analysis of Kamala Harris's presidential announcement speech has her using the word "fight" one time every one hundred words. See *Rhetoric for Good; the Language of Leadership.* Simon Lancaster; Professional Speechwriters Association, March 21, 2021. https://www.youtube.com/watch?v=PRe4PGdTsfQ.

   7. Some of the strategies that have become prominent in contemporary business practice are known colloquially as "gaslighting," where one co-worker subtly undermines the other until all confidence is gone and the manipulated one begins to think the problem lies with him- or herself.

   8. Psalms 32:3–4.

   9. Shankar Vedantam, editor. December 7, 2020. "Screaming into a Void." [April 2, 2021]. https://hiddenbrain.org/category/podcast/?s=screaming+into+a+void.

   10. Howard Thurman. *Jesus and the Disinherited.* p. 88.

   11. See Ronald Arnett, Annette Holba, and Susan Mancino. *Communication Research Trends.* p. 6.

   12. Jeanne Cuzbaroff. "Dialogic Rhetoric: An Application of Martin Buber's Philosophy of Dialogue." *Quarterly Journal of Speech* (May 2000): p. 182.

   13. See Jeanne Cuzbaroff. "Dialogic Rhetoric." 180.

   14. Cuzbaroff, 181.

   15. Cuzbaroff, 180.

   16. Parker Palmer, *To Know as we are Known* (2010). p. 121.

   17. Proverbs 12:18, *The Holy Bible.* NIV.

   18. Ecclesiastes 3:1 & 7b.

Bibliography

Altman, Irwin., & Taylor, Dalmas. A. *Social Penetration: The Development of Interpersonal Relationships.* New York: Irvington Publishers, 1983.

Altree, Wayne. *Why Talk? A Conversation about Language with Walter J. Ong.* San Francisco: Chandler and Sharp Publishers. 1973.

American Psychological Association [January 2, 2016] http://www.apa.org/news/press/releases/stress/2012/generations.aspx; Washington, DC. 2016.

American Society for Acoustic Ecology [February 9, 2022] https://asae.tidyhq.com/.

"Americans View on Mobile Etiquette." (2015) Pew Research Center; [February 8, 2022].

Anderson, Robert, Cissna, Kenneth, and Arnett, Ronald. Eds. *The Reach of Dialogue: Confirmation, Voice, and Community.* Cresshill, NJ: Hampton Press. 1994.

Appel, Edward. "Language as Motive, Perfectionism, Entelechy: Foundations and Prospects for Ecological Disaster." Conference paper presented at Lock Haven University of Pennsylvania, PA. 2003.

Arendt, Hannah. *The human condition.* [Introduction by Mary McCarthy] Chicago: University of Chicago Press. 1958/1986.

Arnett, Ronald. *Communication and Community: Implications of Martin Buber's Dialogue.* Carbondale: Southern Illinois University Press. 1986.

———. Existential Homelessness: A Contemporary Case for Dialogue. Edited by Anderson, R., Cissna, K. & Arnett, R., *The Reach of Dialogue: Confirmation, Voice, and Community.* pp. 229–246. New Jersey: Hampton Press, Inc. 1994.

Association of Internet Researchers [AOIR]. "The Strength of Internet Ties." *Message*, archived at www.aoir.org. January 26, 2006.

Bennett, Stephanie. "Endangered Habitat: Why the Soul needs Silence." NY: *Plough Quarterly*, No.15. 2018.

———. "The Disappearance of Silence in Mediated Digital Culture." Paper Presentation at the 89th annual National Communication Association conference, Miami, FL: 2003.

Berger, M. (2018). "Social Media use increases Depression and Loneliness." *Penn Today*, Penn State University [November 2021] https://penntoday.upenn.edu/news/social-media-use-increases-depression-and-loneliness.

Bivar, V. The Chicago School of Media Theory. The Committee on the History of Culture University of Chicago [June 6, 2019] https://lucian.uchicago.edu/blogs/mediatheory/keywords/senses/.

Bolton, R. (2006). In J. Stewart (Ed.). *Bridges not Walls* (6th edition). New York: McGraw-Hill.

Brummett, Barry. *Rhetorical Dimensions of Popular Culture*. Tuscaloosa: University Alabama Press; revised ed., 2004.

Buber, Martin. *I and Thou.* Trans. Walter Kaufmann. New York: Scribner. 1970.

———. "Genuine Dialogue and the Possibilities of Peace" in *The Reach of Dialogue,* Eds. Anderson, Cissna, and Arnett 3rd edition. Creskill, NJ: Hampton Press. 2003.

Bugeja, Michael. *Interpersonal Divide in the Age of the Machine*. 2nd edition. Oxford: Oxford University Press. 2017.

Buolamwini, Joy. "How Do Biased Algorithms Damage Marginalized Communities?" National Public Radio (NPR), [interview] Manush Zomorodi; October 30, 2020. [May 11, 2021] https://www.npr.org/transcripts/929204946.

Burke, Kenneth. *Language as Symbolic Action.* Berkeley: University of California Press, 1966.

Capizzi, Joseph. "What Am I to Say?" Comment [June 25, 2020] https://breakingground.us/what-am-i-to-say/.

Carey, James W. "McLuhan and Mumford: The Roots of Modern Media Analysis." *Ellul Forum*. 18. FL: University of South Florida. January, 1997.

Carter, Stephen L. *Civility: Manners, Morals, and the Etiquette of Democracy.* NY: Harper Perennial. 1998.

Center for Disease Control [CDC] *Weekly.* August 14, 2020. [January 2, 2021] https://www.cdc.gov/mmwr/volumes/69/wr/mm6932a1.htm.

Chadwick, Owen, ed., trans. *Western Asceticism*. Library of Christian Classics, Ichthus Edition. The Westminster Press, 1958.

Christians, Clifford G. *Media Ethics and Global Justice in the Digital Age.* Cambridge: Cambridge University Press. 2019.

———. *Moral Literacy and Global Justice: A New Theory of Communication Ethics.* Cambridge University Press; 2019. [November 14, 2020] https://www.cambridge.org/us/academic/subjects/politics-international-relations/political-theory/media-ethics-and-global-justice-digital-age?format=PB.

———. "The Ethics of Being." In *Communication Ethics and Universal Values*. Edited by Traber and Christians, Thousand Oaks, CA: Sage Publishers, 1997.

———. "Ellul as Theologian in Counterpoint." Casey M. K. Lum, ed., Perspectives on Culture, Technology and Communication: The Media Ecology Tradition. Cresskill, NJ: Hampton Press, 2005, ch. 5, pp. 117–141.

———. "Ellul on solution: An alternative but no prophecy."

Christians, Clifford G. & Van Hook, J. Eds. *Jacques Ellul: Interpretative Essays.* Urbana: University of Illinois Press, 1981. pp. 147–173.

———. *Media Ethics and Global Justice in the Digital Age.* Cambridge University Press, Cambridge, UK. 1998.

———. "The Sacredness of Life." *Media Development*, 45:2 1998, pp. 3–7

———. "Technology and triadic theories of mediation." In *Rethinking Media, Religion, and Culture,* edited by Stewart M. Hoover, S. M., and Kundby, K, Eds. London: SAGE Publications. 1997.

———. "Utilitarianism in Media Ethics and Its Discontents." *Journal of Mass Media Ethics* 222, 3 (2007): 113–131.

———. "Media Ethics in Transnational, Gender Inclusive, and Multicultural Terms." In C. Christians & K. Nordenstreng, eds., *Communication Theories in a Multicultural World.* New York: Peter Lang. 2014. pp. 293–310.

Cigna Research Study (2018). "Loneliness in the workplace." Info Graphic. [November 2018] https://newsroom.cigna.com/loneliness-in-america.

Cooky, Cheryl. "Success Without Honor: Cultures of Silence and the Penn State Scandal." *Cultural Studies ↔ Critical Methodologies*, vol. 12, no. 4, Aug. 2012, pp. 326–329, doi:10.1177/1532708612446432.

Cross, Cassandra. July 5, 2020. *The Conversation.* "2.5 Billion Lost over a Decade, Nigerian Princes" lose their sheen, but [March 25, 2021] https://theconversation.com/2-5-billion-lost-over-a-decade-nigerian-princes-lose-their-sheen-but-scams-are-on-the-rise-141289

CTIA (2021) Wireless Industry Stats. Cellular Telecommunications Industry Association, Washington, DC. [February 9, 2022] https://www.ctia.org/the-wireless-industry/infographics-library.

Cuzbaroff, Jeanne. "Dialogic Rhetoric: An Application of Martin Buber's Philosophy of Dialogue." *Quarterly Journal of Speech* (May 2000): p. 182.

Durham-Peters, John. *Speaking into the Air: A History of the Idea of Communication.* Chicago: University of Chicago Press. 1999.

Eller, Vernard. "Ellul and Kierkegaard: Closer than Brothers." In Christians, C.G., and Van Hook, J. eds. *Jacques Ellul: Interpretative Essays.* Urbana: University of Illinois Press, 1981. pp. 52–66.

Ellul, Jacques. "Seeing and hearing: Prolegomena." Editors, Anderson, Robert., Cissna, Kenneth and Arnett, Ronald. *The Reach of Dialogue.* NJ: Hampton Press. 1994, pp. 120–125.

———. *The Technological Society.* Trans. John Wilkinson. New York: Knopf, 1964.

———. *Reason for Being: A Meditation on Ecclesiastes.* Translated by Joyce Hanks. Grand Rapids, MI: Eerdmans Publishing Company. 1990.

———. *The Humiliation of the Word.* Trans. Joyce M. Hanks. Grand Rapids, MI: Eerdmans. 1985.

———. "The Ethics of Propaganda." *The Ellul Forum 37.* Berkeley, CA: International Jacques Ellul Society. 2006.

———. "On Dialogue." In *Jacques Ellul: Interpretive Essays*, edited by C. Christians and J. Van Hook, pp. 291–308. Urbana: University of Illinois Press, 1981.

———. *The Ethics of Freedom.* Translated by G. W. Bromiley. Grand Rapids, MI: William B. Eerdmans. 1976.

Eng, Paul. "Dawn of the Avatars?" ABCNews.com Sims Online. January 9, 2003. [3 February 3, 2003] http://abcnews.go.com/sections/scitech/DailyNews/virtual-worlds030109.html

Fasching, D. J. (1997, January). Lewis Mumford, technological critic. *Ellul Forum, 18*, 9–12.

Fox, George. *The Journal of George Fox.* Edited by Rufus Jones. Friends United Press, Indiana. 1976.

Fukuyama, F. (1999, May). The great disruption. *The Atlantic Monthly, 283* (5), 55–80. Retrieved May 22, 2006 from http://www.wesjones.com/fukuyama.htm.

Gergen, Kenneth J. *The Saturated Self: Dilemmas of Identity in Contemporary Life* New York: Basic Books, 1991.

Gergen, Kenneth J., and S. McNamee. "Relational Responsibility and Dialogue." In *Bridges without Walls*, 9th ed., edited by J. Stewart, pp. 141–149. New York: McGraw-Hill, 2006.

Gill, David W. *Doing Right: Practicing Ethical Principles.* Downer's Grover, IL: Intervarsity Press. 2004. p. 293.

Glaser, Chris, ed. *Henri's Mantle: 100 Meditations on Noouwen's Legacy.* Cleveland: The Pilgrim's Press. 2002. p. 67.

Goffman, Erving. *The Presentation of Self in Everyday Life.* New York: Doubleday, 1956. pp. 22–30, 70–76.

Goffman, Erving. *Stigma: Notes on the Management of Spoiled Identity.* New York: Doubleday, 1963.

Graves, Michael P. "A Perfect Redemption from this Spirit of Oppression": John Woolman's Hopeful Worldview in "A Plea for the Poor" in *The Tendering Presence, Essays on John Woolman,* Mike Heller, ed. Roanoke College, Pendle Hill: 2003.

Graves, Michael. P. "The Rhetoric of the Inward Light: An Examination of Extant Sermons Delivered by Early Quakers, 1671–1700." Doctoral Dissertation. University of South California, 1972.

Green, Julian. *God's Fool: The Life and Times of Francis of Assisi.* San Francisco: Harper and Row. 1985.

Gwyn, Douglas. *Apocalypse of the Word: The Life and Message of George Fox.* Richmond, IN: Friends United Press, 1986.

Huxley, A. (1931). *Brave New World.* London: Chatto and Windus. p. 235.

Jacobsen, Wayne, Willis Taylor, Arnita, and Prater, Robert L., 2019. *A Language of Healing for a Polarized Nation,* Torrington, WY: Blue Sheep Media.

Kelly, Paul. "Human Identity: Part 1: Who Are You?" Metropolitan Life, e-lecture: [September 9, 2004] www.web.archive.org/web/200000817195330. www-home.calumet.yorku.ca/pkelly/www.id1. 1997.

Knapp, M. L. *Nonverbal Communication in Human Interaction*, 2nd. ed. New York: Holt, Rinehart & Winston. 1978.

King, M. L., Jr. "Letter from a Birmingham Jail." April 16. Foundation for Economic Education FEE. 1963. [March 3, 2020] https://fee.org/articles/letter-from-a-birmingham-jail/?gclid=CjwKCAiAnfjyBRBxEiwA-EECLFyGQ72Dw9QaP-4wL7rCOWhqWbi529qMBpbizZAerikHXcT1Q69RqWhoCzpAQAvD_BwE.

Lancaster, Simon. "Rhetoric for Good: The Language of Leadership." Professional Speechwriters Association, March 21, 2021. https://www.youtube.com/watch?v=PRe4PGdTsfQ.
Lanier, Jaron. *You are not a Gadget.* NY: Vintage. 2010.
———. *Virtual Reality.* Films for the Humanities and Sciences, 1997.
Lardieri, Alexa. "Study: Many Americans Report Feeling Lonely." *U.S. News and World* Report. [November 17, 2021] https://www.usnews.com/news/health-care-news/articles/2018-05-01/study-many-americans-report-feeling-lonely-younger-generations-more-so. May 1, 2018.
Lehman, Charles Fain. "Deaths of Despair and COVID-19: What we Know so far." [Institute for Family Studies, Charlottesville, VA. [May 9, 2021] https://ifstudies.org/blog/deaths-of-despair-and-covid-19-what-2021.
Makau, Josina and Marty, Debian. *Dialogue and Deliberation.* Long Grove, IL: Waveland. 2013.
Mancino, Susan. "The Intertwined History of Communication and Philosophy." *Communication Research Trends,* 2020. Santa Clara, CA; Vol. 39, Is 2. 2020. Pp 3–14.
McKibben, Bill. *Enough: Staying Human in an Engineered Age.* NY: Henry Holt and Company. 2004.
McLuhan, Marshall. *The Gutenberg Galaxy: The Making of Typographic Man.* Toronto: University of Toronto Press. 1962.
———. *Understanding Media: The Extensions of Man.* Cambridge: MIT Press, 1994.
Merton, Thomas. *The Silent Life.* New York: Dell Books. 1957.
———. *Contemplative Prayer.* NY: Image Books, 1996.
———. *New Seeds of Contemplation.* Cambridge, MA: New Direction Books, 2007.
Meyrowitz, Joshua. *No Sense of Place.* New York: Oxford University Press. 1985.
———. "Television and Interpersonal Behavior: Codes of Perception and Response." Editors: Gumpert, G. and Cathcart, R. *Inter/media: Interpersonal Communication in a Media World.* 3rd. ed. New York: Oxford University Press. 1986.
Nouwen, Henri. *The Genesee Diary.* New York: Image Books, 1981..
———. *With Open Hands.* Notre Dame, IN: Ave Maria Press, 1972.
Ong, Walter J. *Orality and Literacy: The Technologizing of The World.* New York: Routledge, 1982.
———. "World as View and World as Event." *American Anthropologist,* New Series Vol. 71, No. 4 pp. 634–647. 1969.
Palmer, Parker. *To know as we are Known.* NY: Harper Collins. 2010.
———. *On the Brink of Everything.* Oakland, CA: Berrett-Koehler Publishers. June 26, 2018
———. Podcast: *The Growing Edge,* January 6, 2021.
Picard, Max. *The World of Silence.* Chicago: Henry Regnery, 1952.
Pieper, Josef. *Abuse of Language, Abuse of Power.* San Francisco: Ignatius Press. 1992.
Plato. *Phaedrus.* Translated by Reginald Hackforth. 1952.
———. *The Republic.* New York: Oxford University Press, 1967.

Plato c. 429–347 B.C.E, "Phaedrus" c. 360 B.C.E., 274c–275 b, Reginald Hackforth, transl., 1952. Published by the Cambridge University Press in Cambridge, U.K.

Postman, Neil. *Crazy Talk, Stupid Talk: How We Defeat Ourselves by the Way We Talk—and What to Do About it.* New York: Delacorte Press, 1976.

———. *Amusing Ourselves to Death.* Penguin Books, New York, NY: 1985.

———. *The End of Education: Redefining the Value of School.* New York: Knopf, 1995.

———. *Building a Bridge to the 18th Century.* New York: Random House, 1999.

———. *Technopoly: The Surrender of Culture to Technology.* New York: Vintage Books; 1993.

———. "What is Media Ecology?" MEA *Website.* Retrieved November 21, 2005, from www.mediaecologyassociation.org.

Putman, R. 2000. *Bowling Alone: The Collapse and Revival of American Community.* New York: Simon and Schuster.

Rhodes, S. C. (1993). Listening: A relational process. In Wolvin, A. (Ed.) (1993). *Perspectives on listening.* Norwood, NJ: Ablex Publishing.

Riikonen, E. (2006). Relational responsibility and dialogue. London: Sage Publications. In Stewart, J. (2006). *Bridges not Walls* (6th ed.). New York: McGraw-Hill.

Rogers, Fred. "How Do We Make Goodness Attractive?" *Federal Communications Law Journal*: Vol. 55: Issue 3, Article 23. 2003. https://www.repository.law.indiana.edu/fclj/vol55/iss3/23.

Rose, Barbara. "Surrounded by Sound: Personal Music Players Creating New Social Conventions, Challenging Employers." *Chicago Tribune*, Courant.com; 2006. [February 22, 2006] http://www.courant.com/business/hcipods0220.art-feb20,0,7729784.story.

Rose, Ellen. 2010. "Continuous Partial Attention: Reconsidering the Role of Online Learning in the Age of Interruption." *Educational Technology*, July–August 2010, Vol. 50, No. 4 July–August 2010, pp. 41–46 Published by: Educational Technology Publications, Inc. Stable URL: https://www.jstor.org/stable/44429840.

Runcorn, David. *Center of Quiet.* Downers Grove, IL: Intervarsity Press, 1990.

Schultze, Quentin. *Communicating for Life.* Ada, MI: Baker Academic, 2000.

———. *Communicating with Grace and Virtue.* Ada, MI: Baker Academic, 2020.

Shachtman, Thomas. *The Inarticulate Society.* New York: Simon and Schuster, 1995.

Smith, James K. A. 2021. "The Intelligence of Love." *The Christian Century*. March 10, 2021. Chicago, p. 35.

Soukup, Paul. "Looking Is Not Enough: Reflections on Walter J. Ong and Media Ecology." In *Proceedings of the Media Ecology Association* 6 (2005).

Spath, Thomas and Dahnke, Cassandra. "What is Civility?" Houston, Texas. [April 24, 2021] https://www.instituteforcivility.org/who-we-are/what-is-civility/.

Stewart, John (2006) *Bridges not Walls*. McGraw-Hill Education.

Tannen, Deborah. *The Argument Culture.* New York: Random House, 2018.

———. *You Just Don't Understand: Men and Women in Conversation.* New York: William Morrow, 2006.

Tannen, Deborah, and Muriel Saville-Troike. *Perspectives on Silence.* Norwood, NJ: Ablex, 1995.

Tannen, Deborah. *The Argument Culture.* Random House. 2018.

———. *You just Don't Understand: Men and Women in Conversation.* William Morrow and Company. 2006.

Thurman, Howard. *Jesus and the Disinherited.* Boston, MA: Beacon Press, 1996, reprint, originally published 1949.

Turkle, Sherry. *Reclaiming Conversation.* New York: Penguin Books. 2015.

Walker, D. (2004) Right to Silence? BBC News. [November 2021] http://news.bbc.co.uk/2/hi/uk_news/magazine/3738652.stm.

Walther, Joseph. B. "Computer-Mediated Communication: Impersonal, Interpersonal, and Hyperpersonal Interaction." *Communication Research.* February, 1996.

Watts, Eric King. "Voice and Voicelessness in Rhetorical Studies." *Quarterly Journal of Speech*, 87, 2 (2001): pp. 179–196.

Wilkinson, Loren. "The Master and His Emissary: A Theological and Theopoetic Review." *CRUX.* Canada: Regent College; Vancouver. Winter 2015. Vol. 51, No. 4, pp. 2–11.

Wood, Julia. *Communication Theories in Action.* Beverly, MA: Wadsworth, 2004.

Index

acoustic ecology, 50, 61, 71nn16–17
activism, 30–33, 38, 41n11, 71n15, 175
addiction, to technology, 58
Age of Industry, 79–80
Age of Information, 104
algorithms, 157n3
American Evangelicalism, 29
American Society for Acoustic Ecology (ASAE), 50, 61
Analects (Confucius), xi
Anthony, Susan B., 31
Anthony the Great, 22
anxiety, 57–59, 71n9, 71n10
Appel, Ed, 85
Apple, 71n9
Areliss, George, 66–67
Arnett, Ron, 132, 144
ASAE. *See* American Society for Acoustic Ecology
Attention Deficit Syndrome, 93
attentive silence, 3; emedia fasting for, 52–63; focus with, 47–48; isolation in, 67–70; listening to, 46–47, 66–67; for multi-tasking, 63–66; in neuroscience, 72n21; noise and, 48–52; philosophy of, 45
awareness, 124

The Bachelor (TV show), 134

Bakhtin, Mikhail, xi
behavior, 147
Being and Time (Heidegger), xii, 36
Benedict, 41n16
Benedict of Nursia, 27
Bernardone, Giovanni di Pietro di (Saint Francis), 27–29
Bolton, Robert, 55
boredom, 53
Bowling Alone (Putman), 107–8
brains. *See* neuroscience
Brave New World (Huxley), 113
Buber, Martin, xii, 36, 60, 82–84, 89–92; philosophy of, 136, 173; *la technique* and, 158n24
Buechner, Frederick, 45
Burke, Kenneth, xii, 15, 36, 99n17, 100n23; humanity for, 85–86, 99n19, 100n20, 153; language for, 84–85; symbols for, 86–87

Camino de Santiago, 97, 100n31
Capizzi, Joseph, 86
Carey, James, 5
Carter, Stephen L., 115
Cartesian subjectivism, xiii
Cassirer, Ernst, xi, xiii, xiii–xv
Catholicism, 34–35
cellphones. *See* personal mobile media

Center of Quiet (Runcorn), 24
children, 131–32, 171–72
choice, 115–16
Christ. *See* Jesus Christ
Christianity, 40n1, 40n4, 41n16, 42n27; Guyon for, 33–37; monasticism in, 23–29; paradigm constructions in, 35–36; Protestant reform for, 37–38; Quakers for, 30–33; tradition of, 21–23, 27
Christians, Clifford, 5, 90, 94–95, 115, 141–42, 145, 148
Church of England, 24
Cigna, 59–60
civil society, 2–3, 160; community and, 106–9; in Digital Age, 10–11, 59–60, 105–6; for humanity, 9–10; normativity in, 14–15; public discourse in, 14, 115; in U.S., 161–62, 171–72
CMC. *See* Computer Mediated Communication
co-creation, 88n6
coding, 157n3
cogitation, xvii
cognition, of sound, 48–49
coherency, 124, 132
collaboration, 134
communication: for Christians, 90, 94–95; coherency in, 124; in conversations, 15–16, 54; digital, 80–81; ethics in, 90; for existence, 81–82; with God, 34–37; history of, 78; for humanity, 68–69; influences in, 151–52; interpersonal, 75–82, 93–97, 122–23, 134–35, 138, 139n5; intrapersonal, 26–27, 121–23; listening for, 55–56; as meaning-making, 123–25; metacommunication, 152; philosophy of, 3–4, 70, 96–97; with PMM, 4–5, 7, 14, 52, 65, 100n23, 139n13; for Postman, 68; power in, 8–9; printing press for, 11; proximity-bound, 15; relational silence for, 121–22, 128–36; scholarship on, 77, 114, 139n6, 149; silence for, 46, 70n6; skills, 76; with sound, 12–13; technology for, xiii, 2, 5–6, 11–12, 71n15; on Twitter, 70n7; understanding, 83–84
community, 106–9, 131–32
Computer Mediated Communication (CMC), 2
conflict, 47–48, 50–51, 123–24, 132–33, 158n20
Confucius, xi
consciousness, 51
Constantine (emperor), 22–23, 40n4, 40nn1–2
contemplative prayer, 3, 40n1
contemplative silence: activism from, 30–33; for Guyon, 33–37; history of, 21–23, 40n4; listening in, 37–40; for Merton, 23–29, 41n5; spirituality from, 19–21
conversations: communication in, 15–16, 54; conflict in, 123–24; in Digital Age, 15–16; distractions in, 57–58; face-to-face, 126, 158n19, 166; frustration in, 56; meaningful, 131; on PMM, 60–61, 128, 154; for Postman, 68–70; quality of, 81; scholarship on, 112, 116–17; silence for, 111–12; on social media, 57; stupid, 68–69; trust in, 154–55; on Zoom, 114–15
Cooley, Charles Horton, 77
co-presence, 76
coronavirus pandemic, 19
cortisol, 135–36
crazy talk, 68–69, 77–78, 152
culture: Constantine for, 22–23; crazy talk for, 68–69; cultural sanity, 46–47; digital, 37–40, 128, 142; equanimity in, 10–11; FOMO in, 135–36; Google for, 108; honor, 177n1; in-office, 118n11; language for, 94; marriage in, 92–93; meaning-making for, 130; media

for, 1, 39, 116–17; in Middle Ages, 28; news in, 79–80; oral, 13–15; phantom silence for, 106–9, 111–12; for Picard, 80; PMM for, 85–86, 93, 106–7, 133, 152–53; public discourse for, 58–59; of Quakers, 42n25; respect for, 146–47; rhetoric in, 169–70; silence for, 2–3, 79–80; social media for, 1–2; spirituality for, 32; technology for, xvi; television for, 62–63, 66–67, 87; unhealthy silence for, 159–60; of U.S., 99n16
Cuzbaroff, Jeanne, 173–74

Dahnke, Cassandra, 10
Davies, William Henry, 64–65
death, 34–35
deep listening, 56–57
democracy, 10
depression, 59
Descartes, Rene, xvi, 119n34
Desert Fathers and Mothers, 21–23, 155
Dialogic Imagination (Bakhtin), xi
dialogic impulse, 170–72
dialogic listening, 97, 136–38
dialogic rhetoric, 173
dialogue, 93–97, 137–38, 145–48, 172–77
Digital Age: Age of Industry compared to, 79–80; civil society in, 10–11, 59–60, 105–6; conversations in, 15–16; dialogue in, 177; distractions in, 52–54; for Europe, 99n16; FaceTime for, 130; mobility in, 136–37; online interactions in, 158n25; phantom silence in, 104–6; scholarship on, 93–94; silence in, 144–45; social media for, 112; speech in, 14; violence in, 143–44
digital books, 71n8
digital communication, 80–81
digital culture, 37–40, 128, 142
digital media, 5, 38, 52–53, 107
disappearing silence, 70n2
Disraeli, Benjamin, 66–67

disruption, 92–93
distractions, 48–49, 52–54, 57–58, 60, 63–64

efficiency, 109–10
Egypt, 21–23
Einstein, Albert, 106
Ellul, Jacques, xii, xv, 25–26, 100n23, 145; existence for, 87–88; *la technique* for, 109–10, 113, 119n22, 164; technology for, 5, 116, 118n18
emedia fasting, 52–63
empathy, 94–95
encouragement, 175–76
Enquiries Concerning Human Understanding (Hume), xvi
environmentalism, 38
Environmental Protection Agency (EPA), 61–62, 72n18
epistemology, 15
equanimity, 10–11, 40, 126–27
ethical silence: for dialogue, 145–48; philosophy of, 155–57; for psychology, 141–45; scholarship on, 148–54; unethical silence, 9
ethics: for Christians, 141–42, 145, 148; in communication, 90; ethos, 165; media, 148; ontology and, xvii; philosophy of, xv–xvi; with PMM, 141; in relationships, 145–46; scholarship on, 86; of silence, 155–57; for society, 154–55; of *la technique*, 41n12, 168; with technology, 142; unethical silence, 9
eudaimonia, xv–xvi
Europe, 37–38, 50, 99n16
Evagrius, 22
evil, xvi
existence: communication for, 81–82; for Ellul, 87–88; humanity and, 85; language for, 46–47; love in, 12–13; for Ong, 49; ontology of, xi; with PMM, 89–90; telos and, 76
existential reality, xiv
exploitation, 153–54

external sound, 48–49

Facebook, 1–2, 118n11, 126, 132–33
FaceTime, 114, 130, 136
face-to-face conversations, 126, 158n19, 166
faith, 16, 24–25, 30–35, 40n2, 41n21
faith-based scholarship, xvii
false self, 26–27
Farnsworth, Philo, 87
Faro Fashion, 114
Fasching, Darrell, 142
fear of missing out (FOMO), 135–36
First Discourse (Rousseau), 119n22
"Five Rings of Information Immediacy" (Wurman), 71n10
FOMO. *See* fear of missing out
Fox, George, 29–33
France, 33–34
Francis (Saint), 27–29
fraud, 103–4, 117n1
freedom, 8–9
friendship, 13, 32–33, 122
frustration, 56
Fukuyama, Francis, 99n16

Gadamer, Hans-Georg, xii–xiv
gaming, 5
general anxiety, 59
Gergen, Kenneth, 58–59
ghost in the machine theory, 116, 119n34
God, xii; communication with, 34–37; listening to, 23–29; for Quakers, 30–33. *See also specific topics*
Goffman, Erving, 26, 129, 139n6
Google, 108, 118n11
Guyon, Jeanne, xii, 33–37, 42n29
Gwyn, Douglas, 31

Habermas, Jürgen, xi, xvi–xvii
Harris, Kamala, 178n6
Harris, Michael, 39
healing, 157n14, 176
healthy relationships, 128–29

hearing deeply, 128–29
Hegel, Georg, 98n12
Heidegger, Martin, xii, xvi, 36, 86–87, 98n12
hermeneutics, xii–xiii, xvii
Holocaust, 155, 166
honor culture, 177n1
humanity: for Buber, 90; for Burke, 85–86, 99n19, 100n20, 153; choice for, 115–16; civil society for, 9–10; communication for, 68–69; conflict in, 50–51; contempt for, 41n14; digital media for, 52–53; eudaimonia for, xv–xvi; existence and, 85; Facebook for, 1–2; for Gadamer, xii–xiii; human behavior, 147, 156; human consciousness, 51; imagination for, 46–47; information overload for, 118n17; intimacy for, 153–54; Jesus for, 22–23; language for, 78–79, 88–89; literature for, 15; for neuroscience, 113–14; normativity for, xiii–xiv; ontology and, xvi; rules for, 83–84; self-reflection for, 40; silence for, 9–12; society for, 108; spirituality for, 32–33
Hume, David, xvi
Huxley, Aldous, 113
hyper-individualism, 38, 93–94

I and Thou (Buber), 90
Idhe, Don, 130–31
ILA. *See* International Listening Association
imagination, 46–47, 64–65, 105–6
India, 177n2
industrial sound, 16
info/action ratio, 21, 59
information overload, 118n17
in-office culture, 118n11
Instagram, 1–2
Institute for Civility in Government, 10
intentionality, 47–48, 56–57
interiority, 84–93

Index   189

International Listening Association (ILA), 58, 71n10
international politics, 8
Internet language, 54
interpersonal communication, 75–82, 93–97, 122–23, 134–35, 138, 139n5
Interpretation Theory (Ricoeur), xiii
intimacy, 7, 127, 147, 153–54
intrapersonal communication, 26–27, 121–23
iPhones, 71n9
isolation, 67–70

Jackson, Maggie, 116–17
Jacobsen, Wayne, 157n14
Jaspers, Karl, xi
Jaworski, Adam, 123
Jesus Christ, 22–23, 30, 32
John of the Cross, 27
Julian of Norwich, 27

Kellerer, Ulrich, 114
King, Martin Luther, Jr., 162, 172
knowing silence, 55–56
Kuhn, Thomas, xv

Langer, Susanne, xi, xiii
language: for Burke, 84–85; for crazy talk, 77–78; for culture, 94; for Ellul, 145; for existence, 46–47; of healing, 157n14; for humanity, 78–79, 88–89; Internet, 54; metaphors in, 88; for Ong, 90; philosophy and, xi–xvii, 96; silence for, 52–53; for society, xvi–xvii; telos of, 92; truth in, 149–50
Language as Symbolic Action (Burke), 99n19
leisure, 164
"Letter to my brothers" (Moore, B.), 163
linguistics, 61, 85
listening: to attentive silence, 46–47, 66–67; best practices, 55; coherency in, 132; for communication, 55–56; conflict from, 47–48; in contemplative silence, 37–40; deep, 56–57; dialogic, 97, 136–38; to God, 23–29; ILA, 58, 71n10; psychology of, 45; for race relations, 176–77; relational, 128–36; for relationships, 127–28; secondary orality, 132–33; sound and, 71n16; speech and, 125; for spirituality, 23–24; willingness for, 54–55
Listening to Your Life (Buechner), 45
literature, 15, 71n8
"Literature as Equipment for Living" (Burke), 99n17
Littlejohn, Stephen, 11
living speech, 82
logic, 123–24
The Logic of the Humanities (Cassirer), xiv–xv
loneliness, 59, 103–4
Louis XIV (king), 34
love, 12–13

Macarius of Egypt, 22
marriage, 92–93, 99n16
McGroarty, Beth, 38
McKibben, Bill, 38
McLuhan, Marshall, 5, 113–14
meaning, 145–48
meaningful conversations, 131
meaning-making, 123–25, 130
media: for culture, 1, 39, 116–17; digital, 5, 38, 52–53, 107; ecology, 13–14, 37–40; emedia, 52–63; ethics, 148; for human consciousness, 51; news, 112–13; phantom silence in, 3; scholarship on, 92–93, 113–14; *The Social Dilemma* for, 6n1; for society, 5. *See also specific topics*
Medieval Christianity, 29
meditation, 24–25
Merton, Thomas, xii, 23–29, 41n5, 41n11, 155–56
messages, 129–30, 136, 150–51
message transmission, 76–77, 111
Meta, 117n9

metacommunication, 152
metaphors, 88
Meyrowitz, Joshua, 129
Middle Ages, 23, 28
mindfulness, 49, 64–65
Mr. Roger's Neighborhood, 98n1, 99n2, 99n4
mobility, 136–37
Modern Age, 16, 172
monasticism, 23–29
monastic silence, 155–56
Moore, Beth, 163, 178n4
Moore, G. E., xvi
Moral Consciousness and Communicative Action (Habermas), xvi–xvii
Mott, Lucretia, 31
multi-tasking, 63–66
music, 48–50

Netflix, 1–2, 6n1
neuroscience, 72n21, 113–14, 118n14, 135–36
Neville, Morgan, 1
news, 79–80, 112–13
New Seeds of Contemplation (Merton), 24
noise: for acoustic ecology, 61; attentive silence and, 48–52; for EPA, 61–62; health risks from, 71n17; ONAC, 72n18; phantom silence and, 112–17; sound compared to, 65–66; technology and, 4; in U.S., 70n3; white, 50
normativity, xii–xiv, xvii, 14–15
Nouwen, Henri, 4, 144

objectification, 134
Office of Noise Abatement and Control (ONAC), 72n18
Old Testament, 168
ONAC. *See* Office of Noise Abatement and Control
Ong, Walter, xiii, 11–12; existence for, 49; intimacy for, 147; language for, 90; ontology for, 75; secondary orality for, 132–33; sound for, 84
online gaming, 5
online interactions, 158n25
ontological silence: for dialogue, 93–97; interiority in, 84–93; philosophy of, 73–82; spirit from, 82–84
ontology, xi–xii, xvi–xvii, 75, 81, 90–91
oppression, 9, 42n29, 165–66
oral culture, 13–15
Orality and Literacy (Ong), 132
the other, 124–25

Palmer, Parker, 107–8, 150, 155, 174
paradigm constructions, xv, 7, 11, 15, 35–36
Pascal, Blaise, 20
Penn, William, 31
perseverance, 47–48
personal mobile media (PMM): anxiety from, 57–58; Attention Deficit Syndrome from, 93; communication with, 4–5, 7, 14, 52, 65, 100n23, 139n13; conversations on, 60–61, 128, 154; for culture, 85–86, 93, 106–7, 133, 152–53; distractions from, 49, 60; ethics with, 141; existence with, 89–90; exploitation on, 153–54; human behavior on, 156; interpersonal communication on, 134–35; iPhones, 71n9; for messages, 129–30, 150–51; for Postman, 38; public discourse on, 169; relationships on, 51, 67–68; research on, 63, 156; white noise on, 50
persuasion, 164
phantom silence, 3; for culture, 106–9, 111–12; in Digital age, 104–6; noise and, 112–17; philosophy of, 16, 103–4; *la technique* related to, 109–10
philosophy: of attentive silence, 45; of Buber, 136, 173; of communication, 3–4, 70, 96–97; of empathy, 94–95; of ethical silence, 155–57; of

ethics, xv–xvi; of false self, 26–27; hermeneutics in, xiii; history of, 75, 100n23; language and, xi–xvii, 96; of monasticism, 23–29; of ontological silence, 73–82; of phantom silence, 16, 103–4; Plato for, 115; of relationships, 5–6; religion and, 20, 34–37; scholarship for, 81; of silence, 148–54; of telos, 109–10; thinking and, 11–12

Philosophy in a New Key (Langer), xi, xiii

Philosophy of Symbolic Forms (Cassirer), xi, xiii

Picard, Max, 78–81, 89, 91, 98n14, 111–12, 122

Pieper, Josef, 149–50, 163

pilgrimages, 97, 100n31

Plato, 85, 115, 119n31

PMM. *See* personal mobile media

politics: of democracy, 10; international, 8; of Louis XIV, 34; propaganda in, 117; psychology of, 47; religion and, 139n3; in society, 22–23; unhealthy silence in, 177n2, 178n6; in U.S., 142–43, 171; violence in, 169–70

Postman, Neil, 5, 42n34; conversations for, 68–70; info/action ratio for, 21, 59; PMM for, 38; technology for, 104; technopolies for, 125, 139n3

power, 8–9, 12–16, 26

The Power of Silence (Jaworski), 123

Prater, Robert L., 157n14

prayer, 3, 20

presence, 12–16, 36, 76, 91

Principia Ethica (Moore, G. E.), xvi

printing press, 11

privacy, 151–52

progress, 25

propaganda, 111, 117

protest, 175

Protestant reform, 37–38

proximity-bound communication, 15

psychology: of conflict, 158n20; dialogue in, 137–38; ethical silence for, 141–45; imagination for, 64–65; of listening, 45; of politics, 47; reflection for, 125; sanity, 46–47; silence for, 53–54, 65–66; of technological overload, 62

public discourse, 2, 10, 98n15, 169; in civil society, 14, 115; for culture, 58–59; silence for, 39–40; on television, 95–96

public space, 133–34

public sphere, 169–70

Putman, Robert, 107–8

Quakers, 30–33, 41n21, 42n25, 155

The Question Concerning Technology (Heidegger), xvi

Quiet Communities Act, 61–62

quietism, 42n27

race relations, 160–63, 170–71, 176–77

Reclaiming Conversation (Turkle), 112

reflection, 125

reflective silence, 122, 170

relational development, 124

relational listening, 128–36

relational silence: for communication, 121–22, 128–36; dialogic listening with, 97, 136–38; meaning-making from, 123–25; overlap in, 122–23; for speech community, 126–28

relationships: concepts of, 158n20; ethics in, 145–46; friendship, 13, 122; healthy, 128–29; listening for, 127–28; meaning in, 145–48; philosophy of, 5–6; on PMM, 51, 67–68; romantic partnerships, 122; scholarship on, 134; silence for, 94; on social media, 108–9; stress in, 124–25

religion: in Europe, 37–38; faith in, 30; history of, 21; in Modern Age, 172; Old Testament for, 168; philosophy and, 20, 34–37; politics and, 139n3; progress for, 25; religious studies, 4. *See also specific religions*

Religious Society of Friends.
  See Quakers
respect, 56–57, 146–47
The Responsive Chord (Schwartz),
  65–66, 72n24
rhetoric, 140n16, 169–70, 173, 177
Rhetoric of Religion (Burke), 99n19
Ricoeur, Paul, xiii–xiv
ritualized oppression, 165–66
rituals, 36
Rodriguez, Clemenica, xvi
Rogers, Carl, 128–29
Rogers, Fred, 1, 98n2
Roman Catholicism, 34–35
romantic partnerships, 122
Rose, Barbara, 92
Rousseau, Jean Jacques, 119n22
rudeness, 9–10
Runcorn, David, 24

safety, 98n4
sanity, 46–47
scams, 103–4, 117n1
Schachman, Thomas, 132, 143
Schafer, R. Murray, 49–50, 71n16
Schultze, Quentin, 123, 131
Schwartz, Tony, 65–66, 72n24
secondary orality, 132–33
Seeds of Contemplation (Merton), xii
segregation, 170–71
self-actualization, 37
self-disclosure, 126
self-reflection, 40
A Short and Easy Method of Prayer
  (Guyon), 34
silence: as balm, 160–63; for Buber, 92;
  for communication, 46, 70n6; for
  conversations, 111–12; for culture,
  2–3, 79–80; in Digital Age, 144–45;
  disappearing, 70n2; equanimity
  from, 126–27; ethics of, 155–57; in
  friendship, 32–33; healing and, 176;
  for humanity, 9–12; knowing, 55–56;
  for language, 52–53; monastic,
  155–56; philosophy of, 148–54;
  for Picard, 89, 91; prayer and, 20;
  for psychology, 53–54, 65–66; for
  public discourse, 39–40; reflective,
  122, 170; for relationships, 94;
  scholarship on, 5–7; on social media,
  167; speech and, 50–51, 83, 97,
  123; spirituality and, 121–22; with
  technology, 12–16; in U.S., 8–9. *See
  also specific topics*
slavery, 160–61, 171–72, 177n2
small talk, 150
smart technology, 71n8
Smith, James K. A., 142
social anxiety, 59
social challenges, 25
The Social Contract (Rousseau), 119n22
The Social Dilemma (documentary),
  1–2, 6n1, 157n3, 157n5
social identity, 162
social media: for activism, 71n15;
  conflict on, 132–33; conversations
  on, 57; for culture, 1–2; for
  Digital Age, 112; in neuroscience,
  118n14; relationships on, 108–9;
  research on, 59–60; scholarship
  on, 157n3, 157n5; silence on, 167;
  technology for, 117n9; telegraph
  compared to, 104–6
society: coronavirus pandemic for, 19;
  digital media for, 38; efficiency for,
  109–10; encouragement in, 175–76;
  equanimity for, 40; ethics for,
  154–55; for humanity, 108; hyper-
  individualism for, 93–94; in India,
  177n2; language for, xvi–xvii; media
  for, 5; paradigm constructions for,
  7; politics in, 22–23; public space
  in, 133–34; scholarship for, 3–4;
  technology for, 13–14, 25. *See also*
  civil society
solace, 160–63
Soukup, Paul, 114
sound, 12–13, 16, 48–49, 65–66,
  71n16, 72n24, 84
Spath, Thomas, 10

Speaking of the Language of Healing (Jacobsen, Prater, and Taylor), 157n14
speech: community, 126–28, 131–32; in Digital Age, 14; freedom and, 8–9; listening and, 125; living, 82; for Picard, 78–79, 111–12; power of, 26; silence and, 50–51, 83, 97, 123; in U.S., 20; writing and, 54
spirituality, 19–24, 32–33, 82–84, 88n6, 89, 121–22
Stanton, Elizabeth Cady, 31
Stewart, John, 122, 135, 139n13
stress, 43n40, 124–25, 135–36
The Structure of Scientific Revolutions (Kuhn), xv
stupid conversations, 68–69
stupid talk, 152
symbols, 85–87, 91, 123–24
Syncleticato, 22

Tannen, Deborah, 61, 164
Taylor, Arnita Willis, 157n14
la technique, 41n12, 109–10, 113, 119n22, 158n24, 164, 168
technology: abuse of, 86–87; addiction to, 58; anxiety and, 71n9, 71n10; coding for, 157n3; for communication, xiii, 2, 5–6, 11–12, 71n15; for culture, xvi; disruption from, 92–93; distractions from, 48, 63–64; for Ellul, 5, 116, 118n18; ethics with, 142; face-to-face conversations and, 158n19; *ghost in the machine* theory for, 119n34; history of, 104–6; hyper-individualism from, 38; imagination with, 105–6; in Modern Age, 16; noise and, 4; for objectification, 134; for paradigm constructions, xv, 11; for Postman, 104; printing press, 11; scams with, 103–4, 117n1; silence with, 12–16; smart, 71n8; in *The Social Dilemma*, 1–2; for social media, 117n9; for society, 13–14, 25; techno-determinism, 152–53; technological overload, 62; telegraph, 42n34; for VideoChats, 136
technopolies, 125, 139n3
telegraph, 42n34, 104–6
television, 15, 50, 62–67, 72n24, 87, 95–96, 115
telos, 76, 88n5, 91–92, 109–10
The Theology of Culture (Tillich), xvii
Theresa of Avila, 27
thinking, 11–12
Thurman, Howard, 171–72
Tillich, Paul, xvii
toxic silence, 165–68
trust, 144, 154–55
truth, 149–50, 172–74
Truth and Method (Gadamer), xiv
The Tuning of the World (Schaefer), 49–50
Turkle, Sherry, 39, 112
Twitter, 1–2, 70n7, 126, 132–33

Understanding Media (McLuhan), 113–14
unethical silence, 9
unhealthy silence, 177n2, 178n6; for culture, 159–60; dialogic impulse for, 170–72; dialogue for, 172–77; persuasion and, 164; in public sphere, 169–70; strategy for, 160–63, 178n7; toxic silence and, 165–68
Union with God (Guyon), xii, 34
United States (U.S.): civil society in, 161–62, 171–72; culture of, 99n16; EPA in, 72n18; Europe and, 50; history of, 8; noise in, 70n3; politics in, 142–43, 171; Quiet Communities Act in, 61–62; race relations in, 160–63, 170–71, 176–77; silence in, 8–9; slavery in, 160–61; speech in, 20; stress in, 43n40

Vedantam, Shankar, 169–70
VideoChats, 136
violence, 143–44, 169–70

visual distractions, 66–67
voice, 13, 30

Walker, Duncan, 50
Walther, Joseph, 60
Wayne, John, 66–67
white noise, 50
Wiener, Norbert, xvi
Wiesel, Elie, 155

Won't You Be My Neighbor (Neville), 1
Wood, Julia, 60–61
Woolman, John, 31
The World of Silence (Picard), 98n14
writing, 54, 119n31
Wurman, Saul, 58–59, 71n10

Zoom, 114–15, 130, 136, 147
Zuckerberg, Mark, 117n9

About the Author

Stephanie Bennett, PhD, is professor of communication and media ecology at Palm Beach Atlantic University in South Florida where she has spent the last 20 years teaching, mentoring, researching, and writing around the interplay of interpersonal relationships, faith, and digital media. Her doctoral dissertation (2005) focused on the social theory of French philosopher, Jacques Ellul, and is entitled: "The Disappearance of Silence: A Dialectical Exploration of the Interpersonal Implications of Personal Mobile Media." Author of the trilogy *Within the Walls*, Bennett employs fiction to envision a future America in which the choices between progress, technology, and efficiency compel the reader to run toward all that is organic, relational, and situated in human community. This, her second work of creative non-fiction, focuses on the significance of silence as an integral part of speech and the dialogic necessity of holding both in creative tension.

www.ingramcontent.com/pod-product-compliance
Lightning Source LLC
Chambersburg PA
CBHW020119010526
44115CB00008B/897